STICKS & STONES

THE *Richard Hampton Jenrette* SERIES

IN ARCHITECTURE & THE DECORATIVE ARTS

STICKS & STONES

THREE CENTURIES
OF NORTH CAROLINA
GRAVEMARKERS

M. RUTH LITTLE

Photography by Tim Buchman

The University of North Carolina Press

Chapel Hill & London

Manufactured in Japan by

Toppan Printing Company

Designed by Richard Hendel

Drawings on pp. viii, 5, 10, 11, 13,

and 21 by J. Daniel Pezzoni

Set in Bell, Meta, and Castellar types

by B. Williams & Associates

The paper in this book meets the guide-

lines for permanence and durability of

the Committee on Production Guidelines

for Book Longevity of the Council on

Library Resources.

Library of Congress

Cataloging-in-Publication Data

Little, M. Ruth (Margaret Ruth), 1946–

Sticks and stones: three centuries of North

Carolina gravemarkers / M. Ruth Little.

   p. cm.

Includes bibliographical references and

indexes.

ISBN 0-8078-2417-8 (alk. paper)

1. Sepulchral monuments—North Carolina.

2. Epitaphs—North Carolina. 3. North

Carolina—Social life and customs. I. Title.

GT3210.N8L57   1998

736'.5'09756—dc21   97-32589

                CIP

02   01   00   99   98

5   4   3   2   1

Grateful acknowledgment is made to

the Historic Preservation Foundation

of North Carolina, Inc., for its role in

bringing this book to fruition.

CONTENTS

PREFACE

Eleanor Rigby died in the church
And was buried along with her name.
Nobody came.
—*John Lennon and Paul McCartney, "Eleanor Rigby"*

Old North Carolina cemeteries hold many forgotten people and forgotten names. It was their names that initially drew me to their stones, then I stayed to admire the stones themselves. The subtitle of this book, "Three Centuries of North Carolina Gravemarkers," deliberately avoids the term "gravestones" because this term does not begin to encompass the rich diversity of shapes and materials in Tar Heel cemeteries. Gravestones are only one of a number of ways that North Carolinians marked their graves since initial European settlement.

When I first began to look at North Carolina's historic resources I regarded gravemarkers as an extremely useful genealogical tool. During my first historic architecture survey, of Caswell County in 1972, whenever we found an old house I carefully inspected the family graveyard in order to document the names and dates of the long-dead owners of the house. At the end of the survey, Caswell County gravemarkers remained merely archival records. One bright October day in 1974, I had a riveting experience that led to my long quest to understand North Carolina gravemarkers. I was surveying an antebellum house near the Cape Fear River in Harnett County, one of the inland Coastal Plain counties where thousands of Highland Scots had settled in the eighteenth century. The house was unremarkable, but in the family graveyard nearby stood a tiny headstone (Fig. P.1), crudely cut out of thick reddish-brown sandstone in the abstract shape of a human figure, with a large nose and lips, small eyes, and a large heart. The inscription was illegible, but the lettering indicated that the stone was very old, perhaps eighteenth or early nineteenth century. There were other jobs to do that day, and I didn't even take a photograph of the stone. But it would not let me go. After several weeks of being haunted by the memory, I returned one weekend to photograph the stone and found that it was gone. In that brief time, someone had removed it from the graveyard, whether to save it or to destroy it I never learned.

The Scottish face was gone, but it had given me two gifts: an emotional understanding of the perishability of old gravestones, and a hint of their significance as artifacts of material culture. In 1981, assisted by a two-year grant from the National Endowment for the Humanities to study North Carolina gravestones as sculpture, I approached the stones as keys to culture and ethnicity. The result is the North Carolina Gravemarker Survey, a collection of field notes, transcriptions, drawings, and photographs of 1,200 gravemarkers in 550 graveyards in 34 of the state's 100 counties. The collection is part of the Southern Folklife Collection at the University of North Carolina at Chapel Hill.

In addition to the fieldwork devoted exclusively to gravemarker study, I've

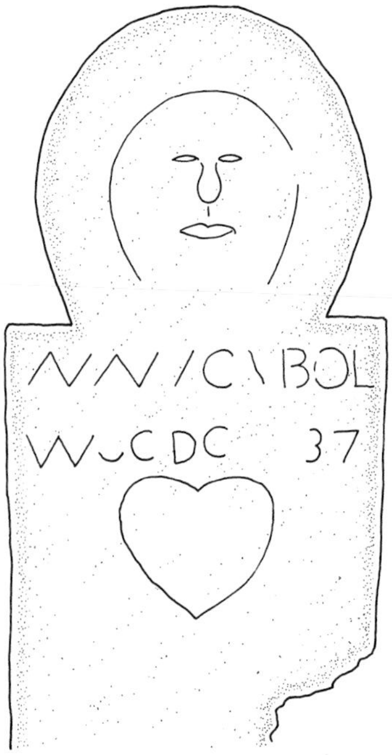

Figure P.1.
Headstone for unknown person,
eighteenth century [?],
Johnson family graveyard,
Buies Creek vicinity,
Harnett County.
(Drawing from a photo
by Buddy Brown, ca. 1971)

roamed nearly every county in North Carolina for twenty-five years conducting field documentation of historic buildings for the State Historic Preservation Office, and taken many a side trip to look at family graveyards and church and public cemeteries to deepen my understanding of architecture and cultural traditions. Lenoir County, where my mother was raised, is one area in which I've searched cemeteries. Impressions stored throughout these years inform the following analysis of the state's monumental heritage.

Figures P.2 and P.3 map the major topographic regions, immigrant groups, and the extent of gravemarker fieldwork conducted in North Carolina. My two years of fieldwork focused on the regional differences in gravemarkers of the three primary early ethnic groups in North Carolina—the British, Germans, and Africans. I began with a reconnaissance survey of each region in which the groups settled and determined which counties promised the highest survival of early graveyards. In the heavily English- and African-settled Albemarle region of northeastern North Carolina, I explored Gates, Hertford, Pasquotank, Perquimans, Chowan, and Bertie Counties. In the English and African-settled Pamlico Sound region I explored Craven and Carteret Counties. In the multicultural Lower Cape Fear, I searched New Hanover, Pender, and Brunswick Counties. In the Highland Scots–settled Upper Cape Fear region, I studied Cumberland, Hoke, and Harnett Counties. In the northeast Piedmont, settled by English and Scots-Irish, Caswell, Orange, and Alamance Counties were studied. In the German and Scots-Irish central and western Piedmont, I explored the counties of Guilford, Forsyth, Davidson, Rowan, Iredell, Mecklenburg, Catawba, Lincoln, and Gaston.

From these I selected the four counties that best represented the major culture groups and changes in tradition and craftsmanship. I documented every historic cemetery in New Hanover County, in the southeast corner of the state at the mouth of the major river, the Cape Fear, because of its British and African settlement and

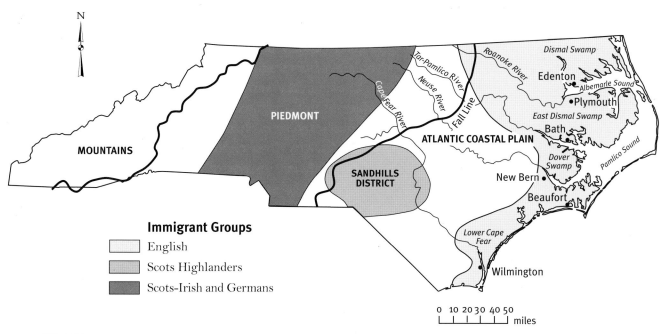

N

Immigrant Groups

☐ English

▨ Scots Highlanders

▨ Scots-Irish and Germans

0 10 20 30 40 50 ⊢⊢⊢⊢⊢⊢⊣ miles

Figure P.2.
Topographic regions and eighteenth-century immigrant groups
in North Carolina.

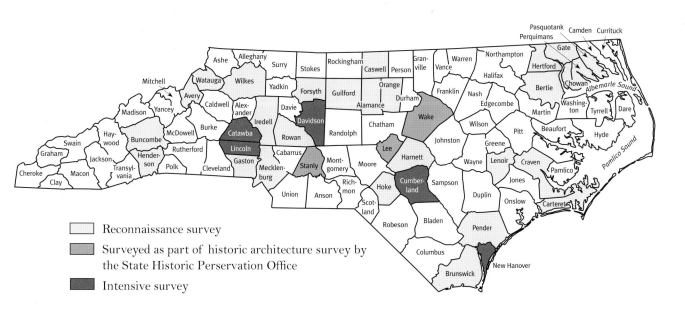

☐ Reconnaissance survey

▨ Surveyed as part of historic architecture survey by
the State Historic Perservation Office

▨ Intensive survey

Figure P.3. North Carolina gravemarker survey, 1981–1996.

because it contains the large and cosmopolitan nineteenth-century port city of Wilmington. Likewise, I recorded every historic cemetery in Cumberland County, at the head of the Cape Fear River, because it was the center of the Loyalist Scot settlement in the late eighteenth century in this Sandhills region and because Fayetteville was an important antebellum trading center. The third county I studied intensively was Davidson County in the western Piedmont; it had been settled by Pennsylvania German Lutherans in the eighteenth century, and had a remarkable collection of early gravestones standing in church cemeteries. Finally, I investigated the tri-county northern Catawba River region of Catawba, Lincoln, and Gaston Counties in the western Piedmont because of its intermixture of Scots-Irish and Germans who had moved to this area from Pennsylvania and its strong tradition of craftsmanship.

In the 1990s I did a study of Wilkes County in the northern foothills and four counties in the Blue Ridge Mountain region, the multicultural counties of Watauga and Avery in the northern mountains, and Buncombe and Henderson in the southern mountains. My discovery during earlier fieldwork that mountain artisans created markers from local stone for several generations after Piedmont craftsmen abandoned this sideline sent me to the Blue Ridge with a fresh appreciation of the mountain gravemarker heritage.

My understanding of gravemarkers has been broadened by three county surveys of historic architecture conducted in recent years by architectural historians who cast their keen powers of observation on cemeteries in addition to buildings. Kelly Lally's Wake County Survey, J. Daniel Pezzoni's Lee County Survey, and Donna Dodenhoff's Stanley County Survey recorded regional gravemarker traditions as integral elements of the built environment.

This study does not treat so-called folk gravemarkers in a vacuum. I set out to study the cultural patterns formed by gravemarkers, thus my original focus was traditional or folk markers, that is, those locally made. The term "traditional" refers to the continuation of custom, often to a continuation of the vernacular. "Vernacular" refers to the native speech, language, or dialect of a country or place: vernacular gravemarkers are the native forms of marking graves in a place. Yet fieldwork revealed that traditional or vernacular gravemarkers coexisted with commercial gravestones from the beginning of North Carolina's monument history, in the late seventeenth century. The entire spectrum of vernacular and imported gravemarkers tells the story of North Carolina's sticks and stones. In cemeteries of the gentry in eastern North Carolina, imported monuments gradually yielded to locally carved imported stones; among the rest of the populace, wooden sticks and brick and other local materials served to mark graves.

In my treatment of North Carolina graveyards and gravemarkers in the following chapters, I have synthesized the cultural geography model, which treats graveyards as important repositories of material culture, and the New England art historical model in which the gravemarker and its maker are primary.[1] The work of gravestone scholars in other parts of the country has provided the context for this study.

The major focus of gravestone studies in the United States has been New England. In 1927 Harriet Forbes wrote the pioneering American tombstone study, *Gravestones of Early New England.* Allan Ludwig wrote the next major study, *Graven Images,* in 1966. Since the 1960s, scholars have exhaustively studied early New England gravestones to identify the major individual stonecutters and their followers and to interpret the symbolism. Scholars have linked the variations in death's heads and soul effigies of seventeenth- and eighteenth-century Puritan headstones to differences in doctrinal philosophy from one church or region to another.[2]

Despite all of the New England activity, researchers have neglected the gravestones of other regions of the United States, particularly the South. Diana Combs published the first southern gravestone study, *Early Gravestone Art in Georgia and South Carolina,* in 1986. In a close analysis of eighteenth-century iconic or imagistic headstones (stones with pictorial carving), Combs demonstrates that New England stonecutters dominated the market in Charleston and Savannah in the eighteenth century. These graveyards contain some of the only signed stones by such New England stonecutters as William Codner and Henry Emmes, showing that these artisans proudly advertised their achievements in these distant colonies. Combs gives evidence of a sophisticated anglophile community in these southern markets for which New England carvers produced baroque-style tombstone portraiture that was closer to contemporary urbane British tomb sculpture than to the tombstone tradition in New England. Her book documents what is New England about southern gravestones and does not deal with traditional gravemarkers in the Piedmont and mountain regions or later nineteenth- and twentieth-century gravestones.

Until *Sticks and Stones,* researchers had never systematically studied North Carolina gravemarkers, nor those of most other southern states. Bradford Rauschenberg's 1977 study of the German pierced soapstone gravestones in Davidson County is the earliest analytical study of a group of gravestones in North Carolina. He related this group of unique gravestones to the vernacular furniture produced by a school of rural cabinetmakers in the county from the 1830s to 1850s. Daniel Patterson is documenting the work of the Bigham family, which operated an early Scots-Irish stonecutting workshop in the western Piedmont.[3]

In North Carolina, as in most of the South, much work remains to be done. The southern tradition of family graveyards makes it more difficult to find historic graveyards than in New England, where the village churchyard is the tradition. Small clumps of gravestones scatter in densely overgrown thickets in the fields of old plantations and farms. To the eye accustomed to the rich symbolism and deep sculptural relief of New England gravestones, most southern gravemarkers seem plain; they lack the doctrinal Puritan symbolism, but come in a greater variety of forms and represent a greater cultural and ethnic complexity. An incredibly rich collection of gravestone types, from gravehouses to cedar boards to seashell mounds to tomb-tables to pierced soapstones to homemade concrete headstones, populate North Carolina's graveyards. Collectively, they tell the history of North Carolina's people through the eighteenth, nineteenth, and twentieth centuries.

The chapters of *Sticks and Stones* examine the range of traditional and commercial options available to families to commemorate graves since initial European settlement. Questions such as the following show why both ends of the spectrum were investigated: In the sandy Coastal Plain where no native stone existed, where did early settlers obtain gravestones? How could a family show its respect if it could not afford to purchase a stone monument? What comparisons can be drawn between the graveyards and gravemarkers of English settlers, the Scotch Highlanders, the Scots-Irish, the Germans, and African Americans—through time and through the flat, hilly, and mountainous regions of North Carolina? Do overall cemetery designs, as well as those of individual gravemarkers, reflect culture?

Chapter 1 provides a general introduction to gravemarker form, symbolism, design sources, and stonecutters. The next two chapters analyze the state's gravemarkers geographically; the last three chapters work thematically, treating traditional nineteenth-century stonecutters, commercial stonecutters during the heyday of the local monument industry in the nineteenth and early twentieth centuries, and, finally, traditional gravemarkers that persist in white and African American communities in the twentieth century despite the standardization of the commercial monument industry after the 1920s. Commercial monuments, inherently more standardized and less revealing, are not treated with equal depth as traditional markers. Nevertheless, the interwoven history of traditional and commercial production, with special emphasis on the antebellum era when the local monument industry began, patterns the book. By the railroad era, when nearly every town had a marble yard, and particularly after the 1920s, when commercial monuments were mass-produced and indistinguishable from one state to another, coverage of commercial monuments is quite selective. Appendix A provides an index of gravemarker artisans in North Carolina.

The following guide to North Carolina gravemarkers is not an exhaustive inventory of every historic cemetery in the state but a general overview of chronological and cultural patterns. My own fieldwork allowed me to inspect only a small sample of the hundreds of thousands of gravemarkers dating before 1920 in North Carolina, leaving much work to be done by others. May the surprising variety and richness of this sculptural legacy encourage local historians all over the state to study and photograph the thousands of graveyards that are weathering away in the woods before their English, Scots, German, French, Eastern European, Indian, and African American faces are gone, too.

The title of this book, *Sticks and Stones*, is taken from the old children's rhyme, "Sticks and stones may break my bones but words can never hurt me." The poem sets up an association between sticks and stones and bones and words that makes the title appropriate for a book about graveyards. But more important, the phrase expresses the dichotomy between the impermanent nature of many markers—the wooden "sticks" or headboards and the grave pailings—and the permanent gravestones.[4] If we concentrate on the stones and ignore the sticks, we have put most of the population outside of our field of interest.

During years of transcriptions of thousands of gravemarkers, I had much opportunity to reflect on my own mortality. It is surely not too soon to have selected my epitaph from one that I found on a number of gravestones of women who died during the later 1800s:

She hath done what she could.

From a feminist perspective, this epitaph, surely sometimes chosen by the women's husbands, seems to damn them with faint praise. Actually, it is taken from a biblical passage, Mark 14:8, and refers to the woman who anointed Jesus with costly ointment at Bethany, in the days prior to his Crucifixion. Jesus, touched by the woman's act of love, exclaimed, "She hath done what she could; she hath anointed my body beforehand for its burial." To me, the epitaph expresses my attitude toward life, which is to throw myself wholeheartedly into worthwhile projects, such as this study of vanishing gravemarkers.

Many, many people have aided me in my long study. Charles G. "Terry" Zug and Daniel Patterson mentored me during the original National Endowment grant and have provided continuing encouragement since then. My husband, Bob Upchurch, my children, Gia and Britton Upchurch, and my mother-in-law, Sarah Upchurch, have cheerfully tolerated a gravestone fanatic living in their midst. My faithful dog, Serena, kept me company in the graveyards during fieldwork. My colleagues across the state, Catherine Bishir, Michael Southern, Claudia Brown, Margaret S. Smith, Donna Dodenhoff, Kelly Lally, George Stephenson, Brad Rauschenberg, Rodney Barfield, Dan Pezzoni, Penne Smith, Greg Sekula, John B. Green, and Elizabeth Reid Murray, supplied information and moral support. Local historians Betty Sowers and Jeanette Wilson in Davidson County, Bill Fields in Cumberland County, Mary Jane Fowler in Salisbury, and Emma Yopp Murray and Beverly Tetterton in New Hanover County provided much help. Thanks to James Clarke for his help with W. O. Wolfe and John Green for sharing his research on Greenwood Cemetery, New Bern. People who sheltered me overnight during the fieldwork were my mother, Virginia Little, my mother-in-law, Sarah Upchurch, Paul Greene Sr., Frank and Susan Ainsley, and Frances Alexander. Thanks to all the people who shared their gravemarker stories with me.

Special thanks go to the individuals who read drafts of my manuscript with patience and insight: Catherine Bishir, Michael Southern, Margaret S. Smith, and Kate Hutchins. Because of Tim Buchman's powerful photographs, the full sculptural and spiritual presence of the gravemarkers are expressed in this book. I am profoundly grateful to the Historic Preservation Foundation of North Carolina, Inc., and most particularly J. Myrick Howard and Banks Talley Jr. for organizing support from many individuals and organizations to underwrite the photography. The spirits of the old ones guided Tim and me along the back roads and through the woods to the graveyards. I was privileged to work with Tim to record these markers for posterity.

SPONSORS OF THE PHOTOGRAPHY

When the University of North Carolina Press initially expressed interest in publishing Ruth Little's manuscript, they suggested the need for photographs that would tell the story as well as Ruth's words. The choice of Tim Buchman of Charlotte to take those photographs was an obvious one. Tim's images for *North Carolina Architecture* by Catherine Bishir, published by UNC Press for Preservation North Carolina in 1990, continue to thrill viewers nearly a decade after their taking. Because of that extraordinary collaboration between Tim and Catherine, acquiring the funds for Tim to take photographs to accompany Ruth's manuscript proved to be one of the easiest fundraising tasks imaginable. One round of requests cinched the needed funding, and Tim was on the road with Ruth.

Preservation North Carolina gratefully thanks the following donors, whose support for the photography of Tim Buchman helped make this book a reality.

J. Myrick Howard, Executive Director
Historic Preservation Foundation of North Carolina, Inc.

Grand Patrons
Mary Duke Biddle Foundation, Durham
Suzanne and John Martin, Columbus
The Michel Family Foundation, Greensboro

Sponsors
Anonymous
Virginia S. Atkinson, Fort Lauderdale, Florida, in honor of Virginia A. Stevens
Ms. Iris E. Bailey, Chapel Hill
L. P. Best Jr., Mebane, in memory of Huldah Walston Best and Lucius Pender Best
Catherine W. Bishir, Raleigh
Mr. and Mrs. Edward H. Clement, Salisbury
Mr. and Mrs. James M. Corcoran, New Bern
Davidson County Historical Museum
Gwendolyn Picklesimer Davis, Raleigh
Todd W. and Patricia S. Dickinson, Hillsborough
Renee Gledhill-Earley, Raleigh
Susanna Revelle Gwyn, Huntsville, Alabama
Lawrence S. Holt Jr. Endowment Fund
J. Myrick Howard, Raleigh
Tabitha Hutaff McEachern, Wilmington
Elizabeth Matheson, Hillsborough
Suzanne G. Millholland, Hickory
Elizabeth Reid Murray, Raleigh, in memory of Dr. Lillian Parker Wallace

Jaquelin Drane Nash, Tarboro, in memory of Pembroke Nash

Mr. and Mrs. Charles S. Norwood Jr., Goldsboro

Mr. and Mrs. Emmett Judson Pope Jr., Mount Olive,
in memory of Mr. and Mrs. Francis M. Manning

Dr. Annemarie S. Reynolds, Emmetten, Switzerland

Mr. and Mrs. E. L. Siler, Asheville, in memory of Mr. and Mrs. C. R. Johnson

Mrs. Elizabeth B. Sink, Winston-Salem, in memory of Carl Jackson Sink

Jim Smith and Pam Troutman, Raleigh

Dr. and Mrs. Paul V. Stankus, Chapel Hill

Mary Arthur Stoudemire, Chapel Hill

Laurie and Sam Sugg, Raleigh, in memory of Natalie J. Sugg

Tanya S. Sykes, Overland Park, Kansas

Mrs. Marvin E. Taylor, Smithfield

W. Michael Trogdon, Asheboro

Theron P. Watson, Forest City

Emeritus Professors Charles M. and Shirley F. Weiss, Chapel Hill

Mr. and Mrs. J. Lanier Williams, Lewisville

Sarah Denny Williamson, Raleigh

STICKS & STONES

In Memory of M.rs
MARY WALKER
the Wife of M.r
George Walker,
who Died Oc.tr
y 22.nd 1763 Aged
26 Years.

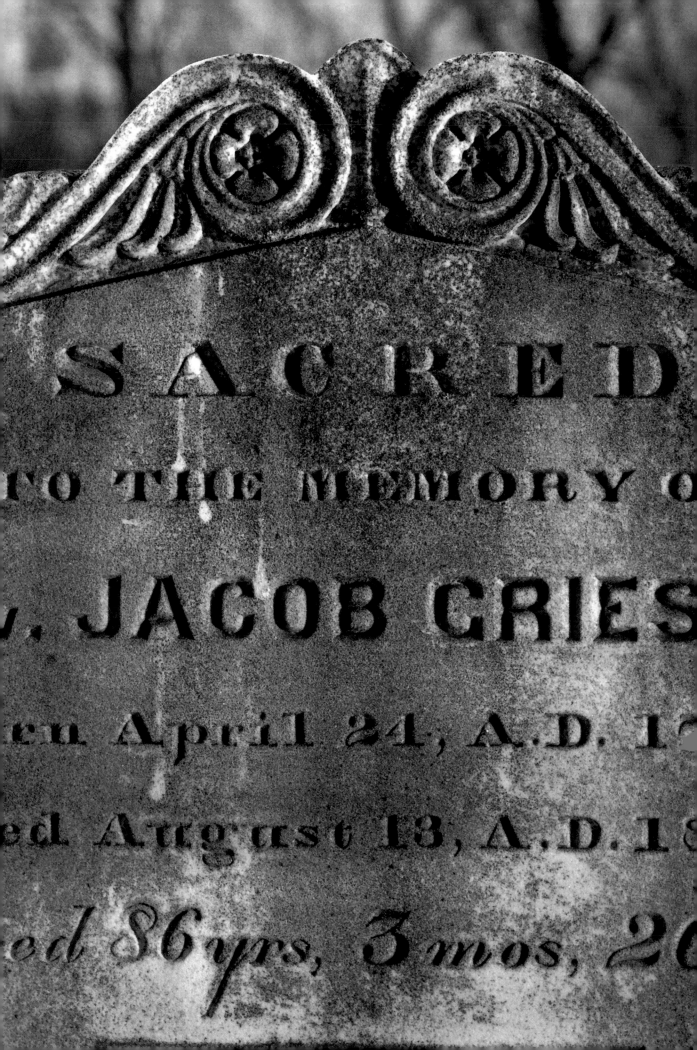

An old graveyard is a cultural encyclopedia. Genealogists, historians, and others eagerly copy the names and birth and death dates inscribed on the stones, and if not for this vital information many a family tree would lack a trunk. Often ignored by genealogists are the revealing sentiments expressed in inscriptions, whether Bible verses or praises of a life well lived. Analysis of the marker as an object made by a particular artisan, and of the graveyard as a cultural statement by a community, reveals much about the people who are buried there. The arrangement of graves in the graveyard reveals community traditions and cultural connections. Some families arrange graves in square plots, others in rigid rows, and still others by age and sex. Some graveyards are laid out with geometric regularity, while in others the arrangement of graves is informal and additive. Some graveyards are neatly grassed, some have scraped earth, and some lie in scrub woods. Graveyards in the Blue Ridge Mountains may be on top of bald knobs, higher than anything around them; those in the Coastal Plain may be private yards on family farms; those in the Piedmont tend to be in churchyards.

The markers, too, contain clues about the culture. The stone reveals much about the family members and their community. Its design, material, and size often indicate a family's economic standing in the community. The source reveals their trade connections: rural people usually bought gravemarkers from a local artisan; city dwellers often ordered a gravestone through the local cabinetmaking and undertaking establishment, or visited the stonecutter at the local marble yard. Some families spent extra money on decoration that ranged from pure ornamentation to an expression of deepest feelings. A bereaved husband might have chosen a carved rose to symbolize his wife's untimely death in the bloom of life, or grieving parents perhaps ordered the symbol of a lamb for the stone of a child. The symbols on many stones reveal religious orientation: Catholics and Episcopalians were more likely to use crosses than Presbyterians, Baptists, and Methodists.

Gravemarkers across the state fall into two basic categories, traditional and commercial. Traditional gravemarkers, sometimes called vernacular or folk markers, are the work of friends, family, or part-time artisans in the community, are generally made of locally available materials, and have deeper personal significance than commercial monuments. Most traditional markers, such as wooden headboards or brick vaults, are plain, but even these reflect local values, craft, and materials. Symbols meaningful to the local community, such as a Scottish thistle, a German heart, or African American mirrors and seashells, often animate traditional markers. At the other end of the spectrum, professional stonecutters working in North Carolina towns as well as large out-of-state cities produced commercial monuments. They copied books, catalogs, and each other and produced the same designs throughout the country. (Custom designs tailored to an individual are the exception.)

A 1906 physiographic map of the state which diagrams the substrata of each geographic region shows that the Coastal Plain contains no usable stone; the Piedmont contains predominantly three types of rocks: slates and schists, granites, and

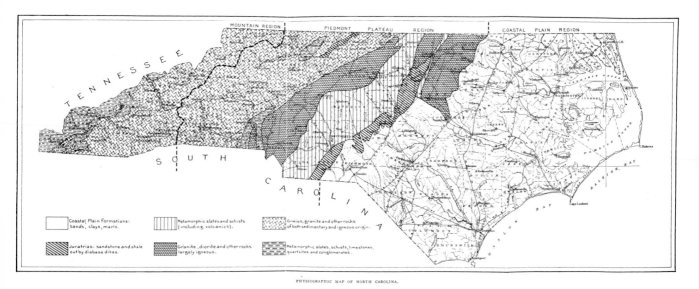

Figure 1.1.
Distribution of
stone in North
Carolina. (From
Watson, Laney,
and Merrill,
*The Building
and Ornamental
Stones of North
Carolina*, 1906)

sandstones; and the mountains contain predominantly gneiss and granite, with some limestone and marble (Fig. 1.1).[1] Much of the granite was too coarse-grained and hard for gravestones, although a granite quarry opened in the 1830s near Raleigh, in Wake County, supplied both building and monumental granite during the nineteenth century.[2] Most of the sandstone was not capable of fine detailing and did not weather well, and its general use was for walls, foundations, and chimneys, but local stonecutters quarried some sandstone and brownstone along the Deep River in Lee and Chatham Counties for gravestones.

Types of Gravemarkers

A place of interment has variously been termed "cemetery," "graveyard," "burying ground," and "churchyard"; a sculpture that marks a place of interment is known as a tomb, gravestone, tombstone, monument, gravemarker, and headstone. In this book, larger, public burial plots usually owned by the community, town, or city are called "cemeteries." Burial grounds located adjacent to church buildings are called "churchyards"; small private ones are called "graveyards." The term "cemetery" refers collectively to all types. Here the terms "gravemarker" or "monument" refer to all markers regardless of their form or material; "gravestone" or "tombstone" refers only to those fashioned of stone; and "headstone" refers to gravestones of that particular type.

Four basic materials, wood, clay, stone, and concrete, formed North Carolina gravemarkers from the eighteenth to the twentieth centuries. The major types of gravemarkers in North Carolina are shown in Figure 1.2. Artisans fashioned each material into a remarkable variety of forms that reveal ethnicity, culture, and historical era. They used wood for railings, graveboards, and gravehouses; brick for vaults; cast or turned clay for slabs or finials that were glazed to serve as gravemarkers; stone for head and footstones, ledgers, box-tombs, tomb-tables, obelisks, and pedestals; concrete for both upright and recumbent monuments. Family members recycled found objects, such as ballast stones, into monuments.

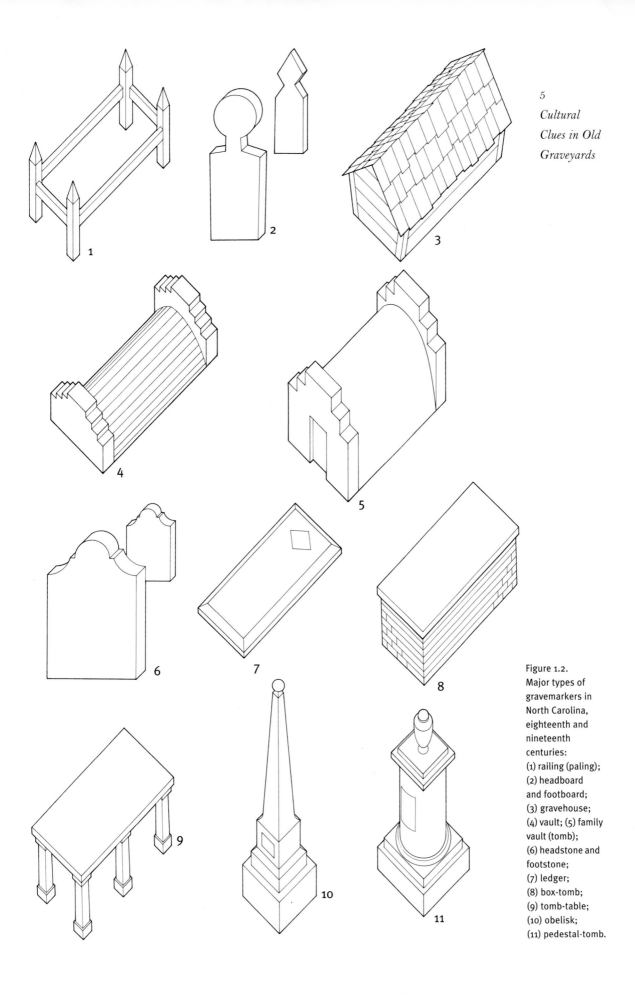

Figure 1.2.
Major types of
gravemarkers in
North Carolina,
eighteenth and
nineteenth
centuries:
(1) railing (paling);
(2) headboard
and footboard;
(3) gravehouse;
(4) vault; (5) family
vault (tomb);
(6) headstone and
footstone;
(7) ledger;
(8) box-tomb;
(9) tomb-table;
(10) obelisk;
(11) pedestal-tomb.

The use of wooden gravemarkers is a European tradition as well as an American one. The graveboard (post and rail gravemarker) was common in Great Britain and New England from the seventeenth century into the nineteenth century. In two regions of England where there is no local stone, East Anglia and Surrey, wood was the most common gravemarker material until the twentieth century.[3] Wooden markers were never much valued; a historian of Scottish headstones dismissed the graveboard as "a mere gravedigger's marker," and there is evidence in North Carolina estate records that it was indeed often the case that the gravedigger not only made the coffin, but supplied the gravemarker as well.[4] Wood was the most easily available and relatively inexpensive material in North Carolina for gravemarkers, thus various wooden markers probably populated North Carolina cemeteries from the earliest settlement to the early twentieth century. Few wooden gravemarkers survived in 1981 when this fieldwork commenced, since wood is a perishable material, and most wooden markers succumbed to rot, fire, or replacement by a more permanent marker.

Wooden "Railings" ("Pailings"). One of the humblest forms of wooden gravemarkers until the mid-nineteenth century is a railing, also known as a pailing, paling, or wooden fence, and it marked graves of the gentry as well as those less well off. It was formed by setting a pale, a piece of wood, vertically in the ground and nailing it to a horizontal rail to form a fence.[5] Often additional pales enclosed the entire grave. Its usage must date to earliest settlement. In 1799 the Philanthropic Society, one of the student literary clubs at the University of North Carolina at Chapel Hill, stipulated that the graves of their brethren who died at school and were buried in the university cemetery should be enclosed with thick oak or yellow poplar railings painted black with white top edging, and the name, death date, and society name lettered in white on the headboard.[6] References to railing graves appears in numerous estate expenses in the first half of the nineteenth century. In 1824, the estate of Jane Clark, Lincoln County, paid Gabriel Brown, probably a coffin maker, $3 for "Pailing in her and Cornelius Clarks Graves." In 1846 Nathan Parks, one of the busiest coffin makers in Davidson County, received $8, presumably for the coffin, and another $1.50 for "Railing grave" of Lucy Byerly.[7] Several nineteenth-century grave pailings stand at Black River Presbyterian Churchyard in Sampson County, in the Coastal Plain (Fig. 1.3). In the later years of the century, wooden railings gave way to cast-iron or wrought-iron fences around individual graves. These offered a more permanent solution to the same goal—defining the boundaries of the grave to help with future burials as well as to keep out animals.

Headboards and Footboards. Artisans often fashioned wood into substantial wooden markers: headboards, footboards, and graveboards. Graveboards, having the shape of the headboard of a bed, are not known in North Carolina.[8] Headboards and footboards are narrower, having the proportions of a headstone. The typical headboard is 6 inches wide, 16 inches high, and 1½ inches thick. In the Coastal Plain, woodworkers preferred cypress, cedar, or heart pine, the same rot-resistant

Figure 1.3.
Nineteenth-
century grave
railing, Black
River Presbyte-
rian Church-
yard, Sampson
County.
(Photo by
Tom Butchko;
© 1981 North
Carolina
Division of
Archives and
History)

woods used for fence posts, for gravemarkers, and a number of head and footboards still exist in rural graveyards, some with traces of white paint.[9] Although people probably erected head and footboards more often than any other type of grave-marker in the eighteenth and nineteenth centuries, few have survived because of destruction by weathering, fire, or replacement with a gravestone (Fig. 1.4).

The wooden headboard and footboard have flat surfaces capable of carrying an inscription, either carved or painted. Family members probably made most of the boards, but numerous artisans also made them. The largest known headboard in North Carolina, at Longstreet Presbyterian Church, Hoke County, is 10½ inches wide, 39½ inches high, and 2 inches thick. Those with money could buy them from craftsmen like William R. Hughes, who operated a chair and bedstead manufactory but stipulated in his advertisement in the Salisbury *Western Carolinian*, 27 May 1833: "In connection with his business, he will also make head and foot boards for Graves, complete; lettered or plain." Itinerant limners and coach painters probably painted boards as one of many sidelines.

Gravehouses and Grave Shelters. The gravehouse, a gable-roofed wood-framed structure approximately six feet long, three feet wide, and three feet high at the roof peak, shelters and protects the entire grave, and the body is interred below ground level (Fig. 1.5). Wooden gravehouses appear to be unique to the South, particularly the Upland South from North Carolina westward to Oklahoma, where they were constructed in European, African, and Native American graveyards.[10] In 1770 a traveler described a grave near Fayetteville as "neatly enclosed . . . with cedar clapboards."[11] In Cabarrus County one gravehouse with its gable roof, covered with wood shingles, has the date 1895 carved on the end rafter. Another has a Masonic emblem carved into its gable.[12] Still others exist in Stanly County.

Figure 1.4.
Headboard
measuring
7" wide,
27" high, and
2 ³/₄" thick,
Old Burying
Ground,
Beaufort.
This probably
dates from the
nineteenth
century.

Figure 1.5. Gravehouses emerge from the mist in the old cemetery at Halifax, ca. 1921. (North Carolina Collection, University of North Carolina at Chapel Hill)

A late-nineteenth-century variation of the gravehouse is the grave shelter, a larger structure consisting of a roof supported on four posts, usually enclosed with fencing or latticework. These are often referred to as gravehouses, and tend to occur in rural cemeteries. They may cover just one grave or several graves. The graves are usually marked with individual markers and the shelter serves the same purpose as a fence enclosing a family plot, to distinguish the grave or graves from others in the cemetery (Fig. 1.6). These once-common types of wooden gravemarkers and shelters, made of perishable materials, have virtually disappeared from cemeteries.

Figure 1.6. Grave shelter, Morrisville Baptist Church, Wake County. This probably dates from the early twentieth century. (Photo by M. Ruth Little)

VAULTS

The vault, almost always of brick, is a burial chamber containing the coffin. Generally the vault consisted of a floor and walls of wood, brick, or marl (a shell conglomerate). The coffin was placed inside this space, in the same way that coffins are placed in concrete vaults today. Generally only the top projects above ground level (Fig. 1.7). Sometimes the vault top exists by itself, the below-ground structure having disintegrated or never having been constructed. The age of the brick and type of mortar generally indicate approximate construction date, but only a few vaults have inscriptions, thus most are impossible to date with precision. Burial in brick vaults occurred in the South by the early eighteenth century, and probably as early as the seventeenth century.[13] This type of monument tends to be located in Episcopalian churchyards and in family graveyards in eastern North Carolina during the eighteenth and nineteenth centuries, and no doubt only well-to-do families could afford its expense. For example, the family of William Dougal, who died in New Hanover County in 1837 leaving an estate of $54,000, paid almost $271 for the tombstone and brickwork on his grave, in contrast to the average $5 to $10 paid for most gravestones.[14]

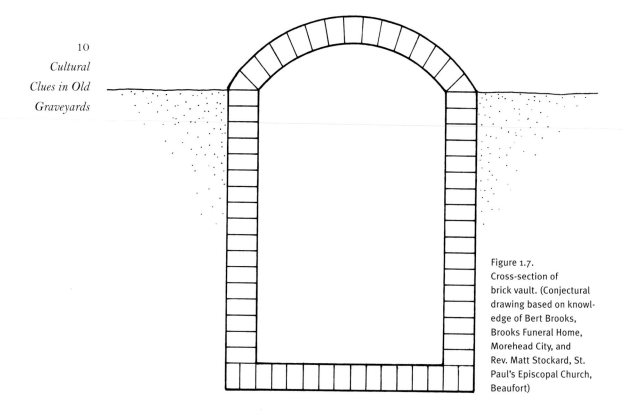

Figure 1.7.
Cross-section of
brick vault. (Conjectural
drawing based on knowl-
edge of Bert Brooks,
Brooks Funeral Home,
Morehead City, and
Rev. Matt Stockard, St.
Paul's Episcopal Church,
Beaufort)

Masons built vaulted brick graves primarily in coastal areas with high water tables, although a few are found as far inland as Cumberland County. There are slight variations in form and construction. Beaufort's Old Burying Ground contains the largest concentration in the state. Row after row of arched and gabled brick vaults, many flanked by head and footstones, crowd this cemetery. Cross Creek Cemetery in Fayetteville contains arched, stuccoed vaults, sometimes enclosing a single grave and sometimes multiple graves. For example, W. H. Tomlinson Sr. (d. 1885) was buried in one of two arched, stuccoed brick vaults attached end to end, with rectangular partitions, each approximately six feet long.

Vaults and gravehouses apparently represent the last vestige of several types of medieval British monuments. The hogback, or coped stone, is a stone mound constructed of two slabs that curve at the ends and meet in a single seam down the spine. The head, foot, and bodystone is a body-shaped stone mound abutted by a head and footstone. The Romanesque shrine-tomb, a gabled stone enclosure for a single burial, is visually even more similar to gravehouses (Fig. 1.8).[15]

A vault large enough to contain multiple burials, even an entire family, was often called a tomb. It follows the same form as the individual vault, but is often submerged wholly or partly in the earth, with walls and a roof. Burial in tombs was a tradition wealthy colonists no doubt brought from Great Britain.[16] In North Carolina, family tombs were used in the eighteenth and nineteenth centuries. The earliest mention of a tomb in North Carolina is that of the deputy royal governor of the Albemarle, Thomas Harvey Sr., a native of Warwickshire, England, who died in

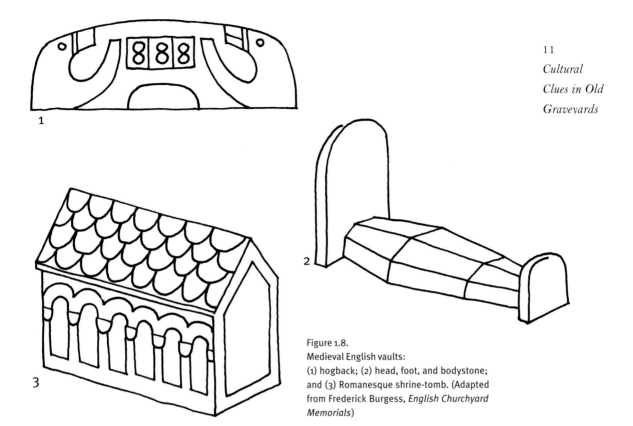

Figure 1.8.
Medieval English vaults:
(1) hogback; (2) head, foot, and bodystone;
and (3) Romanesque shrine-tomb. (Adapted
from Frederick Burgess, *English Churchyard
Memorials*)

1699 and was buried at the family cemetery on Harvey's Neck in Perquimans County, which has since been inundated by the waters of the Albemarle Sound.[17] Most of the other tombs that were located in plantation graveyards have been destroyed, as have the ancestral homes themselves. On the Upper Cape Fear River, Bladen and Cumberland Counties contain several nineteenth-century family tombs: the Robeson Tomb in the Robeson Graveyard near Tar Heel in Bladen County, the Campbell-Mallett Tomb five miles north of Fayetteville on the west bank of the river, in Cumberland County, and the Kelly Tomb on the west bank of the Cape Fear River near Rockfish Creek.[18] The last was an underground tomb built in the 1840s for John Kelly, a wealthy Irish Catholic immigrant. The entrance is a well-built brick segmental arch, surrounded by a massive wall of roughly quarried red sandstone blocks. The Boone Tomb, a large stuccoed brick structure apparently built around 1850, stands at Cross Creek Cemetery in Fayetteville. Finished with stepped ends, the building is 6 feet high, 13 feet long, and about 10 feet wide. The west end contains a cast-iron door and three marble plaques; the earliest commemorates the Reverend William English Boone (1830–1858) (Fig. 1.9). A stuccoed vault with stepped ends and a marble plaque in the west end covers the grave of Mary Julia Bell (1874–1884) beside the Boone Tomb. Use of the family tomb, generally termed a mausoleum, has continued into the twentieth century among wealthy families in the state.

Figure 1.9.
Boone Tomb,
ca. 1858, and
Bell Vault,
1884, Cross
Creek
Cemetery,
Fayetteville.

HEADSTONES AND FOOTSTONES

The slender headstone—whether of slate, sandstone, schist, or marble and almost always paired with a footstone—constitutes the dominant type of marker surviving in early North Carolina cemeteries. Eighteenth-century versions range from 17 to 23 inches wide and 27 to 48 inches high; nineteenth-century ones are 20 to 31 inches wide and 23 to 59 inches high. Thicknesses range between 1¾ and 4 inches for both these periods. Thomas Harvey Jr.'s 1729 headstone in the family graveyard on Harvey's Neck in Perquimans County is the earliest dated example, and it contains a coat-of-arms, a continuation of the British tradition of identifying graves with the family crest that is rare in North Carolina.[19]

Headstone shapes evolved slowly (Fig. 1.10). Until the 1840s, headstones generally had a baroque shape, influenced by the voluptuous curves of European designs of the seventeenth and eighteenth centuries. The top, known as the tympanum, was curved either into a semicircle or into a combination of inward- and outward-curving shapes with a central finial and flanking caps. The tympanum afforded a prominent location for carved symbols or ornate calligraphy. The discoid, a vernacular variation of this, had a circular tympanum and square shoulders that resembled a schematized human head and torso. By the 1820s the neoclassical precepts in architectural design led to simple, bold shapes—the rectangle, the segmental arch, and the pointed arch.

Headstones and footstones were a comparatively new type of grave marker in the early eighteenth century, but caught on quickly. In Virginia, the oldest-known headstone is a limestone marker with a death date of 1651, in Surry County, which

1

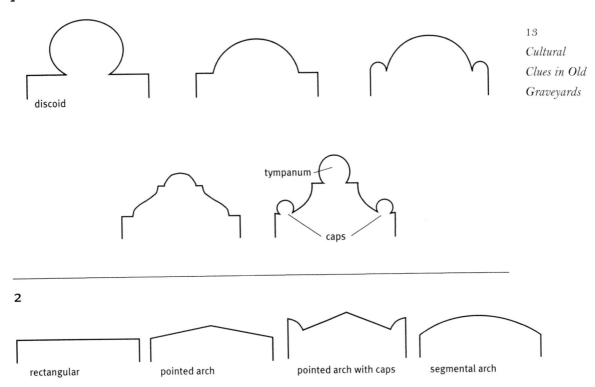

2

Figure 1.10.
Headstone
shapes in
North
Carolina,
eighteenth
through
twentieth
centuries:
(1)
Baroque
(eighteenth
to early
nineteenth
centuries);
(2)
Neoclassical
Revival
(nineteenth
to early
twentieth
centuries).

was probably imported from England. A vein of sandstone on Aquia Creek in Stafford County, Virginia, provided stone for local craftsmen who made headstones in the late seventeenth and early eighteenth centuries, but after 1750 many of Virginia's headstones came from New England.[20] New England stonecutters established their craft in the second half of the seventeenth century, and were frequently multiskilled artisans, often undertaking carpentry, masonry, cabinetwork, or even shoemaking or merchant seamanship. By the 1730s some were well established and specialized in gravestones.[21]

Head and foot stones began to appear in sizable numbers in the 1750s and 1760s along the North Carolina coast. Sailing vessels delivered these stones to wealthy clients from stonecutters' workshops located along the eastern seaboard. In the eighteenth century, eastern North Carolinians imported stones from Connecticut, Rhode Island, Massachusetts, New York, and New Jersey, and from Philadelphia, Baltimore, and Charleston by the early nineteenth century. Urban cemeteries in the early port towns of Edenton, New Bern, Beaufort, and Wilmington contain groups of eighteenth-century headstones.

In western North Carolina, imported headstones are far less common because transportation networks were less developed. Here, from 1770 onward, an individual who could afford to purchase a tombstone was more likely to patronize a local stonecutter. The resulting headstones are generally roughly shaped markers in the eighteenth century. Those from the nineteenth century are often quite refined.

Figure 1.11. Box-tomb of Col. Wilson Reed, d. 1860, Hertford Town Cemetery, Perquimans County. Signed "T. D. Couper, Norfolk."

LEDGERS, BOX-TOMBS, AND TOMB-TABLES

The ledger is a thin horizontal stone slab covering the entire grave and supported on a low masonry base. If the ledger rests on a high, solid base of brick or stone, it is a box-tomb. If it rests on stone corner posts it is a tomb-table, the most elegant variation of this type. Most North Carolina box-tombs are set on brick bases. Tomb-tables occur more rarely than box-tombs because they required fine stonecutting skills to shape the delicate supports and were thus more expensive. Native stone did not lend itself to cutting slabs of ledger size, and most of the examples in North Carolina were likely imported. Eighteenth-century ledgers are almost exclusively of slate and sandstone, while nineteenth-century ones are almost invariably of marble. Until the early nineteenth century, ledgers generally have a refined molded border; after this date they are plain. The earliest dated ledgers in the state are the 1704 and 1705 "Governors Stones" at St. Paul's Episcopal Churchyard, Edenton, but appreciable numbers of them did not appear until the late eighteenth century.

Like other gravemarkers, the ledger had a long history. In medieval England, where it was termed a grave slab, the ledger had been the preferred gravemarker of the upper classes. These slabs, often with an effigy of the deceased and an elaborate epitaph carved into the surface, were laid into the church floor over the graves of royalty, knights, and other high-born individuals throughout the Middle Ages and Renaissance. As churches became overcrowded, and as a middle class prosperous enough to purchase gravestones began to mark its graves in the burying grounds around the churches during the post-Reformation period of the latter sixteenth century, ledgers became a prominent form of gravestone in churchyards.[22]

The North Carolina elite's preference for ledgers, box-tombs, or tomb-tables, undoubtedly a continuation of English tradition, explains why such monuments are numerous in plantation graveyards during the colonial and antebellum period. These largely disappeared after the Civil War, superseded by newly fashionable types of monuments. One reason for their popularity was that the surface, generally 36 inches wide by 72 inches long, provided a large expanse for lengthy inscriptions that extolled the family connections and personal virtue of the deceased. A distinguished group of antebellum box-tombs with granite bases, probably from the state capitol quarry, stand in the Raleigh City Cemetery. Stonecutter T. D. Couper of Norfolk executed one of the most splendid box-tombs in the state for Col. Wilson Reed (d. 1860), in the Hertford Town Cemetery. The paneled marble base contains carved classical wreaths, and the ledger is a marble facsimile of a wooden coffin, with such realistic details as screws and handles (Fig. 1.11). An inscribed marble obelisk stands adjacent.

OBELISKS AND PEDESTAL-TOMBS

Outgrowths of the neoclassical movement, these imposing upright markers represent the most elite type of monument in nineteenth-century North Carolina cemeteries. The obelisk consists of a column or shaft set upon a base; the pedestal-tomb consists of a high base with an urn. Both types appeared in the early nineteenth century.

Inscriptions and Epitaphs

The endlessly varied shapes of the letters and numbers that make up North Carolina inscriptions contribute to the visual impact of every monument. By the seventeenth century, in England, the Roman alphabet, with a mixture of upper and lowercase lettering, using the classical norm of spacing and proportions, became standard on gravestones, and later became the ideal to which all North Carolina stonecarvers aspired. Earlier monuments were often inscribed in Latin or a mixture of Latin and the local vernacular. Eighteenth- and early-nineteenth-century carvers often continued the medieval tradition of separating words with dots and scoring between each line. A vast array of lettering styles distinguishes North Carolina gravestones. The comparative polish of the lettering, the accuracy of spelling, grammatical correctness, and arrangement of the information on the stone indicate the educational background of the stonecutter. Most part-time carvers lacked both the tools and the training to cut anything other than a minimal amount of information, generally only the name of the deceased and the death date, in an uppercase script. Some backcountry and presumably self-taught carvers even achieved lettering of pleasing, often elegant proportion in the nineteenth century. They may have used writing manuals containing samples of lettering styles, but the majority probably used the cemetery, where lettering samples could be studied and emulated, as their classroom. The handsome Gothic lettering on numerous early German American stones suggests that German American artisans needed only to study *Fraktur* certificates commemorating births, deaths, and marriages. Such *Frakturs* contained ornate lettering that was produced by community artists or printed by commercial printers.

Commercial stonecutters, such as Ebenezer Price of New Jersey in the late eighteenth century and John Caveny of South Carolina in the early nineteenth century, signed their stones with the title "engraver" to indicate their training as metal-engravers in addition to stonecarvers. Their inscriptions possess a crisp elegance not often achieved by traditional stonecutters. Most inscriptions are modestly competent exercises in Roman lettering, and few American carvers indulged in the calligraphic excesses of many of the English nineteenth-century carvers, combining different lettering styles and flourishes on a single stone. Scottish-born and trained master-stonecutter George Lauder's essays in combinations of ornamental lettering styles on North Carolina stones of the 1830s to 1850s reflect the general nineteenth-century fascination with stylistic richness (Fig. 1.12).

Epitaphs, short poems, or sentiments beneath inscriptions generally appear only on commercial stones and on stones carved by the most competent backcountry stonecutters. The epitaphs are wide ranging and appear on the markers in English, Scottish, German, and African American cemeteries; they are drawn from literature, religious theology, popular music, and community beliefs.

The Identification of Stonecutters

Ninety-nine percent of all gravestones are unsigned, so most artisans are anonymous. The few signatures that do exist are often obscured by dirt and vegetation, because most stonecutters signed their work in the lower right-hand corner of the headstone. Because stonecutters spent their careers in the same location, their work was so well known as to need no advertisement. When a stonecutter shipped a marker to a distant location, he would sometimes sign it as a method of advertisement (Fig. 1.13).

The identity of some stonecutters can be gleaned from the estate files, sometimes called the probate files, kept by the county courts to document the dispersal of money from the estate of the deceased.[23] This often included itemized funeral and burial expenses, even a payment to a particular person for the gravestone. To say that a stone is probated means that such a record exists. Regrettably for scholars, many executors did not purchase a gravestone for many months or even years, long after the estate had been settled. Even if the marker was purchased before the estate was closed, often the executor's notation was too abbreviated, such as a terse

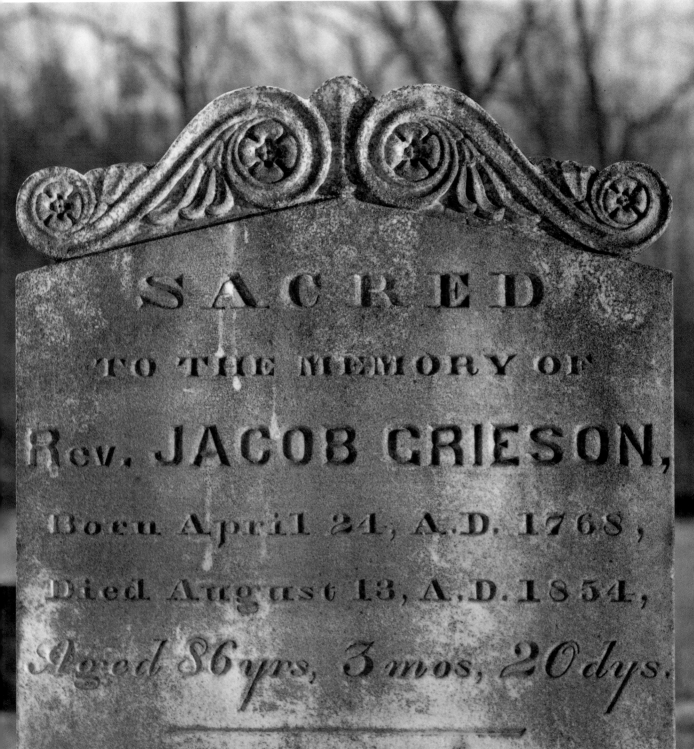

SACRED
TO THE MEMORY OF
Rev. JACOB GRIESON,
Born April 24, A.D. 1768,
Died August 13, A.D. 1854,
Aged 86 yrs, 3 mos, 20 dys.

Figure 1.12.
Inscription cut
by George Lauder
for gravestone of
Rev. Jacob Grieson,
d. 1854, Low's
Lutheran Churchyard,
Guilford County.

Figure 1.13.
Signature
of itinerant
stonecarver
Apollos
Sweetland
from head-
stone of
Mary Munn,
d. 1820,
Philippi
Presbyterian
Churchyard,
Hoke County.
(Photo by
M. Ruth Little;
Southern
Folklife
Collection,
Wilson Library,
University of
North Carolina
at Chapel Hill)

"$7.50 for gravestones." The estate of Elizabeth Ferguson, of Lincoln County, for example, contains a rare find: a receipt from stonecutter Alexander Brown of Columbia, South Carolina, stating that he had been paid $8.00 for "One sett of grave Stones" on 29 March 1847 by the executor.[24] A stonecutter's name that turns up in a receipt or an estate expense account was likely a commercial stonecutter. Local artisans often left no written records, and were as likely to have been paid in potatoes or eggs as in cash, operating in the barter economy outside the domain of court records.

Signed gravestones or gravestones equated with a cutter by an estate record make it possible to attribute other gravestones of similar form, date, style, and geographic location to this same artisan. Attribution is the act of placing a particular object or work of art into the production of a particular craftsman or artist based on the visual similarity of undocumented work to documented work. For example, the headstone of Mary Evans in Bath (Fig. 1.14) is attributed to William Codner of Boston because of its stylistic similarity to signed stones by Codner. Attribution is generally a reliable tool of identification for eighteenth- and nineteenth-century gravemarkers because artisans had distinctive and identifiable styles.

BACKDATING

Although an artisan typically produced a gravemarker a short time following the death of an individual, some markers were made much later, and backdating, the practice of making a marker for an individual who died a number of years earlier, confuses gravestone research that is based solely on the death dates. This practice is more common in some areas of North Carolina than in others. Approximately one-quarter of the twentieth-century gravestones of concrete, marble, and granite in Cumberland County, in eastern North Carolina, for example, are backdated, yet less than a tenth of the markers in the Piedmont appear to be. Backdating generally occurred either because a family delayed ordering a gravemarker, or because a family ordered a replacement for the original marker. Gravemarkers were often ordered in groups, after the deaths of several family members over a period of years. Parents were often preoccupied with raising their family and did not have time or could not afford to mark the graves of children who died young until many years later. Graves of the parents themselves sometimes did not receive permanent markers until the children grew up and purchased monuments fitting to their memory. Most backdating is due to economic change or to the advent of a new artisan into an area.

Figure 1.14.
Portrait
tympanum
of Mary Evans
headstone,
d. 1758, Palmer-
Marsh Grave-
yard, Bath.
Artist Linda
Reeves, 1977.
The stone is
attributed to
stonecutter
William Codner,
Boston.
(North Carolina
Division of
Archives and
History)

Sometimes backdating seems to be the result of the appearance of a gravemarker artisan in an area that formerly had no such craftsman. About 1850, Duncan Mc-Neill commissioned a stonecutter to carve a commemorative monument at Old Bluff Presbyterian Churchyard in Cumberland County for his father, the senior Duncan McNeill, who died in 1791. McNeill's original marker may have been a fieldstone or a wooden marker, but the current marker is a marble headstone of refined craftsmanship. Based on the strong resemblance of the McNeill monument to signed stones, the monument is attributed to Fayetteville stonecutter George Lauder, who established his marble yard in 1845.

Many rural families could not afford a gravestone during the hard years of the late nineteenth century, and by the early 1900s there was a large pent-up demand. When inexpensive mass-produced concrete markers became available during the 1930s, families bought many of them to mark old graves. In the 1970s, when Joseph Bass began to manufacture concrete headstones in a backyard workshop in east Cumberland County, most of his original orders were for old graves.[25]

Stonecutting Tools

The types of tools needed to quarry, shape, and inscribe stone varied with the type of stone and were generally dependent upon its hardness. Slate, marble, and granite are hard stones that required specialized axes, hammers, points, chisels, and saws. The tools used by marble cutter William O. Wolfe at the height of the monument era, the late nineteenth and early twentieth centuries, were virtually identical to early stonecutters' tools, since the technology had not changed (Fig. 1.15). By contrast, soapstone, a form of schist with a high talc content that is quite soft and easily worked when freshly quarried, was the most common type of local stone carved into gravestones in North Carolina. Soapstone could be cut with common woodworking tools that were in many a cabinetmaker's tool collection: iron

Figure 1.15.
W. O. Wolfe's turn-of-the-century stonecutting tools,
Thomas Wolfe Memorial, Asheville. Wolfe's saws, mallets,
picks, hatchets, calipers, and chisels represent standard
stonecutting tools used throughout the nineteenth century.
(Photo courtesy of James W. Clarke Jr., Department
of English, North Carolina State University)

wedges, for extracting blocks at the quarry; a crosscut saw, for sawing it into thin slabs; molding planes, augers, and a compass saw for finishing and decorating the stones; and chisels to form the lettering.

Symbolism

Gravemarkers are a logical repository for symbolism because they commemorate the life of an individual. Since ancient times such markers have contained images representative of the life and afterlife of the interred. The symbols used give powerful cultural clues about the culture of the region where the stone was made, the spiritual beliefs of the artisan, or the beliefs of the client who ordered the marker (Fig. 1.16). Yet few historic gravemarkers in North Carolina contain symbols. The

Figure 1.16.
Symbols from English culture, German culture, and popular culture on North Carolina gravestones
to the mid-nineteenth century.
English culture: (1) skull and crossbones (Sarah Brunlow, d. 1770, Cross Creek Cemetery, Fayetteville);
(2) winged death's head (Morris Nichols, d. 1796, Nixon-Foy Graveyard, New Hanover County); (3) winged-soul head
or soul effigy (Mary Walker, d. 1763, St. Paul's Edenton); (4) coat-of-arms (Robert Campbell, d. 1975, Steele Creek Presbyterian
Church, Mecklenburg County).
German culture: (5) heart (footstone of Peter Lopp, d. 1827, Pilgrim Church, Davidson County); (6) fylfot cross or swastica
(Daniel Wagoner, d. 1827, Bethany Lutheran and Reformed Church, Davidson County); (7) sunburst (Susannah Reichard,
d. 1846, Emanuel Church, Davidson County); (8) tree-of-life (David Reinhardt, d. 1861, Trinity Lutheran Church, Lincoln County);
(9) compass star (unidentified headstone, n.d., Old Shiloh Lutheran Church, Forsyth County); (10) tulip (Elisabeth Bodenhamer,
d. 1824, Abbott's Creek Church, Davidson County.
Popular culture: (11) urn and willow (Jane Munroe, d. 1826, McIntyre Graveyard, Cumberland County).

reason is simple: the extra effort required for an artisan to add a pictorial image in addition to the minimal necessary name and death date either made the project too difficult for an inexperienced artisan or too expensive if the family hired a commercial artisan. Yet another impediment to symbolism was the form and material of the marker. One less-obvious explanation is that the absence of symbols might itself symbolize a certain antimaterialism or even iconoclastic view of life and death. The simple Moravian markers stand in stark contrast to other decorative Moravian crafts, such as pottery, and convey a message in their plainness.

SYMBOLS FROM ENGLISH TRADITIONS

Eighteenth-century headstones imported to North Carolina from New England and the mid-Atlantic states possess a variety of types of emblems representing, initially, the mortal body and later the immortal soul. Scholars of New England stones interpret these images as representations of Christian expectations of resurrection, and their presence is a link to British culture. The grim death's head, or skull, so common in early New England cemeteries, is rare in North Carolina graveyards because the motif had lost favor by the second half of the eighteenth century when headstones became numerous in North Carolina's coastal cemeteries. Likewise, the grim skull-and-crossbones emblem occurs rarely in North Carolina. The headstone of Sarah Brunlow (d. 1770) at Cross Creek Cemetery, Fayetteville, contains one of the few examples of this symbol in the state. The winged death's head symbolizing the hope of resurrection is more common. The headstone of Morris Nichols (d. 1796), in the Nixon-Foy Family Graveyard, New Hanover County, contains a prominent winged death's head. The winged soul, in which the skull has evolved into a human face, symbolic of a stronger belief in eternal life, represents the highest stage of this soul emblem in New England funerary sculpture. The headstone of Mary Walker (d. 1763), St. Paul's Churchyard, Edenton, displays a realistically sculpted winged soul head.

The importation of these carved images into North Carolina, whose Anglicans (later Episcopalians), Presbyterians, and other major denominations held almost no theological beliefs in common with New England's Puritans, Unitarians, and other denominations, invalidates the design's meaning. It might be possible in New England to interpret the theology of the deceased through the symbol on his gravestone, and to label a Puritan as progressive because he is commemorated by a soul figure rather than a death's head. But it is likely that the person who ordered Morris Nichol's grim winged death's-head stone late in the eighteenth century had no substantively different belief in resurrection than the person who ordered Margaret Davieson's more optimistic mid-eighteenth-century winged-soul stone. The buyer probably simply ordered a generic stone with an image, perhaps a "soul" stone, and whether it arrived as a winged skull or a winged angel head was determined by the geographic location and up-to-dateness of the stonecutter who shipped it.

Coats-of-arms, or family heraldry, rarely appear on North Carolina gravestones. The aristocratic continuity that would be expected in seventeenth- and early-eighteenth-century colonial settlement, which came largely from the mid-Atlantic region, Virginia, and directly from Great Britain, did not include a widespread use of heraldic gravestones. In the Albemarle region there are a few from the early eighteenth century. In the late eighteenth century in central North Carolina, the Scots-Irish Bigham family created customized coats-of-arms representing the occupations and patriotic spirit of the deceased, in the spirit of trade guilds, rather than demonstrating high status and an ancestral pedigree.

Only a handful of portrait headstones exist in North Carolina. It is likely that, as with coats-of-arms, the taste for such expensive, customized monuments was absent in the state. Such carved images were popular among upper-class clients in New England and in South Carolina in the late eighteenth century. In North Carolina, one of the few is the portrait stone of Mary Evans (d. 1758) at the Palmer-Marsh Family Graveyard, Bath. Portrait stones generally reflect English culture, but Scots-Irish stonecutter Hugh Kelsey cut a profile portrait on one of his late-eighteenth-century North Carolina headstones for James Blear, a Presbyterian buried in the Piedmont.

SYMBOLS FROM GERMANIC TRADITIONS

The Germans, unlike the English, did not reserve certain symbols for use only in the graveyard, but decorated their gravestones with the same symbols for love, peace, plenty, and everlasting life that they used on all of the objects with which they came into contact every day.[26] The dual symbolic and decorative functions were inseparable in the arts of the German Americans. As with any image that is suffused so deeply into the everyday existence of a population, the meaning of any of the symbols on German American artifacts is both self-evident and inscrutable. All can be traced backward through the medieval period to the Near East, and exist in some form in the decorative arts of every early culture. The peculiar forms assumed by these symbols in Germany, Austria, and Switzerland are the predecessors of German American symbolism.[27] The only documented example of a human image on a German gravestone in this state is the schematic face carved into the finial of a soapstone headstone, dated 1842, in a family graveyard in Davidson County.

In German areas of settlement in North Carolina, stonecutters drew gravestone symbols from abstract or naturalistic rather than anthropomorphic imagery. Traditional Pennsylvania German folk motifs—heart, fylfot cross, sunburst, tree-of-life, compass star, and tulip—appear on gravestones in the Piedmont from the late eighteenth to the mid-nineteenth century.[28] The heart, symbolizing human affection and love, has a distinctive two-lobed turnip shape, the result of relying on a compass to draw it. The fylfot, variously interpreted as symbolizing a cross, a sun, and eternity, also occurs on painted furniture, metalwork designs on pie safes, and in quilts of traditional German design in North Carolina. The sunburst, symbolizing life and renewal, occurs in many different forms but most often as a half- or quarter-sun. The tree-of-life, another ancient symbol, alludes to the cycle of birth, growth, decay, death, and rebirth, and on gravestones it is often shown growing out of an urn or vase that supposedly contains the waters of eternal life, or the heart. The two lowest branches are often drooping. As with other symbols of German folk art, the tree-of-life has incredible variety from one region and one stone-cutter to another. On Catawba Valley gravestones, the tree-of-life represents the particular life span of an individual, from seedlings for infants to many-branched trees for the elderly. Some Davidson County stones contain an unusual form of the symbol—an evergreen tree. The compass star (so named because it was produced with the use of a compass), always has points in even multiples—usually six or twelve—and is a generalized talisman. The tulip, which occurs occasionally on Piedmont stones, was introduced into Europe from the East in the sixteenth and seventeenth centuries. By the eighteenth century, the tulip was one of the most ubiquitous motifs in folk art. Because of its simple contour, it lent itself readily to craft usage. It supplanted and often obscured earlier forms of the tree-of-life. Among its meanings are life, love, and immortality.

Other geometric and abstract designs formed by the use of the ruler and compass, such as patterns of squares, rectangles, hexagons, circles, spirals, and interlaces, abound on gravestones as well as every other decorated artifact used by the Germans. Many symbols are executed in such abstract forms on North Carolina gravestones that they cease to convey a specific meaning and become simply decoration.

SYMBOLS FROM SCOTS-IRISH TRADITIONS

Scots-Irish stonecutters in the Piedmont developed a distinct vocabulary using their own traditional symbols, diverse decorative motifs from the British and German tradition, as well as new and distinctly "American" symbols. Traditional symbols they often combined to achieve highly eclectic headstone designs include the hourglass, celestial symbols, the dove-of-promise (from the biblical story of the flood, in which a dove bears a branch to Noah as proof that the waters have receded), fraternal emblems, patriotic motifs, and coats-of-arms. The headstone of Robert Bigham (d. 1791) at Steele Creek Presbyterian Churchyard, Charlotte, attributed to the Scots-Irish workshop of the Bigham family, contains a coat-of-arms with a shield bearing the thirteen stars representing the American colonies and the motto "ARMA LIBERTATIS," an obvious reference to the newly created flag of the United States.[29]

SYMBOLS FROM NEOCLASSICAL AND
ROMANTIC REVIVAL MOVEMENTS

In the late eighteenth century, the neoclassical revival style in the arts swept away both the overt English soul imagery and the German and Scots-Irish symbolism and replaced them with classical motifs and images of mourning, blurring cultural distinctions in graveyards. The neoclassical movement brought the vogue of mourning art, which included embroidery, silk, and velvet mourning pictures, and mourning jewelry, scarves, and decorated pottery.[30] The widely popular urn-and-willow motif, which appeared on all types of decorative arts, consisted of a mourning woman leaning on a funeral urn, with an overhanging weeping willow tree. On North Carolina stones either the urn or the willow was generally used separately, and the female mourner appears only rarely. Urn-and-willow imagery, executed first in New England slate and later in marble, appeared in eastern North Carolina graveyards by about 1800 and was being incorporated into traditional German headstones in the Piedmont by the 1830s. A good example of the former is the elegantly thin slate headstone of Capt. Ephraim Symonds (d. 1808) of Salem, Massachusetts, who is buried at St. James Churchyard, Wilmington. The imported stone contains an urn-and-willow tympanum and delicately fluted side borders. Another eastern example is the marble headstone of John Maccoll (d. 1819), at Longstreet Presbyterian Churchyard, Hoke County, with its urn tympanum with flanking fan motifs. The stone is signed by itinerant Connecticut carver Apollos Sweetland. An example of the latter is the headstone of Allen Delane (d. 1846), at Old White Church, Lincolnton, containing a willow tree surrounded by German compass stars.

Beginning in the mid-nineteenth century, a succession of exotic stylistic revivals influenced gravestone imagery. As elsewhere, commercial stonecutters in North Carolina made some use of Gothic Revival imagery, particularly the use of the Gothic arch itself for the overall headstone. This was followed at the turn of the century by an explosion of religious and secular symbolism that was carried by the expanding commercial monument industry along railroad lines and by the accompanying design catalogs that big marble and granite companies supplied. These marble monuments were often decorated with floral motifs such as roses; biblical imagery such as gates of heaven; clasped hands and lambs; and emblems of victory such as crowns and wreaths. At this point North Carolina gravestones lost their regionality and cultural distinctiveness, and, in this book, the exotic imagery will not be examined.

Design Sources

Gravestones produced by commercial shops as well as those produced by part-time carvers had particular shapes during each historical period. The standardized imagery on early tombstones indicate that the stonecutters were drawing some motifs from widely disseminated printed materials such as religious, patriotic, and fraternal books. In the early eighteenth century, no gravestone design patternbooks existed, so the death's-head and winged-soul imagery on stones imported from New England are probably reflective of shop traditions. The stonecutters copied traditional emblems from one generation to another and one workshop to another, modifying it upon occasion to incorporate refinements gleaned from printed material such as broadsides, engraved funeral invitations, book woodcuts, and engravings that used such death emblems as the hourglass, gravediggers' tools, the grim reaper, and other symbols of mortality (Fig. 1.17).

Nineteenth-century commercial stonecutters in North Carolina had access to neoclassical imagery through patternbooks, mourning pictures and other materials, and had no need of monument design catalogs to produce simple headstones (Fig. 1.18). In the North Carolina Piedmont, backcountry stonecutters often used this imagery freely, combining formal and folk symbols. A carver working in Lincoln County in the 1830s added a sun to the mourning scene on a headstone.

Figure 1.17.
Funeral invitation of
Rebekkah Sewall, d. 1710, Boston.
(Reproduced courtesy the
Trustees of the Boston Public
Library)

Figure 1.18.
Advertisement for marble yard
of James Foster in Fayetteville.
(From *North Carolinian*, May 1839)

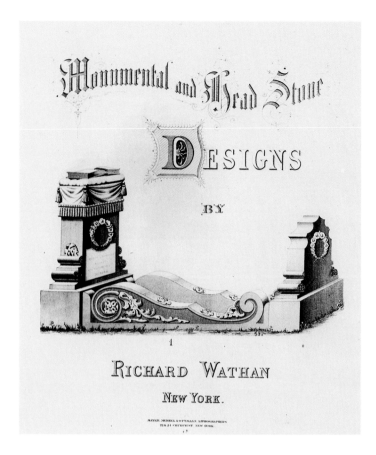

The first funerary monument catalogs available were produced in England in the eighteenth century. The designs in these were drawn by architects and aimed at producing elaborate monuments, such as memorial wall tablets and floor tombs, for wealthy British families, inside churches. Some of these catalogs found their way into American libraries, but were of limited benefit to most American stone-cutters because the catalog designs were for large expensive monuments, such as obelisks, rather than the simple headstones that most clients could afford.[31]

By the mid-nineteenth century, architects in Boston, Philadelphia, and New York began to produce funerary monument catalogs. These featured elegant Gothic and Renaissance Revival tombs, obelisks, and large headstones.[32] One such monument catalog was *Monumental and Head Stone Designs*, published in New York in 1875, which contains scaled elevations, sections, and enlarged details that enable a stone carver to create a full-size monument from the drawings (Fig. 1.19). Such catalogs caused the appearance of new monument shapes, such as obelisks and bedstead monuments—with a footstone and side rails imitating the form of a bed—in North Carolina cemeteries.

By the early twentieth century such marble-cutting firms as the Vermont Marble Company of Proctor, Vermont, and Nichols & Company of Chicago published catalogs, which instructed stonecutters in how to cut monuments in a wide variety of sizes and finish, and published trade catalogs with price lists of precut monuments.[33] Even Sears & Roebuck in Chicago entered the mail-order monument market, publishing in 1902 a special tombstone catalog containing designs for small tombstones and monuments of simple, popular designs affordable to a family of

Figure 1.19. Cover from *Monumental and Head Stone Designs*, by Richard Wathan, New York, 1875. (Reproduced courtesy the Winterthur Library, Printed Book and Periodical Collection)

OUR SPECIAL $20.70 HANDSOMELY ORNA-
MENTED TOMBSTONE.

Delivered on the Cars at Our Quarry and Marble Works in Vermont.

The illustration will give you some idea of the immense amount of artistic work necessary to produce a tombstone of such beauty and quiet elegance.

AT $20.70 we represent a saving to you of from $30.00 to $35.00, even after you have paid the low rate of freight, fully explained on page 4. $20.70 is the actual cost of material and labor, with but our one small profit added. Ordinary sunk inscription letters, 6 cents per letter; sunk verse letters, 2½ cents per letter; 2-inch letters, raised ⅛ inch in panel, 15 cents per letter, and other sizes in proportion. See pages 60 and 61 for some popular verse inscriptions.

This tombstone is quarried from the Acme Blue Marble Company's quarry, cut and polished by expert artisans, traced and carved by artists in their line of work, and the result is the beautiful and imposing monument shown in the illustration. The dimensions of this monument are as follows: Bottom base, 1 foot 10 inches by 1 foot 4 inches by 10 inches. Upper base, 1 foot 6 inches by 1 foot by 8 inches. Tablet, 1 foot 10 inches by 1 foot 2 inches by 8 inches. Total height over all, 3 feet 4 inches. Weight, 729 pounds.

Do not be deceived by any attempt on the part of local dealers to claim that our goods are a cheap grade of material. See the back pages of this book for color illustrations of these beautiful marbles.

Do not be deceived when they tell you that the freight charges are so exorbitant that even though the price is low, the freight will make up for the difference.

Remember two things: The rate of freight is very low on marble. The work is the finest in America.

AT REST

No. 22P770 Price, Acme Blue Dark Vein. $20.70
No. 22P771 Price, White Acme Rutland Italian......................... 23.00
Foot stones, 6x2 inches, sand rubbed, each, 50c; foot stones, 8x3 inches, sand rubbed, each, 75c; corner posts, 4x4 inches, for cemetery lot, each, $1.00; corner posts, 6x6 inches, for cemetery lot, each, $1.65.
A small sample piece of marble in either of the above colors will be mailed on receipt of 10 cents.
GIVE US FOUR TO SIX WEEKS IN WHICH TO FINISH, LETTER AND SHIP.

Figure 1.20. The $20.70 "Special" from Sears & Roebuck, 1901 monument catalog. (Reproduced courtesy the Winterthur Library, Printed Book and Periodical Collection)

modest means.[34] Prices started at $4.99 for a small headstone, and for a $5.00 deposit Sears would ship any tombstone or monument to any address east of the Missouri River and north of Tennessee, with a money-back guarantee. All of Sears tombstones were cut from Acme Blue Marble at "our quarry and marble works in Vermont" (Fig. 1.20). Vermont was the center of the marble monument industry during this period, and Sears apparently had an arrangement with one of the Vermont marble works to fill orders at a lower price than would normally be charged in exchange for guaranteeing a certain volume of orders. No doubt Sears undercut local marble yards by selling monuments at a lower price. The form and decoration of the Sears monuments are found throughout North Carolina cemeteries on the turn-of-the-century monuments that have religious motifs, such as the heavenly gates, and floral motifs, such as a rose branch sandblasted in a flat, linear style. Whether these are Sears stones, or stones cut by local stonecutters using the same motifs copied from design catalogs supplied by the marble and granite companies, remains unknown.

Lost Sticks and Imported Stones

COASTAL PLAIN GRAVEYARDS AND MARKERS

Here lies the Remains of Morris Nichols, Son of John Nichols Sen.ʳ who died Oct.ʳ 1ˢᵗ 1796. in the 19ᵗʰ Year of his Age. He was a promising Youth, and his death was much regreted by all his friends, and more particularly by his Patron, Samuel Lowder, who does this in remembrance of him.

Coastal Plain graveyards are a world apart from the generally later Piedmont and mountain graveyards. Their wide variation in size and shape of stones, the dense vegetation that is encouraged by the same humid climate that causes the growth of lichens and mosses on stones, and tall iron fences create a moody, brooding atmosphere, the epitome of a scene from gothic novels of the nineteenth century. But the complete picture of eastern Carolina culture from the eighteenth and nineteenth centuries is largely absent from the cemeteries, for the sticks and brick gravemarkers are gone. Just as time has largely eliminated the architecture of poor whites and blacks, it has also eliminated the markers erected to preserve their memory. The ghostly anthropomorphic sticks in a clearing in the woods of Onslow County that form the Coston Cemetery come as close to the typical yet much smaller yeoman farmer or slave graveyard as can be found in the entire Coastal Plain (Fig. 2.1). The humble wooden markers and slightly more pretentious brick vaults marking the graves of the lower and middle classes survive in isolation amidst the more permanent stone markers, commemorating the affluent families who could commission such expensive items from out-of-state suppliers.

The Coastal Plain was settled largely by the British and the Africans, both of whom had distinctive cultures. The earliest organized churches were the Quakers and the Church of England, reorganized after the American Revolution as the Episcopal Church, and first settlements were at Bath, Edenton, and Brunswicktown in the early eighteenth century. Outside of the few towns, the economic units were the plantation and small farm, and cash came from crops and from water and forest-related occupations such as shipping, fisheries, lumber, turpentine, and tar. Towns were small and few, and more than 90 percent of the population was rural. Because of the widely dispersed population, poor roads, and few churches, burial tended to occur in family graveyards rather than in church and municipal cemeteries. This family emphasis reflects the isolated social life of an agrarian society with a poor transportation network.

Family graveyards have suffered much destruction because of changing land uses and the breakup of the farms and plantations. Natural attrition by the elements is perhaps more rapid in coastal North Carolina than in inland areas, primarily because of higher humidity but also because of violent sea storms and hurricanes. Many of the earliest plantations bordered the sounds and rivers, and as rising water levels inundated the low areas during the past two centuries, an inestimable number are now underwater. Most pre-nineteenth-century Anglo-American family graveyards in the Coastal Plain have been abandoned, destroyed, or moved. Colonial plantation graveyards at Mount Moseley Plantation (Horniblow's Point), Moses Point, Sandy Point, Eden Plantation, Belgray Plantation, and Cabarrus Plantation in Chowan County, containing some of the earliest dated gravestones in North Carolina with death dates of 1704, 1705, and 1722, were washing into the Albemarle Sound, and in 1888 the Edenton chapter of the Colonial Dames moved them to St. Paul's Episcopal Church, Edenton, and erected a plaque to identify these "Governor's Stones."[1] In Perquimans County, the Skinner and Blount

family stones dating from the eighteenth and early nineteenth centuries were moved from the family graveyard on Harvey's Neck to nearby Old Bethel Baptist Churchyard.[2]

In an area with no native stone, the mere possession of a gravestone during the colonial period was a status symbol. On a 1767 map, the name "Tombstone Landing" appears on Salmon Creek in present-day Bertie County on the plantation of Sir Nathaniel Duckenfield, settler from Cheshire, England (Fig. 2.2). Salmon Creek, which empties into the Chowan River and Albemarle Sound, bordered a number of distinguished plantations, and a ferry operated at the landing. The North Carolina General Assembly met at Duckenfield's plantation at one time. In the 1690s William Duckenfield, an ancestor of Duckenfield, had traveled to Virginia to pick up a "toome stone sent for to England to be laid on the body of Seth Sothell Esqr.," one of the Lords Proprietors of the colony and the last governor of the Albemarle region, who had died during the decade.[3] The whereabouts of this English tombstone is unknown, but it may be the monument for which the landing was named.

The plantation economy of North Carolina and active trade with England and

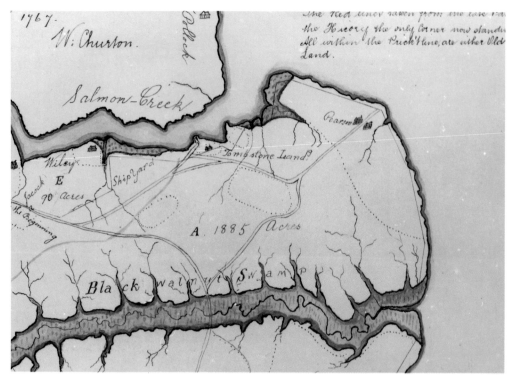

the New England and mid-Atlantic colonies encouraged the wealthiest residents to import stylish gravestones. Initially a few people ordered gravestones from England, either directly, or, in the case of the Sothel tombstone, through an intermediary.[4] Most of the "Governors' Stones" at St. Paul's, Edenton, and Mrs. Mary Quince's box-tomb in St. Philip's Churchyard, Brunswicktown, appear to be English imports. The vast majority of imported gravestones, however, came first from New England, later from the mid-Atlantic region, especially Philadelphia and New York City, and in the early nineteenth century from the southern ports of Charleston, South Carolina, Norfolk, Virginia, and Baltimore, Maryland. Eastern Carolina merchants in port cities such as Edenton and Wilmington and inland river market towns such as Fayetteville advertised in newspapers that they had just returned from a trip to the North, or had just received a shipment from the North, and that they "had in stock all sorts of crockery, china, glassware, cutlery, linsey-woolsey, looking glasses, and other items."[5] A well-to-do North Carolina family would place an order for a custom-engraved monument through such a local merchant, and it would be shipped along with other goods to the merchant.

Figure 2.2. Map of Sir Nathaniel Duckenfield Plantation, Bertie County, 1767, showing Tombstone Landing. (North Carolina Division of Archives and History)

Anglo-American Graveyards

About the mid-eighteenth century, Church of England churchyards became central burying grounds for North Carolina families—town folk and farm folk alike—and most are full of imported gravestones. St. Paul's Churchyard in Edenton typifies Anglo-American graveyards in the Coastal Plain. It contains a tightly packed assortment of marble box-tombs, obelisks, ledgers, and headstones favored by wealthy merchants and planters prior to 1860 (Fig. 2.3). Primacy of the family is

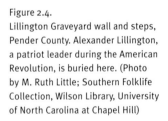

Figure 2.3.
St. Paul's Episcopal Churchyard,
Edenton, filled with box-tombs,
obelisks, and head and footstones.

Figure 2.4.
Lillington Graveyard wall and steps,
Pender County. Alexander Lillington,
a patriot leader during the American
Revolution, is buried here. (Photo
by M. Ruth Little; Southern Folklife
Collection, Wilson Library, University
of North Carolina at Chapel Hill)

evident in the layout of both church and municipal cemeteries in the Coastal Plain—graves are grouped by family in small plots often delineated with ornate brick or stone walls or cast-iron fences.

Anglo-American Tidewater graveyards often have picturesque landscaping, including cedar or other evergreen trees, hardwood trees, shrubs, and grassed lawns and walls. Private and public graveyards were often enclosed with walls of brick or, more rarely, of marl, a type of "shell rock," which was quarried in many coastal locations for buildings and structures. On the plantations, these walls often had no entrance gates; access was gained by steps that went over the wall and down into the enclosure (Fig. 2.4). The function of such gateless walls was apparently to keep animals from foraging around the graves. In addition to the Lillington Graveyard, two other walled examples are the graveyard of Rocky Run Plantation and the Pollock Graveyard, both in New Hanover County along the Northeast Cape Fear River.[6] The most beautiful marl cemetery wall in the state was built in 1854 around Cedar Grove Cemetery, the municipal burying ground of New Bern (Fig. 2.5).[7]

One of the first formally landscaped cemeteries in the state is Calvary Episcopal Churchyard in Tarboro, established in 1842 by the Reverend Joseph Blount Cheshire. Using Andrew Jackson Downing's *Treatise on Landscape Gardening* (1841) as a guide, Cheshire converted the swampy low ground around the church, which already had two or three clusters of graves enclosed with small fences, into an arbo-

Figure 2.5. Marl wall and gates constructed in 1854 for Cedar Grove Cemetery, New Bern.

retum. This enlarged graveyard included the entire churchyard, laid out a radiating pattern of walkways, in which Cheshire planted trees and shrubs of native and foreign stock. Seventeen years later, construction began on a Gothic Revival–style brick church, designed by architect William Percival in a picturesque mode, to complement the arboretum. The result is a church and yard that constitute one of the most sophisticated ensembles of landscape design in the state.[8]

African American Graveyards

Africans were brought as slaves to North Carolina until the early nineteenth century. Many reputed slave graveyards survive in North Carolina: these tend to have either undated and uninscribed fieldstones or no visible markers at all. They may have created gravemarkers and grave decoration out of materials at hand, generally impermanent, and this material culture has long since vanished. Wooden markers and decorative objects probably marked most slave graves in the Coastal Plain, and these have not survived the depredations of weather and insects.

The rare, commercially produced marble markers on graves of black slaves were undoubtedly purchased by their masters, and they are reflective of the burial tradition of the plantation owners, not the slave community. Such an intrusion of marble stones in a slave graveyard occurs at "In Home," the large Jonathan Evans Plantation on the Cape Fear River in Cumberland County. The slave graveyard stands adjacent to the family graveyard, and the only two marked slave graves, for Lucy and Uncle Harry, have small, plain marble headstones (Fig. 2.6). Evans had a reputation as a kindly man, and his monuments to these two slaves, erected at the end of his own life, certainly indicate his great affection for them. Yet the stones per-

haps speak more loudly of the slaves' status as property than of the ties of affection to their master. Evans had the stonecutter engrave the proprietary phrase "My own" above Lucy's given name, and she was not dignified with a last name. Perhaps no one knew the age of Harry, known as "Uncle," a familiar nickname for many elderly slaves, and so it was left blank.

White people continued to erect gravestones for favored servants long after the end of the Civil War. Wilson Swain Caldwell, a servant at the University of North

Carolina at Chapel Hill, died in 1891 and was buried in the university cemetery. Sixteen years later a sandstone obelisk carved in 1835 for the first president of the school, Joseph Caldwell, was replaced by a new monument, and the university staff had the obelisk moved to the center of the African American section of the cemetery and ordered a marble plaque inscribed to Wilson Caldwell, "who served the University faithfully," and inserted at its base. Dilsey Craig, a slave of the Phillips family of Chapel Hill, was memorialized sometime after her death with a polished granite headstone inscribed:

> Dilsey Craig
> 1802–1894
> 60 years a slave
> chiefly in the home of Dr. James Phillips
> whose grandchild erects this in grateful memory
> Well done good and faithful servant.
> Always remembered.

The particular grandchild mentioned in the inscription is unknown, for Dr. Phillips had many. Dilsey might have helped raise this child.[9]

Whether slaves were free to express themselves, even in death, by marking graves in their own way is an open question. Many decisions about burial were made by the master, including the location of the graveyard. Slaves would have likely preferred a graveyard far from that of the master's family at which they could practice their own customs without white surveillance. On some plantations, slaves may have had this freedom. The wife of a Confederate officer, who attended a slave funeral in Charlotte County, Virginia, in 1861 described her experience:

> We had a long warm walk behind hundreds of Negroes, following the rude coffin in slave procession through the woods, singing antiphonally as they went one of those strange, weird hymns not to be caught by any Anglo-Saxon voice. . . . Words of immortal comfort to the great throng of Negro mourners who caught it up, line after line, on an air of their own, full of tears and tenderness,—a strange, weird tune no white person's voice could ever follow.[10]

No antebellum graveyards of free blacks are known to exist in North Carolina, but a small group of antebellum tombstones in Greenwood Cemetery, the major cemetery for New Bern's blacks, represents this distinguished community, which included the largest number of free blacks of any town in North Carolina.[11] A dozen decorative headstones and footstones of sandstone and marble bear death dates from 1805 to 1859 and stand in two crowded rows. These were moved here from Cedar Grove Cemetery, New Bern's city burying ground, which had an African American section before Emancipation (Fig. 2.7).[12] Whether the black graves were moved voluntarily to the new segregated black cemetery or whether these individuals were evicted from their original places of interment remains a mystery.

The craftsmanship and epitaphs on most of the stones raise many questions about the lives and status of these individuals and of the families that erected them. Their elegant neoclassical designs indicate that some stones were ordered from the same New England, mid-Atlantic, or Charleston stonecutters patronized by the elite white community. These stones might have been saved because they were the finest stones in the African American section of Cedar Grove Cemetery.

The earliest headstone commemorates Eliza Johnson (d. 1805), aged thirty years. In 1816 when a sixty-year-old slave named Delia died, she received a headstone with this epitaph: "From her childhood an affectionate, faithful and invaluable servant in the family of Edward Graham." Sarah Rice (d. 1821), aged forty-five, is believed to have been a house slave of the family of Richard Dobbs Spaight, governor during the 1790s. A descendant claimed that the family freed her because of their affection for her.[13] The headstone of Robert Walker (d. 1846) aged twenty-six, was "erected by Charlotte his widow as a tribute of affection."

The tall marble headstone of John Cook, a Methodist Episcopal minister, contains the longest and most impressive epitaph:

> Here lies the remains
> of
> John Cook
> The Colored Preacher. He was a native
> of Africa and was brought to this
> country in the year 1805. He was
> converted and joined the Methodist E.
> Church at this place in 1818 and soon
> after became a Preacher in the Gospel.
> His deep and consistent piety secured
> unbounded confidence in his Christian
> character. Having spent his life in the
> service of God he died in holy triumph
> on the
> 24th of November 1856
> in the 65th year of his age
> This Monument was erected to
> his memory by his brethren and friends
> both white and colored, in token of
> their respect and Christian affection.
> "Soldier of Christ, well done
> Praise by thy new employ,
> And while eternal ages run
> Rest in thy Saviour's joy."

The placement of black cemeteries relative to white cemeteries mirrored the spatial relationship of black and white settlements, from the integration of slavery when blacks lived among whites, to the postbellum period when the races remained mutually dependent, to the strict segregation of the Jim Crow era. At Chapel Hill, in the graveyard for the University of North Carolina, established at the turn of the nineteenth century, one side was set aside for slaves, separated from the white section by a driveway and a stone wall. After emancipation, African

Americans continued to be buried there and in a newer adjacent section. The old Raleigh City Cemetery established in 1798 was a square divided into four quadrants, two for native whites, one for "strangers," and one for African Americans, slave and free. In both cemeteries the white planners created space within the overall plan for African Americans. When Raleigh had outgrown the old cemetery and established a picturesque suburban cemetery, Oakwood, in 1872, planners made no accommodation for black burials. Middle-class African Americans established their own cemetery, Mount Hope Cemetery at the opposite end of town, in the same year. In Wilmington, whites established the first picturesque suburban cemetery in North Carolina, named Oakdale, in 1855. Six years later the city's well-to-do black population created their own picturesque cemetery, Pine Forest Cemetery, on a site adjacent to Oakdale. In New Bern, Raleigh, and Wilmington, as whites moved out of the integrated old districts into segregated suburbs, and out of integrated cemeteries into segregated cemeteries, blacks were forced into separate neighborhoods and separate cemeteries.

Postbellum urban black communities are represented in cemeteries such as Greenwood Cemetery in New Bern, where marble and granite monuments reveal that many in New Bern's black community were well established and affluent during the latter 1800s. The grounds, which occupy about three square blocks, are bisected by a meandering dirt drive running the full length; some family plots are

Figure 2.7. African American antebellum gravestones, Greenwood Cemetery, New Bern.

Figure 2.8. Hank's Chapel American Methodist Episcopal Churchyard, New Hanover County. (Photo by M. Ruth Little; Southern Folklife Collection, Wilson Library, University of North Carolina at Chapel Hill)

edged with brick or granite curbing. But by far the majority of North Carolina's black population lived in rural and small-town areas, and the burial grounds they established contrast strikingly with urban black and white cemeteries. Traditional rural black cemeteries present a more informal, additive arrangement of family groups, with a high incidence of homemade concrete markers and creative reuse of found objects or commercially manufactured materials as gravemarkers. African Americans frequently located their graveyards in overgrown woods or fields, apparently a deliberate practice relating to traditional beliefs. Hank's Chapel American Methodist Episcopal Churchyard in New Hanover County, on the coast, typical of coastal black twentieth-century graveyards, is organized not by family plot but by individual grave, many of which are outlined by concrete blocks and plastic garden fencing (Fig. 2.8).

Vernacular Gravemarkers

WOODEN MARKERS

In both Anglo-American and African American graveyards in eastern North Carolina, vernacular gravemarkers memorialize people from all walks of life. Perhaps the most common type of gravemarkers were wooden markers, but in spite of their former ubiquity, few are left. A portion of a grave railing, a single board approximately twenty-four inches high, with a slot in the upper end, survives in the Nixon-Foy Graveyard in New Hanover County. Three other posts and four rails are gone.

Numerous simple extremely weathered wood head and footboards with a variety of shapes survive in burial grounds throughout the Coastal Plain, usually only one or two in a cemetery. Because few were inscribed, these gravemarkers give almost no clues to their date of manufacture, but the shapes provide a general guide. The earliest ones probably date from the nineteenth century and are small, thin slabs with gently curving tops, similar to the bold curves of baroque headstones popular in the late 1700s and early 1800s. The anthropomorphic discoid headboards are also early nineteenth century in origin, and sometimes the accompanying footboard is either rounded, squared off, or diamond shaped (Fig. 2.9).[14]

By the 1870s, headboard style had shifted to a picket-shaped board. Carrie Deaver's marker, 1876, is the earliest inscribed headboard known in North Carolina (Fig. 2.10). Probably from the same period are two wood headboards, one picket shaped, one round headed, at nearby Old Bluff Churchyard in Cumberland County,

Figure 2.9. Head and footboard, Coston Cemetery, Onslow County, nineteenth century. (Photo by J. Daniel Pezzoni, 1988; North Carolina Division of Archives and History)

which have square recesses with nail holes in the upper ends where plaques containing inscriptions were once attached.

The Coston Cemetery in Onslow County is a rare instance in which an entire rural cemetery of wooden head and footboards survives. There dozens of nearly identical slender discoid headboards stand with smaller picket-shaped footboards. (See Figure 2.1.) The remarkable uniformity of the gravemarkers suggests a once close-knit traditional community.

Figure 2.10. Headboard of Carrie Deaver, inscribed with her name and "Died Feb 11 1876," Hope Mills Cemetery, Cumberland County. (Photo by M. Ruth Little; Southern Folklife Collection, Wilson Library, University of North Carolina at Chapel Hill)

Gravehouses made of wood were once common in the coastal region, but the only remaining examples stand at New Hope Methodist Churchyard in Perquimans County. Some old-timers used the term "doghouses" to describe them.[15] One of these has "ELIZABETH NICHOLSON" (d. ca. 1913) inscribed on the gable end (Fig. 2.11). Beneath its dirt floor the coffin is buried in the earth. Historians of the Albemarle region recall that large numbers of these gravehouses, often of native cypress, survived until the mid-twentieth century. Gravehouses represent a particularly strange aspect of North Carolina's lost memorial traditions.

A gravemarking device unique to the Albemarle region is the use of ballast stones. These large, rounded rocks probably came from New England in the holds of sailing vessels, where they stabilized lightweight loads, in the eighteenth and early nineteenth centuries. During the sailing era when vessels plied the sounds and rivers and dumped their large, smooth rocks along the shore when loading the holds with North Carolina cargo, residents salvaged ballast stones for many uses.[16]

The Quaker population in Perquimans County, who were among the original settlers in the seventeenth and early eighteenth centuries, used ballast stone markers in the Little River Quaker burying ground. Both meeting house and cemetery have disappeared.[17] Ballast gravestones were recorded in the Hertford Town Cemetery in Hertford and in the Whitney Graveyard in Pasquotank County. With a few exceptions, most are unmarked (Fig. 2.12). Being readily portable, most have probably been appropriated for other uses, such as rock gardens, in recent years, but local historians recall their use as grave markers.

"Bricking the grave" is the most frequently found reference to marking a grave

Figure 2.13.
Early-
nineteenth-
century
vaulted brick
graves,
St. James
Episcopal
Churchyard,
Wilmington.

in eighteenth- and early-nineteenth-century Perquimans County estate records and was a frequent method of burial in eastern North Carolina from the initial period of brick making in the late seventeenth century until the early twentieth century.[18] A number of brick grave vaults, either for individual burials or multiple burials, still exist in Coastal Plain graveyards. Many sections of eastern North Carolina have low elevation with a high ground-water level, and this type of grave structure protected the body. Although made of native clay, the craftsmanship necessary to make bricks and construct burial vaults indicates that these represented a burial tradition popular among the elite during the antebellum period. The oldest dated one, identified by a plaque inscribed "Henry Toomer & Charles Jewkes's Family Vault 1786" lies mostly underground close by the foundation of St. James Church in Wilmington. Beside it is a row of three individual barrel vaults built in a row and connected by continuous brick end walls (Fig. 2.13). These are impressive masonry structures reminiscent of early brick cisterns that collected rainwater for household use in coastal North Carolina. The bricks are handmade, and the west ends have red sandstone lintels over the bricked-up openings. A marble plaque inscribed to the memory of Mrs. Lucy Jones Marshall (d. 1818) identifies one vault.

A variation of the individual brick vault is the hogback vault, with rounded ends. A group of these located at St. Thomas Episcopal Churchyard in Windsor, in the Albemarle, probably dated from the late eighteenth or early nineteenth century and had handmade brick with glazed headers, without any visible mortar, laid in rows that curve toward a center spine. These had no inscriptions, nor would there have been any practical place to affix an inscription without erecting a separate headstone (Fig. 2.14). In recent years they have been either removed or rebricked, losing their original form.

Masons built numerous vaulted brick graves for wealthy residents of Beaufort,

Figure 2.14.
Hogback vault grave, St. Thomas
Episcopal Churchyard, Windsor, believed
to date from the nineteenth century.
(Photo by M. Ruth Little; Southern Folklife
Collection, Wilson Library, University of
North Carolina at Chapel Hill)

Figure 2.15.
Brick vaulted graves, Old Burying Ground,
Beaufort, nineteenth century.

(*opposite, above*) Figure 2.16. Vaults of Asa and Sally Jones, 1840, 1838, Cedar Grove Cemetery, New Bern.
(*opposite, below*) Figure 2.17. Family Tomb, Elizabeth City Episcopal Churchyard, Pasquotank County, nineteenth century.

New Bern, and the Albemarle region in the mid-coastal region. At the Old Burying Ground at Beaufort, established in 1731 along the central coast of North Carolina, most of the early-nineteenth-century graves are "bricked" with low vaults projecting from the ground, some domed, some gabled. Most have stepped ends, and some have head and footstones enclosed in the ends (Fig. 2.15). When Sally Jones (d. 1838) and her husband, Asa Jones (d. 1840), died in the nearby town of New Bern, each was interred in a gabled brick vault, with a marble head and footstone at each end (Fig. 2.16).

Grave vaults containing one or several generations of a family are found throughout the Coastal Plain. A gabled version is visible in Figure 2.16. A brick family vault, with the same stepped-end form as most individual brick vaults, stands in the Episcopal churchyard, founded in 1828, in Elizabeth City (Fig. 2.17). Variations on this design include submerged brick vaults with only the top of the vaults visible. This variety of impressive vaulted structures, whose masons are as unknown as most of the individuals buried in the structures, reflects the continuation of an age-old tradition and an ingenuous use of local materials to fashion permanent monuments.

Imported Commercial Monuments

Figure 2.18.
"Governors'
Stones,"
St. Paul's
Episcopal
Churchyard,
Edenton.
Early-
eighteenth-
century
ledgers
originally
located in
coastal family
graveyards.

Of all early gravemarkers erected in the Coastal Plain, wood, ballast stone, and brick markers far outnumbered commercial stone monuments, yet the wood has now rotted or burned, the ballast stone has been carried off, and the brick has often crumbled. Thus the gentry's imported stone monuments often stand alone, sometimes surrounded by a clearing that is all that remains to indicate others were buried there and were given less permanent gravemarkers. The eighteenth-century monuments, generally ledgers, box-tombs, and head and footstones, are almost exclusively of slate or sandstone; the nineteenth-century monuments, of the same shapes, are almost invariably of marble. Ledgers and box-tombs were expensive. Most are found in the graveyards of the very wealthy families and in the cemeteries of the oldest Episcopal churches, whose congregants tended to be the wealthiest residents in any town.

Monuments imported from England can be distinguished by type of stone, designs (often including heraldic devices), and sculptural qualities. The oldest ledgers in the state, the so-called Governors' Stones at Edenton's St. Paul's Episcopal Church, include the slate ledgers of Henderson Walker (d. 1704), "commander of N.C. during the administration of the province," and of "Colonel West of Wilkinson" (d. 1705), and the red sandstone ledger of Charles Eden (d. 1722), governor of the proprietory colony for eight years (Fig. 2.18). Governor Eden's ledger has an elegant coat-of-arms, apparently carved of Portland stone, set into the sandstone ledger (Fig. 2.19). One corner of West's stone retains a delicately engraved fleur-de-lis as a symbol of high station. Another sandstone ledger, whose inscription is so weathered that it is illegible, contains a marble coat-of-arms with a boar. Other aristocratic monuments imported from England probably washed into the sound many years ago.[19]

St. Philip's Churchyard, Brunswicktown, contains a small group of ledgers and box-tombs dating from 1763 to 1838; the three oldest, probably English imports, are the finest box-tombs in the Lower Cape Fear. The box-tomb of Mrs. Mary Quince (d. 1765) contains a slate ledger on an ornate marble base of classical design quite similar to a box-tomb in Hampstead, Middlesex, England, with a death date of 1762 (Fig. 2.20).[20] The marble ledger of Rebecca McGuire (d. 1766) has a Latin epitaph. The marble box-tomb of Mary Jane Dry (d. 1793), wife of William Dry, U.S. customs collector at Brunswicktown, has ornate marble pilasters at the corners of the base.

Figure 2.19. Coat-of-arms on ledger of Gov. Charles Eden, d. 1722, St. Paul's Episcopal Churchyard.

In medieval and Renaissance England, burial within the church reflected both the status and likelihood of resurrection of wealthy parishioners, and this tradition continued in the colonial South. Virginians followed the practice until the 1740s, and hung wall murals, generally imported from England, on the walls of the church to memorialize the deceased.[21] St. Philip's Anglican Church, which was built by British settlers at Brunswicktown, in Brunswick County, North Carolina, under an act of 1751 and burned in 1776, contains twelve floor graves.[22]

The tomb-table became the height of elegance, the counterpart in monuments to the delicate Federal style in architecture, during the first half of the nineteenth century. Oliver Pearce (d. 1815), a native of Providence, Rhode Island, who moved to Fayetteville and became a merchant, is buried beneath a classically inspired tomb-table supplied by "Tingley Bros. Providence, R.I." (Fig. 2.21).

Most of the head and footstones of slate, sandstone, or marble found throughout early Coastal Plain cemeteries were imported from metropolitan centers along the eastern seaboard. Although such stones were valuable advertisements for the stone-cutter, most bear no maker's signature. Throughout most of the eighteenth century, these were imported from New England, although the few early-eighteenth-century headstones may be English imports. Thomas Harvey's headstone, with a death date of 1729, in the Harvey Cemetery on Harvey's Neck, Perquimans County, is the earliest dated one in the state and the only one in the region with a coat-of-arms.

The largest collections of eighteenth-century headstones in the Coastal Plain stand in Episcopal cemeteries in the early port towns along the Atlantic Ocean: St. Paul's Episcopal Churchyard, Edenton; Christ Church, New Bern; and St. James Episcopal Churchyard, Wilmington. St. Paul's Church was begun about 1736, the first Christ Church about 1750, and the first St. James Church about 1751. The earliest death dates on the headstones are from the 1750s and 1760s. In all three cemeteries the headstones are of slate or red sandstone cut in thick slabs to a tripartite form—a central, arched tympanum with flanking arched caps and vertical sides that is typical of eighteenth-century styles. The smooth front and sides contrast

Figure 2.20.
Box-tomb
of Mrs. Mary
Quince,
d. 1765,
St. Philip's
Anglican
Churchyard,
Brunswick-
town, Bruns-
wick County.
Apparently
imported from
England.

Figure 2.21.
Tomb-table of Oliver Pearce, d. 1815, Cross Creek Cemetery, Fayetteville. Signed "Tingley Bros. Providence, R.I."
(Photo by M. Ruth Little; Southern Folklife Collection, Wilson Library, University of North Carolina at Chapel Hill)

strikingly with the roughly finished rear which has prominent chisel marks. The type of stone is a general indicator of its origin, for stonecutters tended to work in stone they could purchase locally—slate for those working in Massachusetts and Rhode Island, red sandstone in New Jersey, Connecticut, and New York.[23] Stone-cutters generally left the tympanum and side panels plain, concentrating their decorative skill on elegantly lettered inscriptions that fill the entire face of the stone. Some headstones have distinctive carved decoration consisting of the skull or soul face, usually with wings, and a naturalistic vine or foliage forming a side and sometimes lower border. On these headstones, American stonecutters carved shallow forms, with linear incised lines, like drawings on stone, rather than the deeper, sculptural forms carved by their English counterparts. The depiction of the skulls and faces vary from humorously primitive skulls, often resembling jack-o'-lanterns, to sweetly angelic faces. Through their visual similarity to documented stones they can be attributed to the workshops of such prominent New England and mid-Atlantic gravestone carvers as William Codner of Boston, Massachusetts, Josiah Manning of Windham, Connecticut, Ebenezer Price of New Jersey, and Richard Hartshorn Sr. of Rhode Island and New York. Such attributions have been aided by the occasional headstone inscriptions that declare the birthplace of the people buried beneath them. Many North Carolinians migrated from the New England and mid-Atlantic areas, and sometimes their tombstones were ordered from their homelands.

Boston's William Codner supplied slate headstones with dramatically three-dimensional soul figures and portraits from the 1730s to 1760s throughout Massachusetts.[24] Codner shipped stones to wealthy South Carolinians and apparently wealthy North Carolina families as well, and one stone attributed to Codner stands in a family graveyard in the early port of Bath. The slate headstone of Mary Evans features a deeply modeled three-quarter-view portrait of a lovely woman in an elegant dress. (See Figure 1.14.) Bath's mercantile families would have had prime opportunity to import a gravestone from Boston. This is one of only a handful of early portrait stones in North Carolina. The tall slate headstone of Isaac Hardee, d. 1770, in the Hardee plantation graveyard, looks like Codner's work, for the soul face carries Codner's characteristic whimsical expression (Fig. 2.22).

North Carolinians also ordered stones from other Massachusetts stonecarvers. The headstones for Elizabeth Bangs (d. 1758) and Josiah Howard (d. 1759) at Christ Churchyard, New Bern, are attributed to the third generation of the Lamson workshop, of Charlestown, Massachusetts, which shipped gravestones throughout New England during the eighteenth and early nineteenth centuries (Fig. 2.23).[25] The winged skull motif on the slate headstone for Morris Nichols (d. 1796), in a family graveyard in New Hanover County, resembles the work of Boston and Charlestown, Massachusetts, stonecarvers of the late eighteenth century who cut skulls with similar shapes (Fig. 2.24). Perhaps the young man had only recently come to New Hanover County, since his "Patron, Samuel Lowder," with whom he may have been living and working, rather than his family, erected the stone.

The shop of Josiah Manning, the most successful one in eastern Connecticut

Here lies buried the Body of Mr
ISAAC HARDEE son of JOHN HARDEE Esc
and SUSANNAH his wife who departed this
Life JANry 9th 1760 Aged 25 Years 7 Mo & 17 D

Could Bloom of Youth, could universal Love
Could Tears of parting Friends to Pity move
Relentless Fate sure Fate had been inclin'd
To spare a man for other Joys design'd
But since one common Death one common Grave
Awaits the youthfull man the generous & Brave
Since nought on Earth but yeilds to Gods Decree
And Heaven declard that short mans Life must be
Let this fair Flower cropt in its freshest Bloom
Teach us that Lifes a Span that Deaths our Doo
That all our Hopes on our Redeemer rely
Like him with him to life like him with him be P.

Figure 2.23.
Headstone of Josiah Howard, d. 1759, Christ Churchyard, New Bern.
Attributed to the third generation of the Lamson workshop, Charlestown, Mass.

(opposite) Figure 2.22.
Headstone of Isaac Hardee, d. 1770, Hardee Graveyard, Greenville.
Attributed to the workshop of William Codner, Boston.

during the latter eighteenth century, carved several of the headstones at St. James
Churchyard, Wilmington. Those for infant Sarah Stone and for William Millor,
who both died in 1788, have semicircular tympana with the winged angel with distinctive coiled hair, "fried egg eyes," and the "Geneva collar" that are hallmarks of
the Manning shop's schematic style. Manning carved large double circles which
look like fried eggs to represent eyes, and between the wings he carved at the neck-

line the distinctive linen strips representing a cleric or academic (Fig. 2.25).[26] The same distinctive winged head appears on the headstone of Frances Wilkinson (d. 1788), at St. James, but the overall shape of this stone is dramatically different—rectangular rather than tripartite—which signals a change to neoclassical form but a retention of the old religious symbolism.[27]

A group of red sandstone headstones from the 1780s and 1790s at Christ Church, New Bern, are attributed to Thomas Gold of New Haven, Connecticut. Levi Gill (d. 1784) and Mrs. Euphamia Gillaspy (d. 1784) have elaborate vernacular winged soul figures set in tall tympana with ornate spiral ornament along the side borders.[28]

Ebenezer Price, who worked in Elizabethtown, New Jersey, from 1747 to 1788, signed "Price, Engravor" across the entire lower face of the red sandstone headstone of William Hunt at St. James Churchyard, one of only two eighteenth-century markers in the cemetery which are signed.[29] (Hunt's parents lived in Elizabethtown, New Jersey, so perhaps they had the gravestone shipped to Wilmington.) Price separated each letter of his signature within a scalloped border, with whimsical flowers sprouting from each edge of the border (Fig. 2.26). Even without the signature, Price's sprightly linear style and whimsical ornament are easily recognizable. His red sandstones have a warmth of material and his soul faces are appealingly three-dimensional with softly rounded features. The headstone of Mary Walker (d. 1763), at St. Paul's, Edenton, is attributed to him, as is the headstone of Nathan Newby (d. 1762), in a tiny family graveyard on the bank of the Perquimans River just outside Hertford.

Richard Hartshorn Sr. of Rhode Island and New York probably carved a number of the late-eighteenth-century red sandstone headstones at St. Paul's and St. James. These are cut of warm red sandstone like Price's, but the markers themselves are elegantly plain, and lack any decoration other than calligraphically embellished inscriptions (Fig. 2.27). A sandstone ledger at St. James with the same lettering style has a partial signature that may be Richard Hartshorn's.[30]

Stonecutter John Stevens of Newport, Rhode Island, signed the slate headstone of Elizabeth Cooke (d. 1784), Cedar Grove Cemetery, New Bern. The tympanum contains a wilted flower bud, flanked by tulips in the borders (Fig. 2.28). Although the port of New Bern had a close trade with Rhode Island in the eighteenth century, this is the only Rhode Island stone from the period known in town.

Most eighteenth-century headstones can be attributed to specific stonecutting workshops or regions of the New England and mid-Atlantic areas, but there are headstones of mysterious origin. Such a stone is the tall marble headstone of Sarah Brunlow (d. 1770), the oldest dated gravestone in Cumberland County, containing a skull and elegantly carved crossbones tied with a ribbon (Fig. 2.29). The stone was moved to Cross Creek Cemetery from the graveyard of the Brunlows, a family of Irish origin who lived near the Cape Fear River.

By the turn of the century, neoclassical-style motifs, often featuring the urn-and-willow motif of mourning, superseded winged skulls and angels. These newly fashionable stones were almost invariably of marble, and were more likely than eighteenth-century stones to have the signatures of the stonecutters. Most of them

Sarah daugh.r to M.r
George T. Stone &
M.rs Lurahah his wife,
who departed this
life Sep.t 10.th 1788.
in the 2.nd Year
of her age

Sleep sweet babe
and take thy rest,
God call'd thee home
He thought it best.

Figure 2.26.
Headstone of William Hunt, d. 1757, St. James Episcopal Churchyard, Wilmington.
Signed by Ebenezer Price of Elizabethtown, N.J.

(opposite) Figure 2.25.
Headstone of Sarah Stone, d. 1788, St. James Episcopal Churchyard, Wilmington.
Attributed to stonecutter Josiah Manning of Connecticut.

Figure 2.28.
Headstone
of Elizabeth
Cooke,
d. 1784,
Cedar Grove
Cemetery,
New Bern.
Signed by
John Stevens,
Newport, R.I.

(opposite)
Figure 2.27.
Headstone of
Mary Bleakly,
d. 1787, St.
James Episco-
pal Churchyard,
Wilmington.
Attributed to
Richard Hart-
shorn Sr. of
Rhode Island
and New York.

worked in Connecticut, New York, and Charleston: "J. Ritter New Haven, Ct." and, later, "D. Ritter & Son, N Haven, Con."; "C. T. Duncomb, Norwalk, Ct."; "Witzel & Cahoon, N.Y."; and "J. Hall," "Thomas Walker," and "John White Charleston." One stonecutter located in North Carolina signed stones during this period as "A. Sweetland, Fayetteville." One of the earliest urn-and-willow stones at St. James Churchyard, for Capt. Ephraim Symonds of Salem, Massachusetts (d. 1808), is

Figure 2.30.
Headstone of
Capt. Ephraim
Symonds,
d. 1808,
St. James
Episcopal
Churchyard,
Wilmington.
Attributed to
a stonecutter
from Salem,
Mass.

carved of old-fashioned slate (Fig. 2.30). Its Adamesque refinement (in the neoclassical style of the Adams brothers of England) is characteristic of the decorative arts of his hometown of Salem, where it perhaps was carved.

Obelisks and pedestal-tombs, usually set on paneled bases with inscriptions, represent the height of neoclassical fashion from the 1820s onward. By about 1850, obelisks had largely replaced ledgers as monuments for wealthy and prominent individuals. Pedestal-tombs, the grandest type of monument in use during the antebellum period, occur rarely. Most were ordered from Baltimore and Norfolk from such firms as "T. D. Couper" of Norfolk and "Gaddess & Benbeen, Balt Md.," although at least one came from "E. Price & Son" of Brooklyn, New York.

(opposite)
Figure 2.29.
Headstone
of Sarah
Brunlow,
d. 1770,
Cross Creek
Cemetery,
Fayetteville.

Highland Scot Graveyards

Thousands of Highland Scots homesteaded the Upper Cape Fear region at the headwaters of the Cape Fear River about one hundred miles inland from Wilmington. The Highlanders landed in Wilmington, sailed up the Cape Fear River, and fanned out from Fayetteville into the Sandhills region from present Lee County on the north to the South Carolina border on the south.[31] These immigrants from the Western Highlands and islands of Scotland formed part of a general exodus from Scotland to North America which peaked just before the Revolution. North Carolina was the most important receiving colony for these Highlanders, and by 1775 there were twenty thousand Highlanders in North Carolina. The settlement of Cross Creek, now the city of Fayetteville, in Cumberland County, has been the urban focus of the Sandhills region since the eighteenth century. The Highland Scots of the Sandhills apparently constituted a relatively unacculturated folk community in the late eighteenth century. During this period they established a number of Presbyterian churches, including Old Bluff and MacPherson in Cumberland County, Longstreet and Phillipi in present Hoke County, and Tirzah (Summerville) and Barbecue in present Harnett County.

Figure 2.31. Longstreet Presbyterian Churchyard, Hoke County.

Stone deposits, unique in the Coastal Plain, contributed to the expression of Highland Scot culture in gravemarkers in the Sandhills, so called for its rolling topography and sandy soil, which supports scrub pine and oak growth. The region

has the same wood and clay for fashioning gravemarkers as the Tidewater, but it also contains deposits of workable sandstone, varying from light to deep reddish brown, in which case it is usually called brownstone.[32] There were small sandstone quarries throughout the area, such as one on the Cape Fear River near Tokay in Cumberland County. This is probably where the stone, which was known locally as "Arsenal Stone," for the U.S. Arsenal built in Fayetteville in the 1830s, was quarried.[33] Although the local sandstone quarried along the banks of the Cape Fear River and the Deep River was not of high quality, it was used extensively before the Civil War for building foundations, chimneys, and walls, and, in some cases, for gravestones.

Sandstone gravestones occur throughout the Upper Cape Fear area and distinguish this region's graveyards from those of the Tidewater. The stone has a coarse grain that does not permit detailed carving; thus it would not have tempted a professional stonecarver to create gravestones. In fact, most of the sandstone gravestones are simply field rocks without shaping or inscription. Others, however, are distinctive headstones of powerful if not refined design.

Highland Scot Presbyterian family graveyards and church cemeteries are characterized by neatly aligned headstones—giving them a more orderly appearance than the wide variety of gravemarkers found in either early Episcopal graveyards or African American graveyards—and are often surrounded by rubble walls created from the fieldstones that were cleared from the site at the time the cemetery was established (Fig. 2.31). The earliest headstones at Philippi and Longstreet Churchyards in Hoke County are of red sandstone. These generally measure about 18 inches wide, 25 inches above ground level, and 4 inches thick. Some have the semicircular tympanum with squared shoulders, but most are jagged slabs. Only two of the dozen local headstones at Philippi have legible inscriptions: to J. McNeill, who died in 1789 or 1800, and to Col. Elis Priest, whose death date is illegible.

Among the late-eighteenth-century sandstones, Longstreet Presbyterian Church has two unique shield shapes that reflect a vestige of traditional Highland Scot gravestone symbolism: one stone, with the date 1773, is inscribed to Laulin McNeil, perhaps a relative of Dugald McNeil, one of the Scottish leaders who brought a large group of countrymen to the area in 1739 (Fig. 2.32).[34] Since this shield shape had significance in Scotland as a continuation of a headstone form which originated in the custom of inserting a slain warrior's shield into his grave as a memorial, these shield-shaped headstones may have been carved by early settlers as a link to their homeland. When Dugald died later in the eighteenth century, his prominent position as one of the founding fathers of the Cape Fear colony of Highlanders may have prompted the fashioning of a shield stone.

Another center of Highlander grave art in the Sandhills is Lee County, on the western edge of the Coastal Plain.[35] Until the 1850s, most Lee County Highlanders buried their dead in family graveyards rather than in church cemeteries, and some of the private graveyards are enclosed with walls of quarried brownstone blocks. Local artisans also cut many headstones from the local brownstone from the 1780s to the 1840s. Some of these are small, discoid-shaped headstones; some have tri-

Figure 2.32.
Shield head-
stone of a
MacNeil, late
eighteenth
century,
Longstreet
Presbyterian
Churchyard,
Hoke County.

partite baroque shapes and neoclassical ornamentation. A family group in the Murchison Graveyard contains a unique bodystone that is reminiscent of a medieval
British tomb: Daniel Murchison, who died in 1788, is buried beneath a gabled
bodystone of brownstone, shaped like a coffin with a peaked lid (Fig. 2.33). Near his
grave is an uninscribed ledger that has small bas-relief carvings of a human figure
and a peaked-lid casket (Fig. 2.34).

The Highlander graveyards of Lee County have a variety of stones from a variety of materials. A number of stones are small discoid headstones cut out of yellow-
green or pink soapstone, perhaps quarried in adjacent Chatham County. The Cam-

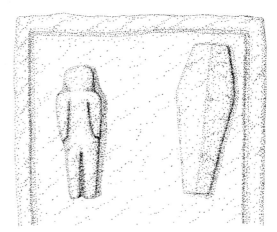

Figure 2.34.
Ledger, decedent unknown, late eighteenth century.
Murchison Graveyard, Lee County.
(Drawing by J. Daniel Pezzoni; reproduced courtesy
Railroad House Museum, Sanford.)

Figure 2.33.
Bodystone of Daniel Murchison, d. 1788, Murchison Graveyard,
Lee County. (Photo by J. Daniel Pezzoni, 1991, North Carolina
Division of Archives and History)

eron family graveyard on Beaver Creek, at the intersection of Moore, Harnett, and
Lee Counties in the Sandhills area, has cairn graves mounded with fieldstones,
which functioned not only as shields from animals and human activity but as powerful cultural links to Scotland. The age and status of the deceased is said to have
determined the size of the cairn, and the head of the Cameron clan has the largest
cairn in the graveyard.[36]

One unidentified Sandhills artisan fashioned at least fourteen gravestones from
the local sandstone for Highlander families in the Cumberland, Hoke, and Harnett
County region. These headstones, with death dates from 1793 to 1835, stand at the
Scots Presbyterian Churchyards of Old Bluff and Longstreet, at two Scottish family graveyards in Cumberland and Harnett Counties, and at Cross Creek Cemetery,
the city cemetery in Fayetteville. His headstones ranged from 10 to 19 inches wide,
13 to 35 inches above ground level, and $2\frac{1}{2}$ to $4\frac{1}{2}$ inches thick. Like some of the Lee
County artisans, the maker cut curvilinear tops and, as closely as the weak, scaly
sandstone allowed, neat lettered inscriptions that conformed to the fashionable baroque marble gravestones being made in Charleston and other centers. The carver
could not cut the light beige sandstone to the elegant thinness possible in marble,
and used no incised decoration besides the inscription. He often ruled the surface,
cut neat upper and lowercase Roman lettering along the lines, and sometimes separated the words with the Gothic dot, a late-medieval style of writing in which
words are separated by a dot or colon. The sandstone has not weathered well, and
most of the group are in poor or fragmentary condition.

Four gravemarkers give the names of the individuals who ordered the headstone as well as that of the deceased, such as:

ERECTED
by
Alexr & Peter
McLean in memory
of their Mother Marian
McLean who died May 6:
1814 aged 62 Years.[37]

Including the name of the patron in the inscription characterizes eighteenth-century headstones in Scotland, and this may be a continuation of the tradition.[38] The stonecutter did not usually go to the extra effort of engraving an epitaph, but the headstone of Alexander McAllister contains a moving instruction to the passerby (Fig. 2.35).[39]

As the nineteenth century opened, most of the Scots in the Sandhills began ordering fashionable marble gravestones from itinerant and, later, resident stonecutters. By the mid-nineteenth century, however, a self-conscious revival of Scottish heritage, perhaps fueled by the popularity of Sir Walter Scott's romantic novels about Scottish history, brought a second wave of Highland Scots culture to at least one Upper Cape Fear graveyard, Old Bluff Presbyterian Church. The son of Duncan McNeill, one of the early Highlander immigrants to the region, who died in 1791, ordered a new gravestone decorated with a thistle, the national symbol of Scotland, for his father's grave (see Figure 5.28). The stone is attributed to Scottish-born stonecutter George Lauder, who owned a Fayetteville marble yard and used the same motif on a nearby obelisk he carved for the 1858 centenary of Old Bluff Church. Lauder was passionately interested in the Scottish Revival movement and even made a pilgrimage to Sir Walter Scott's estate, Abbotsford, in Scotland at mid-century.

Sticks, Bricks, and Stones in the Tidewater and Coastal Plain in Perspective

The late-twentieth-century visitor who pushes through the overgrown thickets surrounding abandoned family graveyards in eastern North Carolina sees only the slates and marbles memorializing the gentry, analogs in death to the grand plantation houses or townhouses where these wealthy farmers and merchants spent their lives. Prominent attorney William Gaston of New Bern lived in one of the most architecturally distinguished houses in town, and since 1844 his resting place has been in Cedar Grove Cemetery beneath a striking marble monument designed by New York architect A. J. Davis. Gaston's house and his gravestone still stand as memorials to his memory. Ordinary residents like Carrie Deaver, in rural Cumberland County, probably spent her life in a small frame house which has now disappeared. Since 1876 a wooden headboard marked with her name and date of death has stood at the Hope Mills Cemetery to perpetuate her memory. Deaver is one of the few of her community and social class whose gravemarker has survived at all.

(opposite)
Figure 2.35.
Headstone
of Alexander
McAllister,
d. 1823,
Old Bluff
Presbyterian
Churchyard,
Cumberland
County.

To the
Memory of
Alexander McAllister
Who was born Feb 4 AD 1766
And departed this life Sept 27
AD 1827.
Tread softly stranger this is
sacred earth
Truth Virtue Magnanimity
and worth
Sleep in silence here.

The well-crafted cedar, cypress, and pine grave railings, white-painted head and footboards, curious gravehouses with cedar shingles, expertly laid brick vaults, and ballast stones reused as memorials, have vanished. Scattered, often hidden examples in present-day graveyards represent these lost folk traditions that reflect both ingenuity in devising memorials in a region without stone and the wide socio-economic and ethnic distinctions between rich and poor, black and white.

In the Sandhills, the southwest corner of the Coastal Plain, the only section that contains native stone, the spirit of the independent Scots Highlanders who settled here lives in the graveyards—in fieldstones piled on graves to create cairn markers, in sandstone and brownstone shaped by artisans to create bodystones, shields and other shapes of headstones, and in the thistle symbols cut by Scottish-born stonecutter George Lauder in the mid-nineteenth century.

3 Fieldstones and Fancy Stones

PIEDMONT AND MOUNTAIN GRAVEYARDS

AND MARKERS

ISRAEL C. WOOD DEC'D THE 14TH OF 8TH 8 MO 1834 AGED 18 M°.

At the fall line, the intersection of the flat sedimentary layers of the Coastal Plain with the rugged granites, slate, and gneisses that underlie the western hills, the traveler leaves behind the remnants of plantation culture—family graveyards sequestered behind walls, ostentatious imported monuments, luxuriant ground covers, shrubs and trees draped with Spanish moss, and slave burying grounds nearby but unmarked and unheralded. In the Piedmont the traveler encounters vestiges of a different world both geologically and culturally, a world with smaller farms, fewer slaves, and flatter social distinctions between regular folk and gentry.

The Piedmont contained the essential ingredients of a traditional culture that created a wide array of decorative arts in the late eighteenth and nineteenth centuries. The intermingling of the Scots-Irish, English, and Germans who moved into the region in the second half of the eighteenth century, after traveling down the Valley of Virginia from Pennsylvania, resulted in folk pottery, quilts, architecture, furniture, and gravestones that have no parallel in eastern North Carolina. The wide variety of local stone deposits, soft enough to work with crude tools, combined with the decorative craft traditions of these ethnic and denominational groups and the cross-fertilization among them while in Pennsylvania, created a flowering of folk art in stone.

The Germans immigrated to Pennsylvania from the Rhenish Palatinate and other areas of the Rhine Valley between 1690 and 1750 because of destructive wars, religious persecutions, and extravagant accounts of America's advantages.[1] Most paused only briefly in Philadelphia before moving to Lancaster, Berks, Chester and Northampton Counties, Pennsylvania. Between the 1740s and the 1780s, they moved south through western Maryland and Virginia along the Shenandoah Valley, and settled in Alamance, Orange, Guilford, Davidson, Rowan, Cabarrus, Stanly, Iredell, Wilkes, Catawba, Lincoln, and several other Piedmont counties of North Carolina, where by 1775 they constituted about one-fourth of the white population of approximately 300,000 in western North Carolina.[2]

The Germans clung to their ethnic identity for several generations.[3] They preferred to settle in their own communities and some spoke German until the mid-nineteenth century. The three principal denominations among the North Carolina German settlers were the Moravians, the Lutherans, and the Reformed. Moravian settlement occupied the Wachovia Tract in the central Piedmont, while Lutheran and Reformed denominations, scattered throughout the Piedmont, had similar beliefs, and congregations frequently built a joint or union church that each used on alternate Sundays. Services were conducted in German until 1825 or 1830. In some German communities, artisans supplied gravestones, often with Germanic symbols, until the 1850s, which indicates that acculturation occurred gradually during the second quarter of the century.[4]

Lowland Scots, English, Irish, and Welsh settlers migrated to the Piedmont from eastern North Carolina, through the Upper Cape Fear Valley and other river valleys. Settlers moved south from other colonies throughout the mid-Atlantic region, many of which traveled down the Valley of Virginia into the state and then moved west to the Blue Ridge.

During the first half of the eighteenth century, thousands of Scots-Irish, known as "Ulster" Scots because of a century-long settlement in Ulster (Northern Ireland), fled repressive trade laws, oppressive landlords, and famine and sailed to Pennsylvania, Maryland, and Delaware. They later traveled down into Virginia and North Carolina because of the cheap, plentiful land.[5] The Scots-Irish were a less distinct cultural group than the Germans. Their church affiliation was diverse, although the majority of them were Presbyterians, and they did not tend to cluster in homogeneous communities. A study of land grants in Rowan County, in the central Piedmont, indicates that the Scots-Irish arrived in considerable numbers before the Germans arrived and thus settled the best land, but there was some intersettlement as Germans bought land between Scots-Irish holdings.[6]

The aristocratic British ledgers and box-tombs—the looming brick tombs that announced class distinctions in Coastal Plain cemeteries—have almost no place in central and western North Carolina. Instead the headstone, usually crafted of local stone by a community artisan, marks the graves of both rich and poor side by side in both church and community cemeteries. The typical gravemarker in the eighteenth and first half of the nineteenth centuries is a small head and footstone of native stone cut by an amateur stonecutter. Dated stones first appear in the 1760s in the Piedmont.[7] A small headstone for two-year-old David McDowell (d. 1767), at the Quaker Meadows Cemetery near Morganton in Burke County, marks the earliest identified site associated with white settlement in western North Carolina. Outside of the few, small towns in the region, Piedmont settlers lived in dispersed farming communities which discouraged the development of full-time craftsmen or the importation of commercial products from industrial centers. Eighteenth-century Piedmont settlers, regardless of their class, lacked the shipping connections enjoyed by planters and merchants in the coastal areas and had little choice but to patronize local artisans. By the 1800s and 1810s, those few who could afford opulent monuments shipped them overland from such cities as Philadelphia, Baltimore, Charleston, and closer stonecutting centers as Petersburg, Virginia, and Columbia, South Carolina. The flow of the Yadkin–Pee Dee and Catawba River systems into South Carolina and the Dan-Roanoke into Virginia controlled Piedmont trade from earliest settlement, and the neighboring states regarded North Carolina as their natural economic domain. In 1834 a Raleigh newspaper editor predicted sourly that the state would become known as the "Virginia and South Carolina Plantations" unless the home markets could be improved.[8]

The first railroads in North Carolina continued the out-of-state dependency: in 1840 the state's only two railroads connected Raleigh and Wilmington with points on the Virginia border, and in 1852 a railroad connected Charlotte to Columbia, South Carolina. Finally in 1856 an east-west trunk line, the North Carolina Railroad, connected Charlotte to Raleigh and to the coast and began to channel some Piedmont trade to ports within the state rather than to neighboring states.

The Piedmont contains the richest concentration of early gravestones in the state. An important reason for this was the tendency of Piedmont settlers, by the second generation, to bury in church cemeteries rather than in family graveyards. Indeed, later generations sometimes moved the graves and gravestones of Piedmont pioneers from the family graveyards to the church cemeteries to insure their protection. The Lange (Long) family is one of many that did this. They moved their eighteenth-century graves and stones from the family graveyard in Davidson County to nearby Bethany Reformed Churchyard in the nineteenth or twentieth century.

The artistry exercised on the gravestones was dependent upon the ethnic background of the settlers and the availability of suitable local stone. The British-dominated eastern Piedmont, Caswell, Durham, Orange, and Wake Counties, used headstones of unshaped or partially shaped field rocks until marble stones became available. Although granites and some slates underlay this region, the early settlers of this area did not nurture skilled gravestone carvers but made do with rough fieldstones with rudimentary inscriptions. The central and western counties of the Piedmont, where the Germans and Scots-Irish settled, are far more likely to have locally quarried stone shaped into artistic monuments.

Rowan County and Salisbury, its county seat, in the central Piedmont, was a trading center from its establishment in 1755. Its early gravestones are the work of many different Piedmont stonecutters as well as out-of-state artisans. A typically made stone of the period is the headstone of a child, Richard K. Barr, who died in 1785 (Fig. 3.1). The oldest gravestone in the Old English Cemetery, established in 1770, shows the influence of New England design on a local carver (Fig. 3.2). Within a decade, some families were turning to Charleston and Philadelphia stonecutters for elegant marble monuments.

Scots-Irish and German families lived in neighboring communities throughout the central and western Piedmont, leading to a fusion of their folk arts in the graveyards (Fig. 3.3). Like the Rosetta stone, a tablet discovered in 1799 with parallel inscriptions in Egyptian and Greek that provided the key to deciphering ancient Egyptian hieroglyphics, the stone for German minister Johann Arends is a sign to Catawba Valley culture, and was cut by the Scots-Irish stonecutting workshop of the Bigham family, from nearby Mecklenburg County.[9] Several of its features represent the extent to which Germans had acculturated by 1807: the typically Scots-Irish shape of the stone, the American eagle holding the motto "E Pluribus Unum," the combination of German and English in the inscription, the use of a Scots-Irish stonecutter, and its location in the burial grounds of a church building shared by Presbyterians, Reformed, and Lutherans (the last of which Arends served as preacher).[10]

The westernmost region of North Carolina, across the Blue Ridge Mountains which marked the Continental Divide, has a different history and culture from the Piedmont. White settlement of rugged western North Carolina, covered by the southern Appalachian Mountains, lagged behind the Piedmont by half a century. Due to the remoteness and isolation of the area, the difficult terrain, and the presence of the Cherokee Indian nation in southwestern North Carolina until treaties in the 1780s and 1790s began to dispossess them of their land, meaningful numbers of settlers did not arrive in the mountains of North Carolina until the late eigh-

Figure 3.2.
Headstone of Capt. Daniel Little, d. 1775, Old English Cemetery, Salisbury.

(opposite)
Figure 3.1.
This small, plain headstone of Richard K. Barr, d. 1785,
of native stone, is representative of Piedmont markers of the period.
Thyatira Presbyterian Churchyard, Rowan County.

Hier ruhet der Leichnam des
heiland wohl ehrwürdigen
JOHANN GODFRIED ARENDS
treu gewesener evangelischer Prediger
er starb am 9ten Juli A.D. 1807 sein Alter
66 Jahre 6 Monate und 28 Tage an einer
auszehrenden Kranckheit nachdem er
32 Jahre das Predigamt mit aller treue ver-
waltet.

Wohl seliger wer stirbt wie du
Der kommt zur ewigen Himmels Ruh.
Remember Man as you pass by,
As you are now so once was I,
As I am now you soon shall be,
Therefore prepare to follow me.

teenth century. Many settlers were Revolutionary War veterans who received land grants in the mountains as payment for their military service.

By 1800, approximately a third of the settlers were English and Irish and a third were Scottish, most of whom migrated west from the Piedmont but also from Virginia and down the Shenandoah Valley from Pennsylvania. Significant numbers of the mountain settlers were of German descent as well as Welsh and a few other national stocks.[11] The mountain Germans scattered among other ethnic groups and thus never achieved the critical mass sufficient to develop distinctive gravestone traditions like those of the Piedmont. Population was sparse and transportation extremely difficult until the twentieth century. Most settlers were subsistence farmers who created a culture that is differentiated from that of the rest of North Carolina only because of the greater isolation and corresponding self-sufficiency. The typical early mountain gravemarkers are small rudimentary head and footstones of native stone similar to the earliest markers in the eastern Piedmont. While such fieldstones nearly ceased to be erected by the mid-nineteenth century in the Piedmont, the relative isolation of the mountains resulted in their persistence early into the twentieth century.

The Stone

The ready availability of stone throughout Piedmont and mountain regions meant that local artisans had access to plenty of raw material for cutting gravestones. The favored local stone for gravestones in the eighteenth and nineteenth centuries was soapstone, a talc schist generally known as steatite among old-timers. It occurs in small deposits (both buried and above ground) throughout the Piedmont and mountains (Fig. 3.4). Soapstone assumes many different forms depending upon the types of minerals predominating in it. It varies in color from white to pink, yellow, green, and gray.[12] Carvers of the archaic period incised petroglyphs of animal and human forms into soapstone outcroppings in western North Carolina; the most famous is Judaculla Rock, located in a soapstone quarry in Jackson County.[13]

The earliest-known published description of soapstone in North Carolina, found in an 1850s geological report on the Piedmont by geologist Ebenezer Emmons, mentioned large deposits of this stone in Wake and Randolph Counties. Emmons reported that its most important uses were as a lining for stoves and in the construction of hearths, backs, and jambs for fireplaces. Emmons did not mention gravestones and he may not have been aware that gravestone carving was a sideline of numerous traditional artisans, but the virtues that he extolled for soapstone also made it particularly suitable for gravestones:

> Its valuable qualities are dependent upon its softness and refactory powers. It enables the mechanic to give it form and shape at a very trifling expense. It is true it is not handsome in itself, as it is not susceptible of a polish; still, when planed and varnished, it makes a very handsome mantle-piece. The varnish brings out lively light green tints which give the surface the appearance of a variegated marble.[14]

(opposite) Figure 3.3. Headstone of Johann Godfried Arends, d. 1807, Old White Union Churchyard, Lincolnton. Attributed to the workshop of Samuel Bigham, Mecklenburg County. The stone, actually a twentieth-century facsimile of the original headstone, is mounted in a granite monument of recent vintage.

Figure 3.4. Soapstone outcropping in front yard of Rev. Alex Wilson, stonecutter, Meat Camp Creek, Watauga County. (Photo by M. Ruth Little)

The small-scale market for soapstone has been recognized over the years in government geological publications. In 1893, state geologist J. V. Lewis, writing about building and ornamental stone, specifically mentioned tombstones as a product of soapstone. He noted that "talcose rocks" (soapstone) were abundant in many North Carolina counties, and that it "is everywhere worked with axes and saws, and the ease with which it is cut is doubtless the chief reason for its very general local use." The report mentioned deposits of it near Burlington, Jamestown, and Greensboro in the central Piedmont, and a two-story house built of soapstone in the mountains of Alexander County in 1890. The geologist observed that it had not been regularly quarried anywhere. Upon exposure, it hardened considerably, he said, and was used for fireplaces, chimneys, foundations, and tombstones.[15] In 1965 state geologist Jaspar Stuckey noted in a summary of the state's geological resources that soapstone occurs in small deposits throughout the Piedmont plateau and mountains and that artisans worked it on a small scale for many years for chimneys, fireplaces, hearths, wainscoting, stove linings, and even as floor tile and stair treads. Stuckey stated that commercial quarries never developed because deposits are small and irregular.[16]

Slate and quartz were used sporadically for gravestones. Slate is plentiful, especially in the Carolina Slate Belt which extends through the eastern Piedmont from Virginia to South Carolina, but was used rarely by local carvers because of its high sedimentary content—thus it flaked easily and was less suitable for carving than New England slate.[17] Quartz occurs as intrusions within the large deposits of granite underlying Salisbury, Lexington, High Point, and northeastern Piedmont counties such as Wake and Franklin. Quartz crystals are most commonly white, yellow, pink, or green.[18] The pink or white glassy rocks used in early gravestones in Guilford and Forsyth Counties are cut from these quartz intrusions. Granite, an extremely hard igneous rock, was often cut into rough blocks for bases of such monuments as box-tombs, but rarely utilized for headstones or ledgers because stonecutters lacked tools and skill to polish and inscribe it.

The Scots-Irish Presbyterian Graveyard

Scots-Irish graveyards are loosely organized by family unit, with gravestones arranged in rows rather than in clusters. Landscaping is simple, with few trees and shrubs planted about the yard. The glory of Scots-Irish cemeteries are the substantial fieldstone cemetery walls and handsome gates of slender iron bars with delicately curved tips made by local blacksmiths early in the nineteenth century (Fig. 3.5).

The traditional gravemarker is a headstone and footstone fashioned of local stone by a skilled community artisan. Scots-Irish stonecutters were less doctrinaire than their English or German counterparts, and borrowed freely from many

Figure 3.5.
Stone and
wrought-iron
gate, Thyatira
Presbyterian
Churchyard,
Rowan
County. Mid-
nineteenth-
century local
craftsmanship.

sources. Among the images on their stones are celestial suns, moons, and stars, emblems of mortality such as the hourglass, abstract decorative patterns, patriotic emblems such as the Scottish thistle or the American eagle, coats-of-arms, and religious symbols such as the winged-soul image and the dove-of-promise. Sometimes these artisans borrowed German folk symbols such as the fylfot cross and the tree-of-life. Sometimes they decorated the rear face of the headstone, perhaps a continuation of the Lowland Scotland tradition, or perhaps because of their more recent exposure to a similar German tradition.[19] Regardless of the influence of particular German features, Scots-Irish stonecutters were engravers, not sculptors; an elegant linearity characterizes their stones.

The largest collection of traditional Scots-Irish gravestones—in Rowan County, a county early settled by the Scots-Irish—stand at Thyatira Presbyterian Churchyard, founded in 1753, the oldest Presbyterian congregation west of the Yadkin River. The stones are carved from local stone in simple baroque shapes. Winged angels and celestial symbols dominate. The slate headstone for Matthew Locke (d. 1801) has a sun and moon etched in the tympanum (Fig. 3.6). An interesting pair of stones, one with a skull, the other with crossbones, probably represents a head and footstone, but there are no names or dates on either marker.

Since they apparently had stronger ties to mainstream culture, Scots-Irish settlements acculturated earlier than German communities, and by the early nineteenth century fashionable marble gravestones imported from commercial urban stonecutters in Charleston, Philadelphia, Petersburg, or Columbia had superseded the traditional gravestones in Presbyterian church cemeteries. The earliest marble

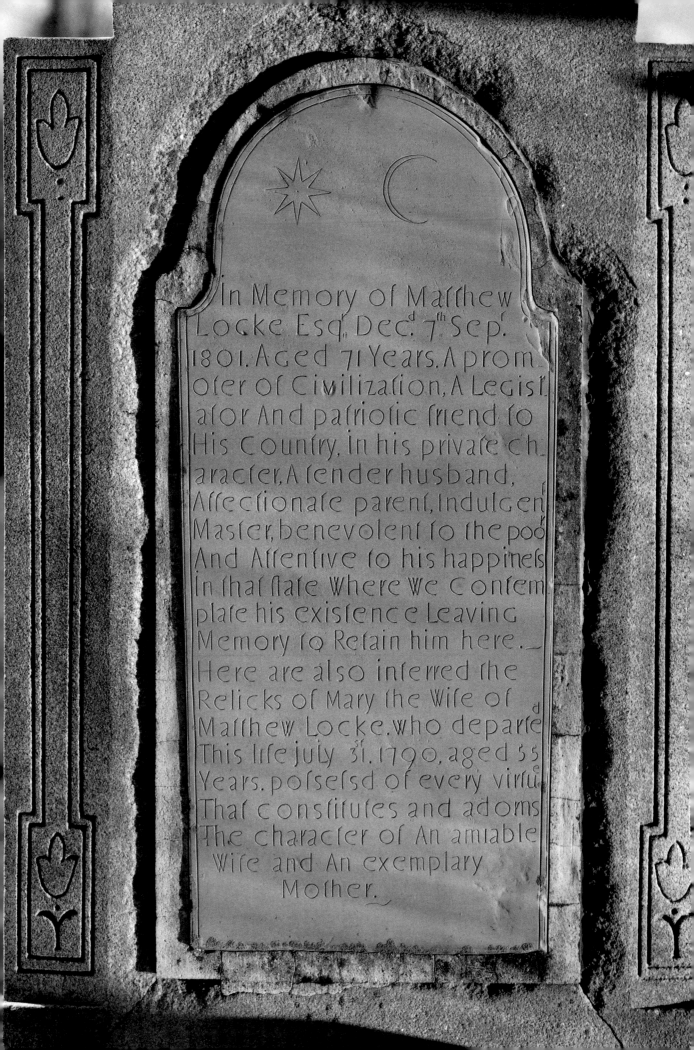

In Memory of Matthew
Locke Esq. Dec.d 7th Sep.t
1801. Aged 71 Years. A prom.
oter of Civilization, A Legist
ator And patriotic friend to
His Country, In his private ch.
aracter, A tender husband,
Affectionate parent, Indulgent
Master, benevolent to the poor
And Attentive to his happiness
In that state Where We Contem
plate his existence Leaving
Memory to Retain him here.—
Here are also interred the
Relicks of Mary the Wife of
Matthew Locke, who departed
This life july 31. 1790, aged 55
Years, possessd of every virtue
That constitutes and adorns
The character of An amiable
Wife and An exemplary
Mother.

Figure 3.7.
Headstone
of Hugh
McCrarey,
d. 1785,
Jersey Baptist
Churchyard,
Davidson
County.

monument at Thyatira Presbyterian Church in Rowan County is a refined ledger with an urn-and-willow, neoclassical fan motifs, and the signature "Rowe & White C.S.C." (Charleston, South Carolina), made for William Locke (d. 1785). At Third Creek Presbyterian Church, Rowan County, founded about 1789, the earliest marble monument is an ornate baroque-style headstone for Jane Graham (d. 1805). The winged angel on the tympanum and the ornate calligraphy link it to a Charleston stonecutter, perhaps Thomas Walker or his workshop. A number of the early-nineteenth-century stones at Third Creek have the illegible signature of a Philadelphia stonecutter, probably Struthers, a favorite of North Carolina's elite during the second quarter of the nineteenth century.

In areas of strong German Lutheran influence, such as Davidson County, Scots-Irish gravestones have Germanic elements and may even have been cut by German carvers. Traditional gravestones at Jersey Baptist Church, established as a Baptist church in a Scots-Irish settlement in southern Davidson, have designs like those found on graves in local German cemeteries, such as a semicircular monogrammed tympanum, tapering sides, uppercase lettering, Gothic dots between words, and closely spaced rows separated by ruled lines. Atypical of the German idiom is the inclusion of a popular eighteenth-century epitaph. Although Hugh McCrarey's stone (Fig. 3.7) was likely carved by a Scots-Irish artisan imitating German stone

(opposite)
Figure 3.6.
Headstone
of Matthew
Locke, d. 1801,
Thyatira
Presbyterian
Churchyard,
Rowan County.

Figure 3.8.
Rear of head-
stone of
Hester Word,
death date
unknown.
Jersey Baptist
Churchyard,
Davidson
County.

style, the headstone of Hester Word (b. 1804, death date not given) (Fig. 3.8) at the same cemetery was almost certainly carved by a German artisan. Its baroque tympanum, molded sunburst, and sides enriched with diagonal molding link it to the antebellum Swisegood cabinetmaking group in Davidson County. To give Hester's stone a personal touch, the German artisan carefully etched a tall thistle, the symbol of Scotland, on the back.

In the mid-eighteenth century, British Quakers, overflowing from Pennsylvania and New Jersey, colonized Guilford, Randolph, and Alamance Counties in the eastern Piedmont. These settlements were widely scattered and remained small, and the design and layout of their graveyards has the same linear arrangement of head and footstones as Scots-Irish graveyards (Fig. 3.9). Their markers were apparently small, simple headstones carved by local artisans (Fig. 3.10). Some were circular medallions supported on low bases, others had clipped corners, still others were rectangular. Most bear neat uppercase lettering and, in keeping with Quaker simplicity, nearly all are plain and unembellished with symbols save one, which has tiny moon and star motifs.

Gravemarkers unique to Quaker cemeteries were made from another abundant local material—clay. The pottery industry in early Randolph, Guilford, and Alamance Counties in the eastern Piedmont was operated largely by Quakers, and by 1850 had made Randolph County the center of salt-glazed pottery in North Carolina. One concentration of Quaker potters in this region was at Snow Camp in southern Alamance County. At Cane Creek Friends Meeting House, established 1751, stand the only two pottery slab markers known in North Carolina, one for infant Israel C. Woody (d. 1834) and the other for "T. Boggs" (d. 1862).[20] The Boggs marker is small and plain; the Woody marker is a larger, skillful imitation of a traditional discoid headstone, with a careful uppercase inscription impressed into the clay in the semicircular tympanum and a small impressed flower design on the front and the back. The potter expressed the infant's age and death date in stan-

Figure 3.9. New Garden Friends Meeting graveyard, Greensboro. Watercolor from "Among the Friends in North Carolina, 1869," written and illustrated by John Collins. (Courtesy Friends Historical Collection, Guilford College, Greensboro.)

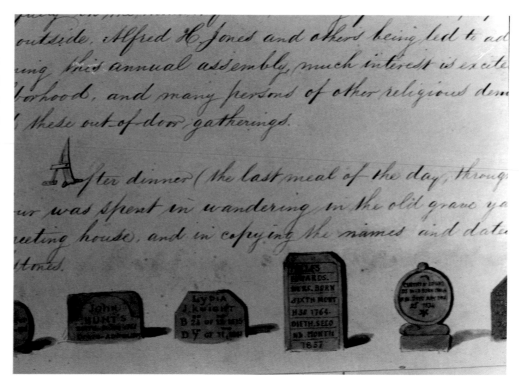

dard Quaker execution (e.g., "the 14th of 8th mo., 1834") in the center (Fig. 3.11).[21] Clay slab construction was inherently difficult; apparently this type of pottery gravemarker was not frequently produced.

In Alamance, Moore, Randolph, and Union Counties in the southeast Piedmont, from the 1830s to the 1930s Quaker and non-Quaker potters turned large numbers of "jug markers" that had open bases and closed tops.[22] These often have a decorative finial or knob at the top that served to keep out water. Some of the surviving jug markers have nipped-in waists, sharp finials on the peak, and heavy glaze coatings on the shoulders that make them outstanding examples of folk pottery, but the majority were simple turned shapes. Most were special commissions, for the potter wrote the name and birth/death dates of the deceased into the wet clay before firing the jug (Fig. 3.12). Many of them were made for members of the potters' families, and would have been inexpensive means of memorializing the dead.

Most pottery gravemarkers were used in graveyards close to the pottery shops of the eastern Piedmont, where generations of potters made utilitarian ceramic vessels from the late eighteenth to the early twentieth centuries. A few examples are known in Buncombe County, in the Blue Ridge Mountains. North Carolina is by no means the only state with a tradition of pottery gravemarkers. Potters in many sections of the eastern United States made them, but the rural southeastern states, especially Virginia, North Carolina, Georgia, Alabama, and Mississippi, may have had the richest tradition of pottery gravemarkers.

Only a handful of pottery gravemarkers still remains in North Carolina cemeteries. This type of marker is extremely fragile, and over the years they have either broken or been removed from cemeteries. The remarkable examples that survive in museum or private collections, old photographs, and oral history provide a tantalizing glimpse of this robust tradition.

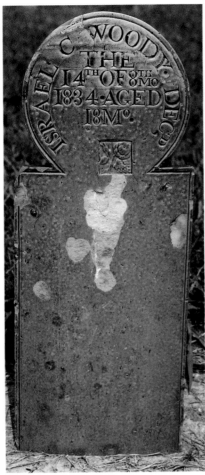 

(left) Figure 3.11. Stoneware grave marker of Israel C. Woody, d. 1834, Cane Creek Friends Meeting graveyard, Snow Camp. Attributed to Alamance potter Solomon Loy. (Photo courtesy Charles G. Zug)
(right) Figure 3.12. Typical salt-glazed stoneware foot and head marker for D. B. Laney, d. 1885, Laney Family Cemetery, Altan. (Courtesy Laney Family Cemetery Committee, Altan; photo courtesy Charles G. Zug)

The Moravian Graveyard

The most cohesive early German settlement in the Piedmont was the Moravian colony of Wachovia in central Forsyth County. Organized by the Moravian Church headquartered in Europe, German-speaking Moravians emigrated from the Czech Republic, Lithuania, Poland, Switzerland, and Alsace to Bethlehem, Pennsylvania, and from there some were sent down through the Valley of Virginia to establish Wachovia, an approximately 100,000-acre tract purchased from Lord Granville, a Lord Proprietor, in 1752.[23] This carefully supervised German-speaking colony established its first town, Bethabara, in 1753 and Salem, which became the center of Moravian government, in 1766. Other Germans (both Lutheran and Reformed), Scots-Irish, and English moved into the backcountry in the second half of the eighteenth century and came within the orbit of Moravians from whom they purchased well-made Moravian guns, furniture, pottery, silver, and textiles. In the early nineteenth century, artisans who trained under Moravian craftsmen moved out to surrounding commercial centers in the Piedmont.

Each Moravian congregation had its own graveyard, called "God's Acre." The Moravians laid out the first God's Acre at Bethabara along with the town in 1753.

God's Acres followed a formula for layout and gravestone design that created a park-like setting of beautiful serenity. The cemetery is located on a hilltop, and is enclosed by a stately border of tall cedar trees. An avenue, often bordered by cedars as well, extends from the village up to God's Acre. The burial ground is laid off in large squares, each square assigned to groups in the church family known as "choirs." Married women and widows are buried, in geometric and chronological precision, in one square; married men and widowers in another; single men and boys in another; and single women and girls in another (Fig. 3.13). The choir system of the cemeteries reflects the groups into which Moravian congregations were organized for activities and mutual support, and sometimes for communal living, since frequently the single men, the single women, and the widows lived in community-owned houses.[24] The centralized church government controlled all aspects of life in Moravian communities.

Each gravestone is a plaque, numbered consecutively according to the order of death, and containing name, date of death, age, and, on the earliest stones, place of birth (Fig. 3.14). The gravestone is laid flush on the ground. The earliest are of local stone, vary slightly in size, and sometimes include a small tulip or sunstar at the top. By the early nineteenth century marble plaques with professional lettering had become standard, as had the dimensions, approximately fifteen inches square. As early as 1790, blanks were stockpiled by the official Moravian stonecutter, who kept a supply of carved stones on hand and filled in the name and dates when a death occurred.[25]

Differences in wealth and social status so obvious in the materials, size, and design of gravemarkers in other cemeteries were intentionally and completely absent from God's Acres. The careful records kept by the Moravians provide both the names of the artisans who cut the gravestones and show how seriously Moravian

Figure 3.14.
Grave
plaque of
Joh Friedrich
Schmidt,
d. 1768,
God's Acre,
Bethabara,
Forsyth
County.

(opposite)
Figure 3.13.
God's Acre,
Bethabara,
Forsyth
County,
established
1753.

leaders enforced the standardized equality of God's Acre. Nonetheless problems did occur.[26] On 16 January 1783, the central authority announced: "We shall carefully maintain the harmony so far kept up with gravestones on our Salem Grave Yard. Mentioning of countries should be in English. We shall also try to find some putty to fill the letters with."[27] But the harmony was not easy to maintain. In June 1786 the leaders reported, "A complaint was raised over the fact that recently our gravestones seem to lose the former equality. They should be of the same size and should have the same type of inscription. For this the English capital letters are to be used."[28]

Apparently the leaders assigned a stonecutter to produce blanks subsequent to this complaint, for in April 1790 they made the following report: "Br. Rud. Strehle is going to Pennsylvania with the next transport. Since he has a stock of grave stones left, it was decided to buy those from him, that are equally well done, for the account of the Community Diaconate, thus the order on the grave yard concerning the equality of the stones will be fostered."[29]

In March of 1792 the leaders discussed the difficulty of keeping up with gravestone demand: "It would be good if the graveyard could be cleared up before Easter, and that the missing grave stones are placed on the graves. Since however, recently many Brothers and Sisters have died this will hardly be possible. Br. Redeken has cut the letters into some of the stones, however, he does not think that he will be able to continue with that. Perhaps Br. Wohlfarth could take this work over. It shall be taken care that the stones and the letters on them are made in one way."[30]

Moravian leaders considered ways to improve the consistency and proportion of lettering in September 1799: "Br. Christ was asked to talk to Br. Wohlfarth about the grave-stones, and tell him how to handle the inscriptions. Br. Schweinitz is going to show him the letters which we want. An alphabet cut from tin would add much to the beauty of the letters on the whole. However, it does not seem to be suiting because of the different lengths of names."[31]

In 1803 the leaders continued to enforce standardization within Wachovia graveyards: "It was suggested that Br. Friedrich Meinung cut the inscriptions on the gravestones. The preacher shall supply the wording, which shall be done in our other congregations also, so that they may be uniform. Dr. Reichel wishes that we could use larger stones, which would give space for more words, but that does not seem possible."[32]

But the central authority allowed a slight loosening of gravestone standards: "In regard to the gravestones, we think that the Brethren and Sisters may choose the type of lettering they prefer, and the color of the paint."[33] But the Moravians never abandoned the basic system, and throughout the 1810s they struggled to maintain graveyard traditions. In January 1820, Brother Will Holland was granted permission to transfer the remains of his children to the Salem Grave Yard, but "it . . . cannot be permitted that the two tombstones, which he brought with him, are put on the tombs of these two children, since—in addition to the customary text— these stones contain several lines of rhyme. He will have to use such stones as are customary with us on our Graveyard, i.e. without any rhymes."[34] And in 1831 the

Congregational Council stated, "It would be a pity if the simplicity and equality which has hitherto characterized our stones in the graveyard were to be marred by the contemplated setting of a stone by Traugott Lineback on the grave of a stranger buried here this year. We therefore passed a motion to dissuade him from this and also to notify the Brethren who make gravestones in future cases of this kind to acquaint people with our customs."[35] Two days later they advised Traugott Leinbach, a Moravian silversmith and stonecutter in Salem, ". . . not to bring the large gravestone on which he has been working for the grave of a gentleman from South Carolina who died here, on the graveyard."[36] Leinbach, a skilled stonecutter, made both standardized Moravian plaques and fashionable neoclassical marble headstones with decorative shapes and urn-and-willow ornament. The gravestone of the South Carolina visitor was probably a neoclassical design that was unacceptable because it was not a Moravian marker.

Dobbs Parish Cemetery, established about 1759 by the Moravians for non-Moravians and Moravians who died of "strange diseases," stands a few miles north of Salem and contains a mixture of Moravian plaques and non-Moravian headstones. Although many of the Dobbs Parish markers appear to have been relocated within the graveyard, it seems that the Moravian separation into choirs by age and sex was not enforced here. The Moravian rectangular plaques are set flush on the ground and are cut with numbers indicating the sequence of burials. Some have well-cut inscriptions; on others the lettering is labored. One plaque of local stone in the cemetery, professionally inscribed with "born" and "died," was probably a Moravian blank completed by a family member, who cut the 1751–1810 dates in an inexpert and tentative hand. A number of the markers are small varied headstones of quartz and soapstone with semicircular tympana, often with a tulip or tree-of-life.

The concept of equality in death and the aesthetic harmony that grew out of Moravian beliefs were such powerful ideas that even non-Moravian neighbors adopted elements of it. There are Moravian-type plaques in graveyards throughout Forsyth and north Davidson Counties, and several non-Moravian churches established in the mid-twentieth century in north Davidson contain standardized plaques laid in rigid rows, although the plaques are larger and graves are arranged by families rather than in the choir system.

The German Graveyard

Non-Moravian Germans who settled Piedmont North Carolina in the eighteenth century established small dispersed farm communities loosely knit by Lutheran, Reformed, and German Baptist Churches. They buried their dead in churchyards and in private family graveyards. In sparsely settled rural areas, Lutheran and German Reformed congregations would often build a single church, known as a Union Church, which they shared. These churches had considerable local autonomy, unlike Moravian churches, which were ruled by centralized government. For the sake of brevity, the term "German" throughout this chapter is used to mean all non-Moravian German denominations, including Lutherans, German Reformed, and

German Baptists. The comparison of a German graveyard, filled with irregular rows of small and large stones of all shapes and decorated with a wide variety of joyous religious symbolism, with a Moravian God's Acre, a serene field of small flat plaques set into neat grass, is a striking visual manifestation of the difference between a laissez-faire and a regimented society.

North Carolina German gravestones followed gravestone traditions in the Rhenish Palatinate homeland of Germany. From the earliest stones of the 1770s to the 1860s, local stonecutters carved distinctive headstones decorated, as were Palatinate German gravestones, with the tree-of-life, often rising out of a sunburst or vase, the compass star, the quarter sunburst, the heart, and the flower.[37] The German gravestone tradition lasted for nearly a century and is marked by variety and spectacular decorative displays. German stones reflect little response to popular culture. Most of the stones are from the locally plentiful supplies of soapstone, slate, and quartz.

Traditional German stonecutters used the German language on stones until the 1820s, although in some areas, such as the Catawba Valley, carvers switched to English by about 1807, while in other areas of the central Piedmont some retained German inscriptions through the 1830s. The content of German inscriptions parallels that of English inscriptions. A lexicon of the most common words includes *Jahr* (year), *Tag* or *Dag* (day), *geboren* (born), *gestorben* (died), *lieb* (body), *ruhet* (rest), *liegt* (lies), and *Himmel* (heaven) (Fig. 3.15).

Germans in Pennsylvania produced traditional gravestones of similar form to North Carolina German stones. In east and southeast Pennsylvania, artisans cut sandstone and occasionally slate in baroque shapes, with German Gothic or Roman lettering and decorative carving in bold relief. Stonecutters often carved a recessed panel filled by a large tree-of-life on the rear face, each branch terminating in a flower, the two lower branches often drooping. Sometimes a compass star filled the tympanum, and quarter sunbursts decorated the corners. Some conservative Pennsylvania German stonecutters produced such headstones as late as 1853, but many stonecutters incorporated English imagery by the early nineteenth century. For example, one otherwise traditional gravestone (Fig. 3.16), decorated with spirals and a tree-of-life, carved about 1800 for an unknown child at Zion's Stone Churchyard in Pennsylvania, displays a winged death's head in the tympanum.[38]

In southwest Virginia, traditional German gravestones persisted from the 1790s to about 1835; here German stonecutters apparently resisted the inundation of popular imagery more than in Pennsylvania. A number of resident and itinerant stonemasons appeared in the area about 1800 and produced not only substantial masonry houses and mills, but also monumental gravestones of striking folk German designs between about 1810 and 1835. Stonecutters cut thick slabs, usually of sandstone although occasionally of slate or schist, into tall discoid shapes with semicircular tympana on square shoulders and bold crimped borders. They employed a flower, star, sun, or fylfot to decorate the center of the tympanum, while covering the entire rear of the stone with folk imagery, sometimes a large tree-of-life, sometimes a triple arrangement of symbols. The stones have no epitaphs, and are inscribed in uppercase, often irregular, lettering. A sole signed stone revealed

(opposite) Figure 3.15. German-language headstone of Daniel Grison, Low's Lutheran Churchyard, Guilford County. English translation: "Here lies the body of Daniel Grison born the 17th of May 1790. He was 30 years, 10 months and 14 days old."

Figure 3.16.
Headstone for unknown child,
ca. 1800, Zion's Stone Churchyard,
Pennsylvania.
(From Barba, *Pennsylvania German
Tombstones*; reproduced courtesy
Pennsylvania German Folklore Society)

the identity of the most talented stonecutter, Laurence Krone, a member of the German Reformed Church who worked in the Valley from about 1815 to his death in 1836.[39] These head and footstones at the McGavock Graveyard, Wythe County, dating from 1817–30, are attributed to Laurence Krone (Fig. 3.17).

The North Carolina cemetery displays are among the very few remnants of the decorative German craft tradition to survive in the state's landscape outside of Wachovia, where the towns of Salem, Bethabara, and Bethania contain whole streetscapes with houses, churches, shops, barns, and cemeteries built by the Moravians and restored in recent years. But in such Piedmont counties as Davidson, Lincoln, and Catawba, the distinctive German gravestones are the principal German artifacts left on the land. Although a few traditional stone houses and churches and massive log barns reflect the once-dominant German culture, the agricultural focus of non-Moravian German groups created a dispersed rural landscape that did not lend itself to restoration as did the Moravian villages.

Except for the designs of gravestones, German graveyards closely resemble those of the Scots-Irish. The graveyards have linear rows of head and footstones, with family members buried side by side rather than in family plots. Cemeteries are treeless and shrubless, with tight rows of headstones including early locally made headstones and commercial marble headstones from the later nineteenth and twentieth centuries (Fig. 3.18). Most of the graveyards have a few unshaped and uninscribed fieldstones that may represent the first generation of settlement, in the

mid-eighteenth century, before artisans found suitable stone deposits and perhaps before they had acquired stonecutting tools. Some of these, such as those found at Organ Churchyard and Lower Stone Churchyard in Rowan County and Beck's Reformed Churchyard in Davidson County, are ingeniously worked (Fig. 3.19). The artisan did not attempt to carve a name or death date on the face of the slab, but incised a pediment in the top of the rough slab.

As early as the 1790s, a number of skilled German artisans were supplying deco-

Figure 3.17. Headstones at McGavock Graveyard, 1817–30, attributed to Laurence Krone, Wythe County, Virginia.

Figure 3.18.
Daniels Lutheran Churchyard, Lincoln County.

Figure 3.19.
Anonymous headstone,
Organ Lutheran Churchyard,
Rowan County.
(Photo by M. Ruth Little;
Southern Folklife Collection,
Wilson Library, University of
North Carolina at Chapel Hill

rative gravestones. Although most of these headstones are quite small, with cramped, careful inscriptions, the styles vary considerably from one region to another, depending upon the type of local stone available and the models followed by the artisan. The richest concentration of traditional German graveyards extends from Guilford, Davidson, and Forsyth Counties in the central Piedmont to the Catawba Valley in the western Piedmont.[40] Their varied and exuberant gravestones range from small to large, unskilled to professional, and plain to ornamental. Individual stonecutters adapted the same basic head and footstone form, local stone, and folk symbolism in many unique ways.

In Guilford and Forsyth Counties, small soapstone, slate, or quartz headstones were cut in discoid shapes and ornamented with exquisitely incised folk motifs including delicate pinwheels, sunstars, or abstract shapes. At Low's Lutheran Churchyard, Guilford County, German carvers created stones of pink, yellow, and white quartz, with a hard glossy surface that permits precise and durable detailing. (See Figure 3.15.) At Shiloh Lutheran Churchyard, Forsyth County, many carvers contributed small groups of stones in discoid and baroque forms, on which the lettering ranges from professionally inscribed German Gothic to unskilled English scrawls. The stones are joyously decorated with relief carved rosettes, tulips, sunstars, abstract symbols, sunbursts, and circles. The several unique markers at Friedens Lutheran Church, Guilford County, include one for Elizabeth Scherer (d. 1826). She is commemorated by a tiny soapstone discoid headstone and footstone with inscription, yet her grave is covered with a thick, roughly hewn native-stone ledger, a rare form in German graveyards. Jacob and Margret Summers (d. 1810) share a massive native granite headstone with a tree-of-life carved in high relief in the shallow tympanum, no doubt the work of a local German artisan who had in mind both the traditional tree-of-life and the neoclassical willow tree (Fig. 3.20).

DAVIDSON COUNTY GERMAN GRAVESTONES

The gravestones reached their fullest development in Davidson County, where the fortuitous combination of one of the purest concentrations of ethnic settlement, a tradition of skilled cabinetmaking, and the presence of soapstone produced the most splendid collection of decorative German stones in North Carolina. During the 1790–1820 period when Guilford and Forsyth County artisans were experimenting with a wide variety of forms, their counterparts in Davidson County created a standardized model: a small tapered shield-like headstone, averaging ten inches wide and eighteen inches high, that has squared shoulders and a semicircular tympanum. Carvers generally centered a monogram or date of birth or death in the tympanum, often in a decorative bracket and then cut the inscription, using ruled lines, and oftentimes Gothic dots to separate the crowded words, on the main body of the stone. The back was left undecorated and uninscribed except for an occasional beaded border (Fig. 3.21). Germanic symbols could be added to the tympanum or base. The tiny headstone of Ludwig Stokinger (d. 1806), at Beck's Churchyard, has a pointed arch tympanum with inscribed sunburst. German hearts etched along the base enliven the headstone of Adam Hedrich (d. 1798), at Beck's

Figure 3.20.
Headstone
of Jacob
and Margret
Summers,
d. 1810,
Friedens
Lutheran
Churchyard,
Guilford
County.

Figure 3.21.
Headstone
of William
Claten,
d. 1807,
Bethany
Lutheran and
Reformed
Churchyard,
Davidson
County.

Churchyard. Traditional stonecutters continued to produce shield-type stones even after a new style emerged in the 1820s, although the idiom became less distinct. The headstone of Conroad Grubb (d. 1842), at St. Luke's Lutheran Churchyard, an irregularly shaped fieldstone inscribed in careful but unskilled lettering, with no added decoration, typifies these late examples of the tradition.

About 1820 a new style was adopted by several stonecutters in Davidson County: a "pierced style," based on the shield shape but incorporating motifs used on locally made furniture and *Fraktur* to create baroque-style headstones with voluptuously molded ornament.

CATAWBA VALLEY GERMAN GRAVESTONES

Although the Catawba Valley counties of Catawba, Lincoln, and Gaston in the western Piedmont had approximately equal numbers of Germans and Scots-Irish settlers in the late eighteenth and early nineteenth centuries, distinctive German gravestones are extremely rare. Lincoln County was an important center of iron manufacture in the late eighteenth century. Open-hearth iron furnaces operated by

Figure 3.22.
Rear of
headstone
of Karlik Lein,
d. 1801,
Old White
Church,
Lincolnton.

German and French Huguenot settlers cast decorative chimney backs and other iron objects, and could have produced cast-iron gravemarkers, but no examples have been found in the region. Indeed, only a few of the earliest gravestones, headstones of local stone, with semicircular tympana with squared shoulders, uppercase lettering between scored lines, words often separated by Gothic dots—Antoni His (d. 1792), Salem Lutheran Church; Maria Haasin (d. 1796), Daniels Evangelical Lutheran Church; and Maria Catrena (d. 1796) and Catharine Riebin (d. 1816), Old White Church—are inscribed in German. On Catharine Riebin's stone, the only decorated German stone, the stonecutter carved a German turnip-shaped heart in the center of the neatly beaded tympanum.

One German artisan carved robustly sculptured headstones ornamented with folk motifs during the 1790–1820 period (Fig. 3.22). His high relief sunbursts on the front and rear of the tympanum and on the upper rear corners achieved a baroque richness in the spirit of European altar pieces and paralleled the use of the fan motif by commercial stonecutters in the same period. Three other headstones that he carved with the same high-relief decoration early in the century stand at St. Paul's Lutheran Church in Newton, Catawba County, about twenty-five miles north of Lincolnton.

The Appalachian Mountain Graveyard

The graveyards planted on the grassy slopes of the Appalachian Mountains possess a composite character all their own and lack the ethnic distinctiveness of those in the Piedmont and Coastal Plain. They often surmount the high knobs that rise in the Appalachian Mountains, sites so steep that they were impractical for building dwellings or for farming (Fig. 3.23). The decision to use those sites achieved a spiritual meaning that parallels burial traditions in such radically different cultures as the American Indians and the German Moravians. Indians of western North Carolina buried their dead in man-made earthen hills known as burial mounds, and white settlers who found these mounds on the land they acquired after the Indians had been driven off sometimes placed their own family graveyards on them.[41]

Mountain graveyards from the late-eighteenth- and early-nineteenth-century settlement period contain rough, uninscribed fieldstone markers and isolated examples of skillfully cut headstones. By the mid-nineteenth century, the discoid

Figure 3.23.
Glenn Cemetery, Ward Branch Road, Watauga County.
(Photo by M. Ruth Little; Southern Folklife Collection,
Wilson Library, University of North Carolina at Chapel Hill)

soapstone form was being used throughout the region. Most families made their own gravestones, just as they made most everything else, and many elderly mountain people recall that their fathers and grandfathers cut soapstone out of the hills with a crosscut saw and hewed them with axes to obtain decorative shapes. No doubt Piedmont people alive during the late nineteenth century recalled such memories as well.

Figure 3.24. Headstone of John A. Finley, d. 1811, Wilkesboro Presbyterian Churchyard, Wilkes County. (Photo by M. Ruth Little)

The earliest appearance of skillfully carved stones varies from locale to locale. Some areas had access to talented local stonecutters as early as the 1820s or 1830s, and others not until the 1850s. The group of small soapstone headstones with baroque shapes dating from 1811–43 at Wilkesboro Presbyterian Church in Wilkes County are probably the work of a local antebellum artisan. The earliest of these is for John A. Finley (Fig. 3.24); one of the last is for John Thomas Martin. Baroque-style headstones at Shaw's Creek Methodist Church Cemetery in Henderson County date from the 1830s and 1840s. The congregation of old Three Forks Baptist Church, established in 1790, had only rough fieldstone markers in the churchyard for more than two generations. Even in the 1840s and 1850s, a stonecutter managed to produce only very roughly shaped discoid stones for church members who died. The churchyard is located on the bank of the New River in Boone, Watauga County, at the extreme western edge of the state.

Some mountain headstones commemorate settlers who died twenty-five to fifty years before the stones were carved, an understandable occurrence in a frontier region that had poor or nonexistent roads in the earliest decades of settlement. Revolutionary War veteran George Gordon (who came to Wilkes County from Virginia in 1770) died in 1800. Although this is the oldest dated stone in the St. Paul's Episcopal Churchyard in Wilkesboro, it could have been carved many years after Gordon's death. This tall, thick soapstone headstone with a semicircular tympanum, flanking caps too attenuated to be stylish, and neat inscription is a masterful design by an anonymous stonecutter.

In 1827 the opening of the newly completed Buncombe Turnpike, connecting Greenville, South Carolina, to Asheville, North Carolina, brought the taste of the gentry in architecture, household goods, and gravestones to the mountainous west. The parish graveyard of St. John's in the Wilderness Episcopal Church at Flat Rock, the Charleston summer colony established in the early nineteenth century in Henderson County, has family plots with box-tombs probably hauled from Charleston, surrounded by walls and iron fences characteristic of coastal Carolina plantation graveyards. A few stonecutters working in the area, probably building the group of South Carolinians' stone summer houses, carved some gravestones for local people. These tall headstones of local stone have simple baroque shapes (Fig. 3.25). The "J.P." who carved one for Thomas Rhodes (d. 1827) was John Pearson, an English stonecutter who lived in the county during the mid-nineteenth century and was probably engaged in stone house construction.[42]

The most dramatic example of backdating known in western North Carolina occurs in Watauga County on the Tennessee border. The first person buried in the Jont Brown Graveyard in Watauga County is Thomas Brown, who died in 1835. Rev. Alex Wilson, a Baptist preacher who began carving gravestones in the 1890s, cut a soapstone headstone of neat shape and lettering for Brown, backdating it by more than fifty years. Another soapstone carver, whose identity is unknown, worked at the turn of the century in the Mitchell and Avery County area. He cut a group of greenish soapstone headstones with exuberant, eccentric lobed shapes that stand at Pisgah Methodist Church in Avery County.

Marble gravestones, like commercially manufactured furniture and stylish architecture, symbolize the march of progress in the western foothills and mountains. By the late 1820s some families in Wilkesboro commemorated their loved ones with marble box-tombs and headstones. By the time Wilkesboro Presbyterian Church was established in 1837, congregation families were ordering marble ledgers and headstones for churchyard graves as well. When Elizabeth Weaver, of Weaverville, in Buncombe County, died in 1843, her family managed to purchase a blank marble headstone of elegant design. But when they took it to a local artisan for the inscription, he engraved her name and birth and death dates in hasty scrawls on the rear of the stone, leaving the decorative front face blank.[43]

As Elizabeth Weaver's backward-engraved monument shows, marble monuments were often purchased as blanks and engraved locally by someone unfamiliar with the conventions of gravestone engraving. At Shaw's Creek Methodist Churchyard in Henderson County lies Polly Summey, who "died in the faith" in 1857 and is memorialized by a tall neoclassical marble headstone that came from the Walker shop in Charleston, South Carolina. At Zionville Baptist Churchyard on the Tennessee border, marble headstones with death dates in the 1840s stand out among the local fieldstone markers.

Western North Carolina people continued to order monuments from South Carolina marble firms until the arrival of railroad tracks from the east allowed access to North Carolina Piedmont marble yards and encouraged stonecutters to set up businesses in the mountains. By 1860 the Western North Carolina Railroad was completed from Salisbury in the Piedmont to Morganton in Burke County, at the eastern edge of the mountains. Twenty years later it was finished to Asheville, in 1882 it reached the Tennessee line, and in 1890 it extended to Murphy in the extreme southwest corner of the state. Rebecca A. E. Snead, a member of St. Paul's Episcopal Church in Wilkesboro, died in 1880, and her family ordered a splendid marble tomb-table for her from a stonecutter named Roble in the western Piedmont town of Statesville. By 1884 a number of marble works had opened in the mountains: J. H. Hemphill's in Marion, A. E. Baum's in Sylva, and William O. Wolfe's in Asheville.[44] Wolfe had been lured to Asheville by the railroad boom. Born in Pennsylvania, Wolfe had learned stonecutting in Baltimore, and owned a marble yard in Raleigh before moving to Asheville, primarily in hopes of improving his wife's health in 1880.[45] He must have counted on gaining a good business for his grave monuments in Asheville, where the railroad enabled his marble to be shipped from Georgia and Vermont quarries.

(opposite) Figure 3.25. Headstone of Thomas Rhodes, d. 1827, Old French Broad Baptist Churchyard, Henderson County. Signed "J.P.," presumably stonecutter John Pearson. (Photo by M. Ruth Little)

Piedmont and Mountain Perspective: A Stone for Every Grave

In the Piedmont, the socioeconomic spectrum of the eighteenth and nineteenth centuries with its predominant middling yeoman farmer class is still visible, for the local stone from which the poor and the wealthy cut their monuments has survived equally well. The locally carved headstones of the eighteenth and nineteenth centuries provide a continuous record of the distinctive Scots-Irish and German cultures of the Piedmont and their artistic cross-fertilization and acculturation. Settlement, railroads, good roads, and skilled stonecutters all arrived much later in the mountains than in the Piedmont. Ethnic groups blended in the valleys and hollows so that the Scots-Irish or Germanic symbolism of Piedmont headstones faded into a more individualized self-expression on mountain gravestones. While part-time stonecutters in the Piedmont put away their mallets and chisels about 1860, when trainloads of commercial stonecutters and blocks of marble began to arrive, the mountain artisans thrived for another fifty years, carving headstones out of local stone. The continuation of traditional gravestone carving in the mountains until the early twentieth century is the most important story that mountain gravestones tell. Touching, often labored headstones carved by family members, local artisans, and the occasional skilled stonecutter animate the cemeteries of the mountains.

4 Backcountry Stonecutters

IN MEMORY OF

Joseph S. Williams

Born Jan. 17th 1822

Died June 10th 1825

Farewell my parents here below
Though much you do me love
. . . s, and I must g . . .

Six individual stonecutters or stonecutting shops, who worked in two distinctive regions of the rolling Carolina Upland frontier known as the "backcountry"—the Catawba Valley of the Carolinas and Davidson County in North Carolina—have emerged from the anonymity of the preindustrial age into the light of historical identity. These stonecutters lived in rural communities that had a rich crafts tradition. The plentiful supply of local stone and the close-knit ethnic communities supported the carving of hundreds of gravestones during the eighteenth and first half of the nineteenth century. The basic economic and social unit of these communities was the family farm, and the combination of a trade with farming was a widespread practice. Artisans, like lawyers and physicians, kept farms in order to raise their own food and gain stability in a world with scattered and unpredictable opportunities for specialized work. The heyday of the traditional farmer-artisan in Piedmont Carolina began in the late eighteenth century, as communities matured beyond the frontier stage into small towns and country neighborhoods and more specialized work roles emerged among all the trades, including carpenters, masons, potters, coopers, silversmiths, and cabinetmakers. Rural artisans commonly worked over a range of two or three counties around a home base, often functioning as jacks-of-all-trades. If a rural artisan could undertake a wide range of tasks, he could get many different kinds of jobs and thus find frequent employment among a scattered clientele. Most specialty craftsmen combined two or three lines of work in order to remain in one location and earn a living, or else lived an itinerant life.[1]

A number of North Carolina artisans crafted gravemarkers as a sideline. The most likely specialty, masonry, did not breed stonecarvers in the Carolina backcountry. The absence of a building tradition in stone usually prevented masons from specializing in stonecutting. Masons generally laid brick, although they might perform minor stonecutting tasks such as cutting and installing door or window sills of stone and constructing an occasional stone chimney. One frequent combination of trades in both urban and rural areas, cabinetmaking, undertaking, and building, sometimes resulted in gravemarker production. A cabinetmaker's staple product was coffins, which led him into making other funeral arrangements, including digging the grave and providing transportation to the graveyard. Nineteenth-century business directories in North Carolina generally listed the two trades together; for example, in the 1860s Raleigh had three "Cabinet Maker and Undertaker" establishments.[2] In the 1870s George J. Smith and his son operated in Guilford County as contractors, carpenters, and coffin makers, and in the early twentieth century John E. B. Shutt of Davie County built a two-story frame building to house his cabinet- and coffin-making, wagon-building, and undertaking businesses.[3] Thomas Tilley operated a large coffin, casket, and furniture factory from about 1930 to about 1960 in the countryside of Stokes County out of a two-story frame building.[4]

Typically, the backcountry gravestone carver cut local stone into traditional forms and decorated it with designs meaningful to the community. He carved in-

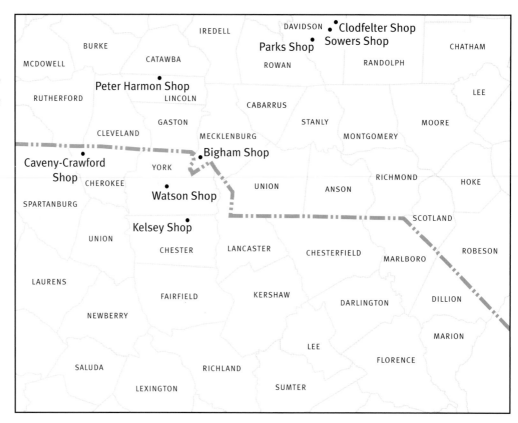

Figure 4.1.
Nineteenth-
century
stonecarving
centers in
Piedmont
North and
South
Carolina.

scriptions that often exhibited uneven lettering, misspellings, and grammatical er-
rors. He rarely thought to sign his work as would an artist, and so is generally
anonymous today. He was usually part-time, his main occupation being farming.
His method of advertisement was word-of-mouth, his clientele generally consisted
of members of his own family or neighbors, and his products were rarely sold outside of his own geographic region.

A few artisan families were able to specialize in gravestones and to supply the
demand over a larger geographic region, even across state lines. The western piedmont counties of North and South Carolina formed a single trade region, united by
the north-south flow of rivers and roads, enabling stonecutters on each side of the
state line to sell their stones throughout the entire area. Stonecarvers flourished in
the frontier of both states in the eighteenth century, although the largest workshops were in York and Mecklenburg Counties in the Catawba Valley, astride the
state line. In the valley Scots-Irish and German settlement was evenly balanced,
but Scots-Irish carvers dominated gravestone production. The initial center of production was in southern Mecklenburg County where the Bigham family worked,
followed in the early nineteenth century by the work of the Caveny and Crawford
families in northern York County (Fig. 4.1). By the 1810s, a group of German cabinetmakers, known as the Swisegood School, emerged in Davidson County. The
Bighams, the Caveny-Crawfords, and the Swisegood School, along with individuals
such as Hugh Kelsey, Peter Harmon, and others who remain anonymous, were accomplished stonecarvers whose work had an impact far beyond the boundaries of
their home counties.

BIGHAM FAMILY WORKSHOP, MECKLENBURG COUNTY,
NORTH CAROLINA, CA. 1765–1810

Samuel Bigham Sr., the earliest identified backcountry stonecutter in North Carolina, settled in the Steele Creek section of southern Mecklenburg County in the 1760s. The Bigham family had probably brought their trade with them from Northern Ireland when they immigrated to Pennsylvania in the 1730s and had carved gravestones with coats-of-arms in that mid-Atlantic colony until 1763, at which point they moved to Mecklenburg County. They quickly became the most prolific stonecutting workshop in the state during this period. Between 1765 and 1810 the shop produced hundreds of gravestones that were shipped by wagon throughout the western piedmont of both North and South Carolina. The stone-cutting trade was handed down through the extended Bigham family for at least two generations, ceasing around 1810.[5]

At least six different carvers worked in the Bigham Shop in Mecklenburg County. Samuel Bigham Sr. founded the workshop. The second generation, who probably began working in the 1780s, included three brothers, Samuel Bigham Jr., William Bigham, and Hugh Bigham, all apparently Samuel Sr.'s sons.[6] Two apprentices, James Sloan and William McKinley, also worked at the shop around the turn of the century. During nearly fifty years of operation, the Bigham Shop produced more than 900 surviving stones, some highly decorated, for graves in some twenty-four cemeteries in the Catawba Valley counties of Mecklenburg, Iredell, Lincoln, Gaston, and Rowan in North Carolina, and York, Chester, and Lancaster in South Carolina, as well as the more distant Haywood County on the Tennessee border. The finest collection of Bigham stones stands in the center of the church-yard of Steele Creek Presbyterian Church.[7]

Throughout the 1765–1810 period, the Bighams continued the tradition of eighteenth-century gravemarker decoration that they had produced in Northern Ireland: family coats-of-arms, religious imagery, and a bird holding a twig cover the fronts, backs, and sometimes sides of their headstones.[8] Most of the Bigham headstones had a standardized shape—an arched tympanum flanked by small caps. The specific symbols the Bighams carved often relate to the religious and social identity of their patrons, particularly to their Ulster Scot heritage. They often selected the dove-of-promise, a Scots-Irish symbol drawn from the Old Testament story of the flood, in which a bird with a twig in its beak is sent by God to prove to Noah that the ark's passengers could soon emerge onto dry land. The dove-of-promise is found on other Scots-Irish gravestones in the Carolina Piedmont and is still used by Scots in Ulster, in Northern Ireland. The Bighams carved a thistle, the national emblem of Scotland, on a number of stones. For many stones they carved the family coat-of-arms, a strong Scottish tradition (Fig. 4.2). These lose their specific family identity over the decades and combine with Masonic emblems or patriotic symbols such as the American eagle, the seal of the United States.

When Robert Bigham, surely a relative of the carver, died during the American

Revolution, he received a coat-of-arms headstone bearing a shield decorated with thirteen stars and the motto "Arma Liber Tatis" that clearly expressed his support for the independence of the thirteen colonies. Delicate thistles engraved in the caps of the tympanum recall his Scottish heritage (Fig. 4.3). A detailed rendition of the seal of the Commonwealth of Pennsylvania dignifies the headstone of Andrew Bigham, another family member (Fig. 4.4). The change from family arms to symbols of larger allegiance illustrates the transition in the late colonial and early Federal period from Old World clannishness to new defining relationships, such as fraternal orders or civic pride.[9]

Although most of the Bigham clients were Scots-Irish, and most of the stones are of Scots-Irish design and stand in Presbyterian churchyards, the workshop also borrowed decorative and symbolic motifs from the English and Germans, including a winged-soul head, the fylfot cross, and tree-of-life (Figs. 4.5, 4.6). They also decorated the rear face of their stones, a custom borrowed from German American and Scottish practices.[10] Most of the images are raised in high relief from the surface of the stones, creating a sculptural effect closer to Germanic gravestones than to the flat engraved style of most Scots-Irish stones.

The tall, slender headstones, carved of a fine-grained light-gray soapstone, demonstrate the high standards of quality to which the shop adhered. The Bighams cut fine moldings at the edges of the round-arched stones, and often finished the border of the tympanum with an additional ornamental pattern resembling tooled leatherwork. Most are decorated with symbolic images. Sometimes they engraved the inscription into the stone, sometimes the inscription is raised from the stone's surface by cutting away the surrounding stone. The letters are slender and of uniform width in comparison to the classical Roman alphabet of varying widths used by New England stonecutters. Although almost never signed, the stones possess a distinctive style that is instantly recognizable as the work of the Bigham Shop.

The only gravestone that a Bigham family carver is known to have signed is the headstone of Dr. Samuel Heron (d. 1798) at Prince George Winyah Churchyard, Georgetown, South Carolina. The stone depicts a rampant lion with flanking deer and a hand grasping a half-moon, apparently the Heron family coat-of-arms. The epitaph continues onto the back of the stone, with an emblem of crossed swords. Perhaps because Samuel Bigham was sending the gravestone outside of his usual market, to coastal South Carolina, he signed it "Engraved in No. Carolina Mecklenburg County by Samuel Bigham."[11] The stone became an advertisement for Bigham's work, which needed no identification within the Catawba Valley where the shop was well known.

The Bighams' work exhibits wide variety in form and decoration. For the stone of Lutheran minister Johann Godfried Arends (d. 1807), the Bigham Shop cut a seal of the United States (see Figure 3.2). For Polly Graham (d. 1801), daughter of ironmaster Joseph Graham, they cut a ledger stone.[12] For John McCaule (d. 1801), at Unity Presbyterian Church, Lincoln County, they used the customary tripartite shape, beaded edge, a tooled border, and, in addition to a verse epitaph, included a vivid account of McCaule's death (Fig. 4.7):

(opposite)
Figure 4.2.
Headstone
of Hannah
Greir, d. 1788,
Steele Creek
Presbyterian
Churchyard,
Charlotte.
Attributed
to the Samuel
Bigham work-
shop. This
is one of
the finest
examples of
the Bigham
workshop's
usage of a
traditional
coat-of-arms.

Figure 4.4.
Headstone of Andrew Bigham, d. 1788, with seal of the Commonwealth of Pennsylvania, from where the Bigham family emigrated. Steele Creek Presbyterian Churchyard, Charlotte. Attributed to the Samuel Bigham workshop.

(opposite)
Figure 4.3.
Headstone of Robert Bigham, d. 1777, Steele Creek Presbyterian Churchyard, Charlotte.
This Revolutionary War–era stone attributed to the Bigham workshop bears a coat-of-arms containing
both personal and national symbols.

(opposite)
Figure 4.5.
Headstone
of Mary Allen,
d. 1776,
Steele Creek
Presbyterian
Churchyard,
Charlotte. This
traditional
English "soul
image" is
attributed to
the Samuel
Bigham
workshop.

Figure 4.6.
Headstone
of Elizabeth
McClellen,
d. 1791,
Steele Creek
Presbyterian
Churchyard,
Charlotte. This
stone bearing
a fylfot cross
and trees-
of-life is
attributed to
the Samuel
Bigham
workshop.

Figure 4.7.
Headstone of
John McCaule,
d. 1801, Unity
Presbyterian
Church, Lincoln
County.
Attributed to
the Samuel
Bigham work-
shop.

Sacred to the memory of
JOHN McCAULE
Who in health left home 10th Nov.
1801 & went to a fair. The even
ing of that same day fell among
the sons of cruelty & in conse
quence of abuse received from
them died the next night in the
35th Year of his age.

Bigham followers Samuel Watson and William McKinley carved a number of headstones during the 1790–1810 period that follow the basic form, style, and choice of symbols of the Bigham Shop. Samuel Watson, a farmer and part-time stonecutter in York County, carved a small number of stones in his own community and for a few individuals in the northern Catawba Valley. His tall, narrow tripartite headstones have high, sharp shoulders, beaded moldings, and flat, tentatively carved images, including a portrait, the American eagle, and the dove-of-promise.[13] He probably carved the small headstone of Elisabeth Davis, an infant who died in 1795, at Olney Presbyterian Church, Gaston County. In the tympanum, the stylized floral design is derived from the Bigham repertory, and the inscription is cut in uneven lettering. William McKinley, an apprentice in the Bigham Shop, probably cut the dove-of-promise headstone of George Bivings (d. 1808) at Old White Church and the headstone of Eliza Higgins (d. 1808), at Olney Presbyterian Church, Gaston County.[14] McKinley's stones are simpler versions of Bigham stones, usually containing a single image set into the tympanum.

HUGH KELSEY, CHESTER COUNTY, SOUTH CAROLINA, 1770s–1817

Another early stonecutter was Hugh Kelsey (1754?–ca. 1817), who lived in Chester County, South Carolina, just south of York County. As a self-sufficient backcountry farmer with multiple skills, Kelsey possessed tools and equipment for shoemaking, stonecutting, tanning, woodworking, spinning, weaving, and general farming. Using local stone, he carved short, thick, round-arched headstones of local stone on which he lavished his surprisingly inventive repertory of symbolic imagery. He formulated unique combinations of Scots-Irish motifs, particularly the dove-of-promise, for his stones.[15]

Most of Kelsey's stones stand in his own community of Fishing Creek Presbyterian Church in Chester County, South Carolina, but he also carved stones that stand at Buffalo Presbyterian Church and Alamance Presbyterian Church in Guilford County. On the smooth slate of Mary Starratt's headstone he depicted a dove, probably symbolizing her soul, flying into the arc of heaven, above the sun, moon, and stars (Fig. 4.8). The stone for Robert Allison has the dove-of-promise (Fig. 4.9). James Blear's has a delicately incised profile portrait, a rare feature on North Carolina gravestones (Fig. 4.10). On yet another stone, Kelsey carved a horse with the globe symbol of earth. Kelsey might have copied engraved book illustrations. Although linearity is characteristic of Scots-Irish stonecarvers, the linear patterns of the dove's wings and tail on Mary Starratt's stone particularly resemble engravings.

CAVENY-CRAWFORD WORKSHOP, YORK COUNTY, SOUTH CAROLINA, AND CATAWBA VALLEY, NORTH CAROLINA, CA. 1800–CA. 1880

As the Bigham Shop ended its long and productive history about 1810, in the Catawba Valley the center of large-scale stonecutting activity shifted to York County, South Carolina, which had been recently settled by Scots-Irish from Penn-

Figure 4.8.
Headstone of Mary Starratt, d. 1775, Buffalo Presbyterian Churchyard, Guilford County.
Attributed to Hugh Kelsey, Chester County, S.C.

Figure 4.9.
Headstone of Robert Allison, d. 1782, Alamance Presbyterian Churchyard, Guilford County.
Attributed to Hugh Kelsey, Chester County, S.C.

Figure 4.10.
Headstone of James Blear, d. 1776[?], Alamance Presbyterian Churchyard, Guilford County.
Attributed to Hugh Kelsey, Chester County, S.C.

sylvania and Virginia. Yorkville, the county seat, was known in antebellum days as the "Charleston of the Upland" because of its strategic position as a trading center on the Catawba River.[16] Two intermarried Scots-Irish families, the Cavenys and the Crawfords, began a three-generation-long business of carving gravestones from soapstone from King's Mountain, located on the North Carolina state line, and from imported marble.[17]

Pennsylvanian John Caveny (1778–1853) was in his early twenties when he arrived in the Carolinas, about 1800, probably as part of a group of Scots-Irish families and neighbors in search of a fresh start. He married Mary Crawford and purchased a 120-acre farm adjacent to the lands of James Crawford, Mary's brother.[18] Caveny was already an accomplished stonecarver. He epitomizes the early-nineteenth-century stonecutter working in the neoclassical mode that was spreading throughout America in architecture and the decorative arts. His marble gravestones with urn-and-willow decoration, which he began carving about 1800, kept pace with the fashionable stones imported from Charleston, South Carolina, the South's style-setting center of the arts during the Federal era, yet most of his gravestones were cut of local soapstone in elegant baroque shapes with refined Roman lettering.

He executed sophisticated tombstones for wealthy clients, sometimes signing his name "J. Caveny, Engravor." The competent script with which he signed gravestone receipts indicates that he was schooled (Fig. 4.11). Caveny signed a number of stones, apparently those of which he was particularly proud. He belonged to nearby Bethany Associate Reformed Presbyterian Church, whose graveyard is full of gravestones cut by him, his brother-in-law, and their sons.

Caveny's gravestones, made throughout his fifty-year career, until his death in 1853, are found in cemeteries in York, Chester, Gaston, Lincoln, and Catawba Counties. At least nine of these he signed. For John McCall (d. 1807), a member of his church, he signed a soapstone headstone with elaborate Masonic imagery. About 1826, the Brevard family of Lincoln County commissioned John White of Charleston (son-in-law of Thomas Walker, the leading Federal-period Charleston stonecutter) to produce the monumental classical pedestal-tomb for Rebecca Brevard (d. 1824) and her daughter Eloise (d. 1826) that stands at Machpelah Presbyterian Church in Lincoln County. In 1829, when her husband, Capt. Alexander Brevard, died, John Caveny added a marble commemorative panel for him, signed "J. Caveny" (Fig. 4.12). In addition to at least three Caveny gravestones identified through receipts and probate records, forty-three are attributed based on style, motifs, and carving. Caveny's son, R. C. Caveny, born in 1808, became an engraver, too.

Figure 4.11. John Caveny's receipt for Mary Baird's gravestone, Lincoln County estate records, 1811. (North Carolina Division of Archives and History)

Caveny's stones emulate the stylish marble headstones cut by Thomas Walker, John White, and other contemporary Charleston stonecutters but are distinguishable because of their reliance on local stone, a certain naïveté of overall stone shape, including dimple motifs in the caps, and a restraint in size and choice of motifs. His stones rarely exhibit the full-blown neoclassical imagery of urns and willows so popular on Charleston gravestones. Instead, he generally used overall shape and lettering to achieve elegance. The headstones of Mary Baird (for which Caveny received two dollars in partial payment in 1811) and of Sarah Butts typify his oeuvre (Figs. 4.13, 4.14). Both are of the light-gray King's Mountain schist or soapstone that Caveny preferred. Both are elegant baroque shapes with a calligraphically simple but elegant lettering of the word "Sacred" in the center of the arched tympanum and half-moon or "dimple" motifs in the flanking caps. Both have their primary inscriptions executed in the same professional upper and lowercase Roman-style lettering.

James Crawford (1775–1842), whose younger sister Mary married John Caveny, lived on a farm next to John and Mary and was also a stonecutter. Indeed, his father, William Crawford, born in 1747 in Ireland, may have been a stonecutter himself.[19] A unique thin headstone cut of greenish stone for Joseph Carrell (d. 1803) may be the work of William Crawford or an early work of James Crawford (Fig. 4.15). The imagery reflects a mixture of the German compass star and Scots-Irish lunar symbolism, yet it is cut in a tentative, experimental style completely different

Sacred to
the
Memory of
MARY BAIRD
Who departed this life
9th 1810.
Aged 61 years.

Once engaged in scenes of life
A tender mother, loving wife
But now she's gone and left us here
The lesson bids us all prepare.

Figure 4.14.
Headstone of
Sarah Butts,
d. 1827, Old
White Union
Churchyard,
Lincolnton.
Attributed to
John Caveny.

from the richly detailed style of the Bigham Shop across the state line in Mecklenburg County. The carver miscarved several letters of the inscription and attempted to carve over them. When James Crawford died in 1842, he left "one-half of my stone Quarry Tract of land lying on part of King Mountain near the memorable hill called the Battleground and the Crow bar" to his oldest sons, Robert M. and William N. Crawford. Crawford's farm tools included one pair of tackles, one single tree and clevis, one ax and log chain, one iron wedge, one pick, and one lot of "worn-out" irons, which could have been used in quarrying the stone, shaping it

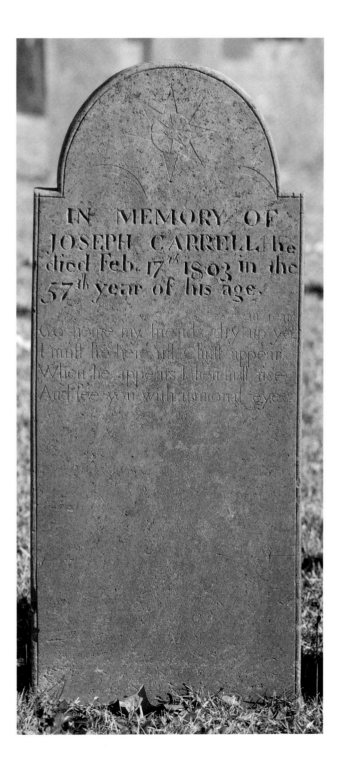

Figure 4.15.
Headstone of Joseph Carrell, d. 1803,
Bethany ARP Churchyard, York County, S.C.
Attributed to William Crawford Sr.

into rough slabs, and hauling it to the workshop. Other tools among Crawford's possessions that might have shaped and inscribed gravestones were a crosscut saw, a handsaw, augers, gouges, chisels, and drawing knives. The inventory of his personal property included "2 Sette Head & foote Stones (unlettered)" valued at $14 and "3 Sette Head & foot Stones (lettered)" valued at $23.[20]

James Crawford, although a skilled carver, apparently never used marble and never signed his gravestones. He cut schist into headstones with arched tympana and high caps that resembled the marble headstones cut by his partner John Caveny and by their Charleston competition. The tall headstone of York County militia leader Col. Frederick Hambright, which he cut in 1818, exemplifies his work.[21]

The next generation of Cavenys and Crawfords expanded the business: John Caveny's son Robert C. Caveny (1808–1890), who married a cousin of the Crawford family; Robert M. Crawford (1803–1865); William N. Crawford (1808–1894); and their brother-in-law Zenas S. Hill (1808–1877), who married their sister Lucinda Crawford. These carvers entered the business in the 1830s but captured an ever-decreasing share of the gravestone trade in York County, due to competition from South Carolina urban marble cutters of Charleston and Columbia. But the Caveny-Crawford Shop's cheaper prices and willingness to cater to local taste enabled them to acquire a large share of the gravestone trade in the Catawba Valley of North Carolina into the late 1860s. In addition to twenty-six documented stones in York County and in the Catawba Valley of North Carolina, there are more than two hundred attributed to this generation. Robert and William were the most prolific of the group. They rarely cut marble stones; however, all but a few of their signed gravestones are of marble, indicating that these were showcase stones. Robert signed five 1840s gravestones in York and Gaston Counties, and at least five of his 1830s to 1850s gravestone receipts survive in Lincoln County estate records.[22] William signed thirteen headstones in York and Gaston Counties, with dates from 1831 to 1879, and three of his receipts, dated 1847, 1851, and 1877, emerged in a sample of the Lincoln County estate records.[23]

Hundreds of gravestones in Lincoln, Catawba, and Gaston Counties dating from the mid-1820s to the mid-1870s are probated or attributed to John Caveny, Robert and William N. Crawford, Z. S. Hill, and R. C. Caveny.[24] Three-fourths of these are in Lutheran and Reformed churchyards, and many of the rest are in the cemeteries of United Church of Christ and Methodist churches. With the exception of a handful of marble stones, all of the Caveny-Crawford stones in the Catawba Valley are cut of a greenish-gray schist with a sparkling crystalline structure.

The earliest signed stones of Robert and William Crawford, with death dates in the 1830s and early 1840s, are fashionable marble headstones cut in identical neoclassical style. Blanks cut by Columbia and Charleston stonecutters were probably frequently on hand in their workshop, for it was by then common practice for local stonecutters to engrave imported blanks cut and shaped by other stonecutters. The executor of the estate of a Lincoln County woman bought a blank set of gravestones from well-known Columbia stonecutter Alexander Brown in 1847 for $8, then took the stones to William Crawford and paid him $2.72 for engraving them.[25]

Figure 4.19.
Headstone of Martha Jane Crawford, d. 1875,
Bethany ARP Churchyard, York County, S.C.
Signed "W. N. Crawford."

Lawson James Crawford, he carved and signed a tall marble headstone with a naturalistic rose bush that recalls the German tree-of-life, flanked by weeping willows representing out-of-date symbolism for the 1870s (Fig. 4.19). Lawson James Crawford, who died in 1912, is buried beside Martha Jane under an identical stone, apparently carved by William as part of the set and inscribed many years later when L. J. died.[27]

The stones that can be assigned to Robert C. Caveny and Zenas S. Hill are fewer in number. R. C. Caveny spent his career in York County and apparently carved no North Carolina stones. His signed stones at Bethany indicate that he worked in the same style as his father. Zenas S. Hill, who was probably living in Gaston County, North Carolina, by the 1830s, carved stones that are almost identical to those of Robert and William, but he cut inscriptions in deeper relief.[28] Only one stone, an 1843 headstone for Hugh Gibson at Olney Presbyterian Church, Gastonia, has been documented as Hill's work.[29] Based on this stone, six other headstones at the same churchyard, dating from 1827 to 1839, are attributed to him.

As mid-century approached, the number of commercial stonecutters in Piedmont Carolina had so increased that the Caveny-Crawford Shop was losing its fa-

vored status. Robert Crawford moved across the state line into the northern Catawba Valley, probably in search of a new market for his stones, and by 1860 was
residing in the county seat, Lincolnton. He and two of his sons, Robert A. and
Anderson M., identified themselves as "stonecutters" rather than farmers, which
was their label in 1850. This may have been necessitated by his move to a town, for
he clearly was away from the family farm down in York County. He continued the
stonecutting business until his death in 1865; in 1866 his estate received a payment
for a gravestone he made for a Catawba County man.[30] William remained in York
County, probably managing the shop, and supplied the South Carolina market.

For Lincoln and Catawba Counties, until the late 1840s, the shop cut baroque
headstones with curvilinear tops, generally absolutely plain, but urn-and-willow
imagery appears on six stones attributed to them with death dates from 1802 to
1847. Either Robert or William Crawford probably carved the urn-and-willow
stones of Allen Delane (d. 1846), at Old White Church, Lincolnton, and John
Miller (d. 1847) (Fig. 4.20), at Daniels Lutheran Church, Lincoln County. Both represent extraordinary linkages of popular and German art, for the carver cut a cluster of four-pointed compass stars around the small willow on the Delane stone,
and, in the tympanum of the Miller stone, added a little German sun to shine on
the sinuous willow tree as if to burn away the dolorous mists of the mourning
scene.

During the last twenty years of his career, Robert moved away from neoclassical
design into a stencil style consisting of eccentric arrangements of popular ornament and German symbolism, cut into the stone with a thin, patterned precision.
From the 1830s to the 1860s the Caveny-Crawford Shop provided German communities in the valley with hundreds of headstones filled with folk German symbolism including trees-of-life, sunbursts, stars, hearts, and flowers.

A series of stones cut in the 1840s illustrates this stylistic transition. On the
stone for Jane Hill (d. 1844), at Olney, Robert cut a small branch or tree-of-life in
the center of a shallow pointed-arch tympanum, with corner sunbursts. Another
early indicator of the style shift is the headstone of James Quinn Sr. at Bethany
Church (Fig. 4.21), Robert's only signed work in local stone, featuring a quaint
combination of neoclassical and folk motifs—including a tree-of-life and quarter
sunbursts. This personal, rather than fashionable, design may have been a labor of
love for a family member. Robert's wife, Margaret, was a Quinn, and this man may
have been his father-in-law. The marble headstone of Nancy C. Holland at Olney,
signed by Robert, illustrates a busy combination of folk and popular imagery (Fig.
4.22). Trees-of-life, seven-point star-flowers, and abstract sunbursts fill a frame-
work of ovals, triangles, and circles.

Robert Crawford is credited with most of the later, German folk phase of the
workshop's production in North Carolina because he lived in Lincoln County in
the later years of his career and because the same sunbursts and trees-of-life that
decorate the folk German stones in Lincoln and Catawba Counties appear on his
signed stones in York and Gaston Counties in the 1840s. None of the Caveny-
Crawford stonecutters signed any of these Lincoln and Catawba County gravestones, but seven stones cut from the 1830s to the 1870s for people who lived in

(opposite)
Figure 4.20.
Headstone of
John Miller,
d. 1847,
Daniels
Lutheran
Churchyard,
Lincoln
County.
Attributed to
Robert or
William
Crawford.

Figure 4.21. Headstone of James Quinn Sr., d. 1846, Bethany ARP Churchyard, York County, S.C. Signed "RMC."

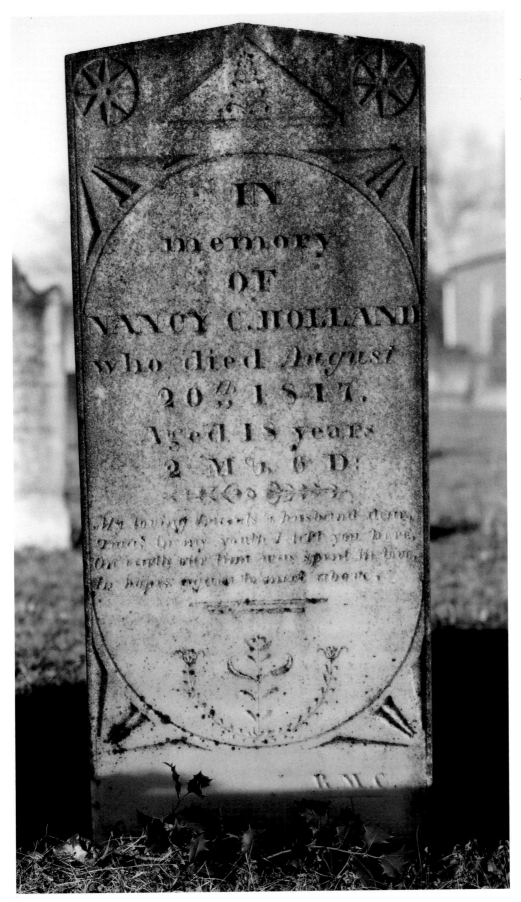

Figure 4.22.
Headstone
of Nancy C.
Holland,
d. 1847, Olney
Presbyterian
Churchyard,
Gastonia.
Signed
"R.M.C."

these two counties are probated to either Robert or William Crawford. Robert's receipt for at least one folk German stone, the headstone of Henry C. Robinson (d. 1854), at Trinity Lutheran Church in Lincoln County, is preserved in an estate record.[31] Robert may have moved to Lincoln County in order to supply the specialized German market that centered in this area.

The Caveny-Crawford Shop's later German gravestones, produced from the 1840s to the 1870s, follow a formula: a tall, narrow rectangular headstone with a star-flower, sunburst, or leafy branch flanked by quarter sunbursts adorning the area above the inscription, and a tree-of-life below the inscription. There are minor variations in the configuration of the rays of the sunbursts, in the points of the compass stars, and in the number of branches and size of the leaves and blossoms on the trees-of-life, yet the total effect of these dozens of folk German stones in each of the Lutheran and Methodist graveyards in Lincoln County is of mass production. The ornament takes on the secular detachment of the stencil-painted decoration on folk German furniture, or the pierced-tin decoration on pie safes. Powerful folk symbols such as the heart and the sunburst often perform a double duty. For example, the quarter sunbursts in the corners also function as Adamesque fans (a popular motif during the neoclassical period), and the heart becomes a string of tiny ornaments dividing the inscription and the epitaph. Yet the shop occasionally used such symbols at full strength. On the marble headstone of infant Chambres Wortman (d. 1861), at Olney Presbyterian Church in Gaston County, are three German turnip-shaped hearts inside squares—a small center heart flanked by larger hearts—symbolic of the linked hearts of this baby and his parents, united even in death.

The most variable symbol, the tree-of-life, usually illustrates the age of the deceased. The Lin infant, who died at birth in 1854, was commemorated by a "tender plant" (Fig. 4.23). Two-year-old John F. Fulbright (d. 1859), also at Trinity Lutheran Church, Lincoln County, has a branch with a single large leaf in the center. Two-year-old M. S. I. Pryor was memorialized with a one-tiered tree and with a rarely encountered epitaph that reinforces the visual symbolism (Fig. 4.24).

Medium-sized trees symbolize the lives of older children and young adults. The marker of eight-year-old David C. Carpenter (d. 1855), at Palm Tree Church, has a single vertical trunk with medium-sized leaves. The stone for fifteen-year-old Franklin Goodson (d. 1860), at St. Luke's Church, Lincoln County, displays the same type of tree with slightly larger leaves at the top. The stones of eighteen-year-olds Samuel E. Lutz (d. 1839) (Fig. 4.25) and Nancy C. Holland (Figure 4.22) display similar single-tiered trees with buds on the base and fairly large leaves on the trunk.

(opposite)
Figure 4.23.
Headstone
of infant
daughter of
W. & C. Lin,
d. 1854, Trinity
Lutheran
Churchyard,
Lincoln County.
Attributed to
the Crawford
workshop.

The most extensive development of the tree occurs on the headstones of those who died in the fullness of life. A small tree with three shoots, terminating in a large leaf in the center and smaller side leaves and blooms (perhaps symbolizing children) expresses the productive life of 47-year-old Elizabeth Lefever (d. 1857), Salem Church, Lincoln County. A large tree with three tall shoots curving almost into a complete circle symbolizes the fruitful life of 57-year-old Mary Robinson (Fig. 4.26). A two-tiered tree, the second tier terminating in blooms and crowned by a large leaf, memorializes the life of 64-year-old David Reinhardt (Fig. 4.27).

The fullest tree of all blooms on the stone of 77-year-old Rebecca Wyont (d. 1862), at Trinity Lutheran Church.

Because the Caveny-Crawford Shop produced a large number of these folk German headstones with similar ornament and a stenciled, mass-produced appearance, it is tempting to dismiss the German stones of the Crawfords as mere commercial products, with no more cultural meaning than the Pennsylvania Dutch hex signs that adorn twentieth-century barns throughout the United States. But these German stones, even though not produced by German craftsmen, were created for particular clients. The hearts and trees-of-life conveyed deep emotion and significance to the lives of those buried beneath the monuments. The Caveny-Crawford Shop had put down deep community roots and could produce gravestones that reflected the traditions of its clients. Just as the Bighams created a synthesis of Scots-Irish

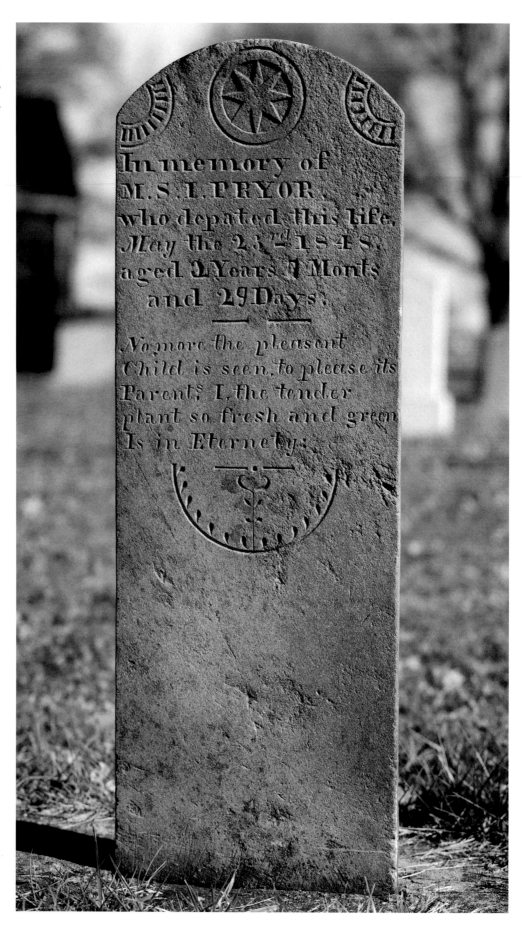

Figure 4.24. Headstone of M. S. I. Pryor, d. 1848, Palm Tree Methodist Churchyard, Lincoln County. Attributed to the Crawford workshop.

Figure 4.25.
Headstone
of Samuel E.
Lutz, d. 1839,
Trinity Luth-
eran Church-
yard, Lincoln
County.
Attributed to
the Crawford
workshop.

(opposite)
Figure 4.26.
Headstone
of Mary
Robinson,
d. 1862,
Trinity
Lutheran
Churchyard,
Lincoln
County.
Attributed to
the Crawford
workshop.

Figure 4.27.
Headstone
of David
Reinhardt,
d. 1861,
Trinity
Lutheran
Churchyard,
Lincoln
County.
Attributed to
the Crawford
workshop.

and German folk art on Catawba Valley stones during the early years of independence, the Caveny-Crawford Shop did so in the nineteenth century with the then-fashionable decorative vocabulary that reflected the communities' tastes. The Germans of the Catawba Valley were fortunate to have a stonecutting shop that would memorialize their joyful beliefs in stone.

Catawba Valley German Stonecarvers

PETER HARMON, CATAWBA COUNTY, 1820s–1850

The Caveny-Crawford Shop may have found success with the traditional German farm families of the northern Catawba Valley during the late antebellum period because the one local German artisan who carved monuments at this time lacked a strong style. Peter Harmon, a German farmer who lived in northern Lincoln County (which became Catawba County in 1842), carved gravestones from the 1820s to about 1850. Harmon, who may have been a blacksmith as well as a stonecutter, belonged to Old St. Paul's Church, where the largest group of his gravestones stand, and died in 1876 at the age of ninety.[32] Harmon's gravestones stand alongside the Caveny-Crawford stones in the German Protestant churchyards of Lincoln and Catawba Counties. Although St. Paul's was organized before 1771, its members must have had no dependable local source for gravestones before Harmon began working, since there are a variety of headstones by different carvers, along with numbers of rough fieldstones, prior to the 1820s. Even in the early 1830s, when stones by the Caveny-Crawford Shop became available throughout the Catawba Valley, Harmon continued to hold a share of the market, probably because of his accessibility and the lower cost of his stones.

Harmon's stones are documented by two receipts, one for the stone of Elizabeth Gross (d. 1828), for which he received $5 in 1829, the other for the stone of George Cansler, for which he received $4 for "Cutting and engraving Grave stones for said deceas'd" in 1832.[33] The Elizabeth Gross marker—a small headstone of eccentric baroque shape that Harmon cut from local schist—is in Old St. Paul's Churchyard (Fig. 4.28). Harmon shaped the center section of the tympanum into a fleur-de-lis form and engraved the inscription in fairly deep-cut uppercase Roman lettering, yet his arbitrary use of upper and lowercase letters, even within the same word, and inconsistent spacing indicate the hand of a self-taught stonecutter. The "I" in the phrase "In memory of" models the elegant calligraphy of neoclassical style headstones but lacks the grace.

Based on the distinctive style of Elizabeth Gross's headstone, twenty-one other schist headstones at Old St. Paul's in Catawba County and eighteen stones at Daniels, Salem, St. Luke's Lutheran, and a few other churchyards in Lincoln County are attributed to Peter Harmon.[34] In addition to the fleur-de-lis tympanum, Harmon occasionally used a curious three-lobed shape. Harmon cut religious epitaphs drawn from the Bible, and perhaps from Lutheran hymns, on a few of the stones, such as "It is finished" for the stone of John Wilson (d. 1831), aged seventy-eight. For the stone of Anna Maria Beissiin (1801–1832), he carved, "So teach us to number our days that we may apply our hearts unto wisdom." Harmon's gravestones

Figure 4.28.
Headstone
of Elisabeth
Gross,
d. 1828,
Old St. Paul's
Lutheran
Churchyard,
Catawba
County.
Probated to
Peter Harmon.

must have represented a comforting consistency to his customers, who were his brethren in rural Lutheran communities in the northern Catawba Valley. Throughout the thirty-four-year range of dates on his stones, Harmon introduced no change in his style or quality of execution. Typical of his work is the headstone of William Rudisill with its stiff, old-fashioned baroque shape and lyrical epitaph (Fig. 4.29).

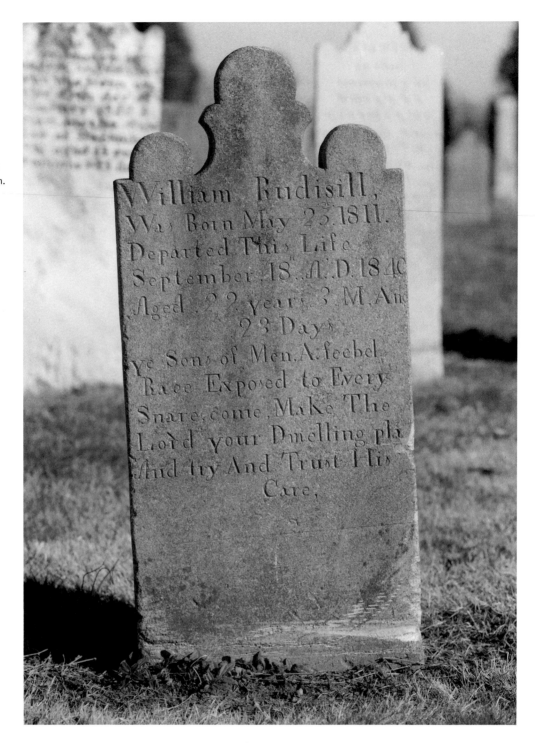

Figure 4.29.
Headstone
of William
Rudisill,
d. 1840,
Salem
Lutheran
Churchyard,
Lincoln
County.
Attributed to
Peter Harmon.

Davidson County German Stonecarvers

DAVIDSON COUNTY CABINETMAKERS AND PIERCED-STYLE
GRAVESTONES, CA. 1813–CA. 1850

The Davidson County school of stonecarving, which flourished during the second quarter of the nineteenth century, produced about forty distinctively pierced headstones, sometimes with footstones, between about 1813 and 1850. These markers stand at four of the oldest Lutheran and Reformed churchyards, Bethany, Pilgrim, Beck's, and Beulah, and at one Baptist churchyard, Abbott's Creek. A second group of approximately fifty stones of similar style, though of lesser quality and not all pierced, were apparently cut by different artisans during the 1830s and 1840s. They stand at the same churches and in the following Davidson County churchyards: Emanuel United Church of Christ, Jersey Baptist Church, Midway Methodist Church, Fair Grove Methodist Church, Piney Woods Methodist Church, Good Hope Methodist Church, Old Mount Vernon Baptist Church, Spring Hill Methodist Protestant Church, and the Wagner Family Graveyard.

Although the stones have death dates from 1797 to 1857, the two dated before 1814 were apparently backdated; the one stone dated after 1849 was probably cut in the 1830s and inscribed many years later.[35] These distinctive and exuberant gravestones are found in no other areas of German settlement in America, or, apparently, the world.[36]

A pierced headstone has a decorative shape perforated through the stone, creating a window that allows sunlight to shine through. In almost every instance, the decorative piercing is in a symbolic shape, most often the fylfot cross, which connotes eternity, but tulips and other flowers, hearts, and abstract shapes were also used. All have decorative molding forming a radiating sunburst, chevron, or quadroon (herringbone) pattern on the front, rear, or sides, and a tympanum shaped like an ornate baroque pediment. Some have trees-of-life, arches, or compass stars carved in high relief or engraved into the surface of the front or rear. They are the earliest headstones in North Carolina to be truly sculpture in the round.

All but one of these pierced stones are of a soft, smooth, light-gray soapstone. Soapstone can be worked with axes and saws, and these headstones do not display the usual marks of picks and chisels used by early-nineteenth-century masons to dress a slab. Instead, they still bear the indentations of compass points used to scribe circles and of ruled lines scratched into the surface to lay out the design. Because of the softness of the soapstone from which they carved the pierced gravestones, these artisans could use the same tools they used to fashion furniture. Their size is larger than the early traditional German stones, varying from 12 to 20 inches in width, 20 to 32 inches in height from ground level, and from 1 to 2¾ inches in thickness. These gravestones were generally created in a set of headstone and footstone, the latter being smaller, with a single pierced shape and sometimes the deceased's monogram. Many of the footstones in Davidson County cemeteries were removed some years ago, probably to simplify the task of mowing the grass.

The fylfot cross appears in at least half of the group as the central focus of the design. On some stones, the cross itself is pierced through the stone (a negative fylfot); on the others, the stone around the fylfot is cut away (a positive fylfot). The direction of the fylfot is not uniform; sometimes the lobes move in a clockwise direction, sometimes counterclockwise. In the most highly developed examples, the carver cut a border of pierced cyma (double-curved leaf forms) around the fylfot.

Occasionally the customers may have requested symbols that held special meaning. On the stone of Elisabeth Bodenhamer (d. 1824), at Abbott's Creek Churchyard, a Davidson School artisan cut a pierced tulip rather than a fylfot (Fig. 4.30). This headstone is also cut from a harder, greenish-gray soapstone with sparkling quartz crystals than most of the other pierced stones. On the headstone of Sarah

Figure 4.30.
Headstone
of Elisabeth
Bodenhamer,
d. 1824,
Abbott's
Creek
Primitive
Baptist
Churchyard,
Davidson
County.
Attributed
to the
Swisegood
School.

Figure 4.31.
Headstone of
Sarah Davis,
d. 1829,
Abbott's
Creek Primi-
tive Baptist
Churchyard,
Davidson
County.
Attributed
to the
Swisegood
School.

Davis (d. 1829) (Fig. 4.31), also at Abbott's Creek, the artisan cut the top and bottom lobes of the fylfot opposing one another to form a symbolic lover's knot, and engraved this epitaph:

> Loving husband children dear
> Sweet were the moments we spent here
> But now I hope to go to rest
> And be forever blest

The parents of little Joseph Williams, who died in 1825, may have helped design his stone. The finial is pierced by a large half-moon, taking the shape of a bird perched

Figure 4.32. Headstone of Joseph S. Williams, d. 1825, Abbott's Creek Primitive Baptist Churchyard, Davidson County. Attributed to the Swisegood School.

on top of the stone, a touching memorial for a three-year-old boy (Fig. 4.32). This remarkable design features the only asymmetrical tympanum in the pierced style.

The Davidson artisans generally shaped the top of the gravestones as a baroque pediment, with a center finial and side turrets. To give a focus, they often shaped the finial like a knob and flanked it with two lobed extensions pierced with half-moon designs. Some have richly concave moldings that accentuate the illusion of motion created by the negative space of the fylfots. On some of the finest stones, moldings radiate from the fylfot out to the tips of the tympanum, sometimes forming a circular sunburst around the fylfot. Vertical, diagonal, or paneled moldings or flutings sometimes decorate the sides of the slab, and another set of moldings may decorate the lower half of the rear. On the rear of some stones, chevron-patterned moldings extend from the fylfot down to the ground level or form tendrils or tree-of-life shapes. On the marker for Sarah Davis at Abbott's Creek Churchyard, a molded vine extends up to the fylfot (Fig. 4.33). A stone for a Koons family member who died in 1834 at Beulah Church bears a large molded leaf. Sometimes these moldings border the edges of the stonelike pilasters, and, on the Henry Grimes stone at Beulah Church, dated 1844, they terminate in bull's-eye corner blocks. On the stone of Elizabeth Garner, at Beck's Church, and the Elizabeth Leonard stone, at Pilgrim Church, these tendrils with toothed edges sinuously flow up the rear of the stones like vines overgrowing the stone.

Linework images play a minor but important role in the pierced style. There would seem to be no room left for more elaboration on the pierced stones, yet a small number of the group have delicate incising that resembles engraved metal-work designs. The lower front of the 1844 Grimes stone at Beulah Churchyard has a complex bracket around a "Momento Mori" script and, on the rear, an elaborately etched tree-of-life growing out of an upside-down flower blossom and terminating in an upright flower blossom (Fig. 4.34). The headstone of Valentine Berrier (d. 1849), at the same churchyard, has a large decorative line-work bracket below the epitaph. The Berrier stone has no piercing and is one of the last dated stones in the otherwise pierced style. The 1824 Elisabeth Bodenhamer stone and the 1828 Kezia Jones stone have calligraphic flourishes that set off the epitaphs. As most of the carvers of the pierced stones excelled in high relief carving rather than engraving, it is likely that the incised decoration and calligraphic lettering of these stones were cut by different artisans specializing in engraving.

Who created these remarkable works of art? Why do the German Protestant cemeteries of Davidson County flower with such distinctive grave sculpture? The answer lies in the happy convergence of a school of local cabinetmakers and an abundance of malleable soapstone. The cabinetmakers of north Davidson County, called the Swisegood School after John Swisegood, their best-known craftsman, were esteemed for statuesque, ornately finished corner cupboards and chests. Their members consisted of local farmers who practiced cabinetmaking as a part-time occupation in workshops apparently at their farms during the first half of the nineteenth century.[37] The top section of a corner cupboard attributed to Mordecai Collins, the earliest-known cabinetmaker in the school, contains all of the essential characteristics of the style—arched door, paneled pilasters, molded caps, rope

Figure 4.33.
Rear of
headstone
of Sarah
Davis,
d. 1829,
Abbott's
Creek
Primitive
Baptist
Churchyard,
Davidson
County.
Attributed
to the
Swisegood
School.

(opposite)
Figure 4.34.
Headstone
of Henry
Grimes,
d. 1844,
Beulah
Church
of Christ
Churchyard,
Davidson
County.
Attributed
to the
Swisegood
School.

molding, baroque tympanum with center finial, and sunburst-like bosses (Fig.
4.35). Wooden moldings decorate every possible surface of the cupboard in a riot-
ous celebration of German folk craft.

Collins moved to Indiana about 1816, leaving behind his former apprentice John
Swisegood, who went on to become the best-known cabinetmaker in the group.
These cabinetmakers continued to make corner cupboards that elaborated the basic form created by Collins. Swisegood's corner cupboards contain comma-shaped
inlay work, a finial plinth reeded in a lozenge pattern, and, on one piece, a delicate
vine motif, and, on another, a tiny pierced heart.

Because these cabinetmakers rarely signed their furniture, researchers generally
attribute their pieces on the basis of style to the known cabinetmakers in the group.
There is some precedent for signatures, however: in 1817 Swisegood signed a desk,
"I John Swisegood his hand and pen this 8th d of March in the year 1817," and in a
Davidson County log house containing a corner cupboard attributed to Swisegood,
he signed "John Swisegood" on the underside of the stairwell.[38] Maybe he only did
finish carpentry rather than the rough carpentry, but he obviously practiced house
carpentry as well as cabinetmaking. He may have had other sidelines as well.
Swisegood's farm was probably no more than twelve miles from Abbott's Creek
Churchyard, which contains some of the finest pierced gravestones in the county,
and his saw and gristmill stood within sight of the churchyard.

Coffins were a staple of cabinetmakers' business in the nineteenth century, and
all three known members of the Swisegood School—Jesse Clodfelter, Jonathan
Long, and John Swisegood, as well as thirty-five other artisans—were paid from

five to ten dollars per coffin in the 1830 to 1863 period, and, as scholar Brad Rauschenberg of the Museum of Early Southern Decorative Arts has convincingly argued, at least a few of them extended their funeral services to the cutting of gravestones.[39] In about 1848, all three identified cabinetmakers in the school emigrated to the Midwest, leaving behind a number of artisans who continued the decorative German craft tradition for a few more years.[40]

The fertile craft atmosphere in Davidson County apparently allowed a substantial group of craftsmen to collaborate in the development of the distinctive pierced style. Each of the three churchyards containing the major collections of pierced stones showcase the work of a different craftsman who probably lived nearby. Bethany Lutheran and Reformed Church, the home church of cabinetmakers Jacob and Joseph Clodfelter, appears to be the birthplace of the style. Abbott's Creek Primitive Baptist Churchyard contains the most inventive variations of the style, with tulips and even a lover's knot pierced through the stones, and it stands near the site of John Swisegood's sawmill. Swisegood lived and worked near Joseph Clodfelter's farm, and cabinetmaker Jonathan Long bought items at Jacob's estate sale. Receipts prove that artisan David Sowers, who attended Pilgrim Lutheran and Reformed Church, created in its cemetery another variation of the pierced style, with dramatic Gothic shapes and delicately engraved trees-of-life, to mark the graves of his family and friends. Once one innovative cabinetmaker, perhaps Jacob Clodfelter, discovered that the decorative German vocabulary of forms and symbols could be cut into the soft soapstone with furniture saws and molding planes, the others quickly followed. Enough variation in technique and decorative forms occurs in the pierced stones to indicate that at least three skilled artisans, and perhaps a dozen less-skilled followers, cut gravestones in the pierced style during this thirty- or forty-year period.

JOSEPH CLODFELTER

The key piece of evidence in attributing some pierced-style stones to a particular individual is the headstone for Josiah Spurgin (d. 1802), Abbott's Creek Church, Davidson County, on which "MAID BY THE HAND OF JOSEPH CLODFELTER" is carved in labored uppercase letters on the back side (Fig. 4.36).[41] Clodfelter is the only German stonecutter in North Carolina known to have signed a gravestone. The act of signing a gravestone is out of character for a traditional craftsman, yet the form of the signature is very much in character. The large size, unusual wording, and location of the signature do not conform to professional stonecutting tradition, which prescribed a small signature at the base of the front face of the stone. In placement, the signature resembles furniture signatures, most often written casually on the back of the piece rather than being a formal element of the design. Furthermore, the misspelling and backward letters are typical of the lettering on many German stones throughout the county.

To create six-year-old Josiah Spurgin's headstone, Joseph Clodfelter masterfully exploited the soft nature of soapstone, cutting an ornately lobed tympanum and piercing a bold fylfot cross through the center. In the same lettering style, and with the same backward letters, he inscribed the phrase "HERE LIES THE CORPSE OF"

Figure 4.36.
Signature
of Joseph
Clodfelter,
rear of
headstone
of Josiah
Spurgin,
d. 1802,
Abbott's Creek
Primitive
Baptist
Churchyard,
Davidson
County.

in a semicircle above the fylfot. That a different stonecutter engraved the remainder of the inscription and the epitaph in a professional lettering style, with upper and lowercase letters, well-proportioned spacing, bold cutting, and no misspellings suggests that Josiah's parents purchased the gravestone from Clodfelter as a blank (Fig. 4.37). Although Clodfelter possessed sufficient skill and creativity to cut a dramatic headstone, he lacked the ability to do professional lettering.

Yet Joseph Clodfelter probably did not originate the pierced style. The earliest pierced gravestones are a pair of identical small soapstone headstones for Sara and Felix Glatfelter (d. 1813 and 1814), so small that they would be easily overlooked by a visitor to Bethany Lutheran and German Reformed Church in Davidson County (Fig. 4.38). Sara and Felix were the great-grandparents of Joseph Clodfelter. Joseph was an adolescent when they died, probably not old enough to have carved their gravestones, and it is more likely that another family member, perhaps Joseph's father, Jacob (ca. 1770–1837), carved them. Both stones have scalloped baroque tympana with small pierced fylfot crosses in the center, surrounded by long German inscriptions in concentric circles continuing down the front and onto the rear surface. Both had footstones with pierced heart designs that have disappeared. It is unlikely that they were a product of Joseph's youth because they are inscribed in tiny German lettering quite unlike Joseph's signature and because their surnames retain the original German spelling, which by the 1830s had been anglicized to Clodfelter. Jacob probably also cut the other early pierced-style markers at Bethany Church, one dated 1799 with a fylfot cross incised but not actually pierced through the stone, and two dated 1819 and 1822 with finials and lobes elaborating the tympanum and English inscriptions.

The Spurgin and Glatfelter stones illustrate the necessity of analyzing each gravemarker within the whole body of work of a particular artisan, as well as within its craft tradition. Josiah Spurgin's stone is a dramatic example of backdating, mentioned in Chapter 1 as one of the pitfalls of gravestone studies. Spurgin died a year after Joseph Clodfelter was born, so Clodfelter could not have carved the Spurgin stone until the late 1810s, when he was grown, thus it is backdated by some eighteen years. Furthermore, the pierced style was not created until the 1810s, thus Josiah Spurgin's stone, certainly carved by Joseph himself, was probably created about 1820.

Felix Glatfelter brought his family to Davidson County from York County, Pennsylvania, about 1765, settling on the Brushy Fork of Abbott's Creek. His grandson Jacob was born there a few years later. In 1801 Joseph was born to Jacob and his wife, Margaret. Jacob was a farmer of comfortable means, who probably also did cabinetmaking. At his death in 1837, he possessed a set of cabinetmaking tools including a bow saw, cross-cut saw, tenant saw, hand saw and mill saw planes, augers, a turning lathe, turning chisels, drawing knives, a set of tongue and grooving planes, a "guaging" rod, iron wedges, one large "compas," a "compas saw," and ten thousand feet of plank and scantling for use in building construction.[42] Jacob Clodfelter's cabinetmaking-tool collection included virtually every tool necessary to produce the pierced gravestones: iron wedges to split large blocks of stone in the quarry, saws to square it into panels, augers to bore holes to start the piercing, a

Figure 4.37.
Headstone of
Josiah Spurgin,
front face.
Signed by
Joseph
Clodfelter.

(opposite)
Figure 4.38.
Headstone of
Felix Glatfelter,
d. 1814,
Bethany
Lutheran and
Reformed
Churchyard,
Davidson
County.
Attributed
to Jacob
Clodfelter.

"compass saw" to cut the curved fylfots, and molding planes to create the relief-molded decoration. Jacob might have used some of his tools to cut the small soapstone headstones for his grandparents Sara and Felix about 1815.

Like his father, Joseph Clodfelter (1801–1872) was a farmer and successful cabinetmaker, and one of his products was coffins.[43] Upon his father's death in 1837, he inherited a 200-acre plantation and a slave named Joseph. Joseph Clodfelter possessed a well-rounded set of cabinetmaking tools, including some all-purpose construction tools: wedges, joiners, dazes, augers, files, drawing knives, saws, chisels, planes, and one "lerrtting [lettering] Box," which he may have used for inscriptions.[44]

A pair of headstones for Joseph Clodfelter's parents and three headstones for his neighbors—Daniel Wagoner (d. 1827), Peter Leonard (d. 1839), and Henry Grimes (d. 1844)—represent the highest development of the pierced style and are probably Joseph's work. He probably carved his parents' gravestones in 1837 when his father died, for they are commemorated by a pair of the finest pierced stones in the county, with a fylfot cross surrounded by a pierced cyma border (Fig. 4.39). Daniel Wagoner was Joseph's next-door neighbor; Henry Grimes and Peter Leonard were buyers at Jacob Clodfelter's estate sale. Chevron-patterned moldings cover the entire lower rear of the Wagoner stone at Bethany Church (Fig. 4.40). The Leonard stone, at Pilgrim Church, lacks piercing but has a molded sunburst tympanum and a molded arch design covering the entire rear surface. The Grimes

(left)
Figure 4.39.
Rear of headstone of Margaret Clodfelter, d. 1857, Bethany Lutheran and Reformed Churchyard, Davidson County. Attributed to Joseph Clodfelter.

(right)
Figure 4.40.
Rear of headstone of Daniel Wagoner, d. 1827, Bethany Lutheran and Reformed Churchyard, Davidson County. Attributed to Joseph Clodfelter.

stone at Beulah Church is adorned not only with a beautiful fylfot and ornate sunburst tympanum, but with unusual molded pilasters with bull's-eye corner blocks bearing a strong resemblance to furniture decoration (See Figure 4.34).

Based on available documentation, it appears that Jacob originated the basic stylistic formula in stones he cut for his family members around 1814, and Joseph and other artisans perfected the style in the 1820s, 1830s, and 1840s. Unlike receipts linking gravestones in the Catawba Valley to such stonecutters as Robert Crawford and Peter Harmon, no receipts identifying the carvers of the pierced gravestones have yet turned up in the surviving estate records for Davidson County. The only payment for a specified service to Joseph Clodfelter found in Davidson estate records was for making two coffins in 1850.[45]

Collaboration among various craftsmen is one of the complicating facts in studying gravestones. Cutting the gravestone and engraving the stone constituted separate steps of production, often performed at different times by different artisans. Just as portrait painters painted standardized torsos and filled in the faces when a customer appeared, so stonecutters kept an inventory of gravestones that could be customized for individual clients. It is obvious in comparing the inscriptions on the pierced stones that considerable collaboration occurred, for a variety of hands of various levels of skill cut them. Indeed, one of the earliest of the pierced-style headstones is a blank, with no inscription, and two of the pierced-style markers at Bethany Church, apparently carved by Joseph Clodfelter, are also blanks. Margaret Clodfelter's stone at Bethany Church was almost certainly cut as a blank and only partially lettered in 1837 when her husband, Jacob, died. In addition to Joseph Clodfelter, at least four other hands carved inscriptions on the pierced-style stones. The same unmistakable lettering style with which Clodfelter signed the Spurgin stone is present on six or seven of the finest pierced stones. The same professional lettering hand that inscribed the main portion of the Josiah Spurgin inscription lettered a dozen other stones of the group, distributed throughout the years of production. An engraver who produced a deeply cut upper and lowercase alphabet of bolder shape than the professional hand on the Spurgin stone lettered the headstones of David Wear (d. 1838), at Bethany Church and the Henry Grimes stone. Two other lettering styles appear. One stonecutter used labored uppercase letters and colons between words, as, for example, on the headstone of Catharine Counse (d. 1823), Beulah Churchyard. Another stonecutter managed to cut bold upper and lowercase letters of competent shapes but divided words between two lines and used a backward "4." Typical of this hand is the headstone of Jacob Long (d. 1824), at Beulah Churchyard.

DAVID SOWERS

David Sowers (Sauer), working about ten miles away in central Davidson County, created a distinctively different variant of the pierced style. Although a member of the Swisegood School, Sowers created his own style with Gothic forms and traditional German symbols. Sowers did not pierce his first gravestone until about 1823, no doubt copying Clodfelter's bold innovation. He did not sign any stones, but his receipt for the stones of Peter Lopp (d. 1827) identify his work with sufficient distinction that allows for the attribution of fifteen other gravestones with death dates from 1812 to 1834 at Pilgrim, Emanuel, and Bethany Lutheran Churchyards.

Peter Lopp's pierced headstone represents the peak of development of Sowers's distinct style. Following the evolution of this style requires ordering these attributed stones from the earliest headstone cut about 1812 through the following fifteen years to the documented Lopp headstone. These dark-gray headstones are characterized by a circular tympanum or a Gothic-arched tympanum with a distinctive S-shaped curve (known as an ogee), squared shoulders, and delicately incised symbols such as the tree-of-life, the star-flower, the heart, and the bracket. They exhibit a clear stylistic development from the earliest stones of the 1810s to the stones carved in the 1830s. Sowers carved inscriptions in German until the 1820s, although three of the earlier stones have English inscriptions.

Sowers's earliest attributed headstones follow the traditional form of eighteenth-century Davidson County German stones: a semicircular tympanum with monogram and date, often within a bracket; tapered sides; a crowded inscription within ruled lines; and the continuation of the inscription on the rear. Words are separated by dots, and spelling is phonetic; *S*'s are sometimes backward. Epitaphs are a rare occurrence on German gravestones in Davidson County, but Sowers carved one for Polley Frits's stone at Pilgrim Churchyard:

(front)

P 1812 F

HERE.LIES.THE.BODY.OF.POLLEY

FRITS.THE.DAUGHTER.OF.JOHN.FRITS

AND.REBECCA.CATHERINE.POLLEY

WAZ.BORN.FEBUWARY.THE.11

DAY.1812.AND.HIR.DEPARTTURE.FROM

THIS.WORLD.WAS.DEAZEMBER

THE.TWENTY.THIRD.DAY.1812

ZHE.WAS.TEN MONTHS.A.17

DAYS.AND.HALF.OLD.WHEN

SHE.DIED.HIR.PARRENTS

WAS.SORLY.TRUBLED.AT

HIR.DETH.BUT.ALL.THAT

COMFORTS.THEM.IS.THE

HOPE.SHE.IS.GONE.TO.REST

(rear)

P 1812 F

WHY.DO.YOU.MORN.DEPARTEND

FRIENDS.AND.SHAKE.AT

DETHS.ALARMS.FOR.IT.IS.THE

VOISE.THAT.JESUS.SENDS.TO

CALL.THEM.TO.HIS.ARMS.OLD

AGE.IS.COMMING.ON.WHEN
BUTY.WILL.DCAY.THE.FAIR
IST.FASE.THAT.EVER.WAS
SEEN.IN.TIME.WILL
TURN.TO.CLAY.AND.MUST
THIS.BODY.DIE.THIS.MOR
TAL.FRAME.DECAY.AND
MUST.THOSE.ACTTIF.LIMBS
OF.MINE.LIE.MOLLERING.IN.THE.CLAY[46]

By 1816, Sowers had achieved a style that took full advantage of the unusually plastic medium of soapstone; he introduced new shapes, new decoration, and a sculpture-in-the-round treatment. He began to decorate all four sides of his stones. Occasionally Sowers ran a triple set of beads or moldings on the sides of the stone reminiscent of furniture decoration. He also introduced his two trademark shapes: the semicircular tympanum with circular foils cut into the shoulders, and a Gothic-arched tympanum with ogee curve. He enriched both faces of his stones with delicately incised symbols, including the tree-of-life (either an evergreen or the more typical tree with blossoms), star-flower (executed with a compass), turnip-shaped heart, and fylfot. Unlike the engraved decoration on the pierced stones of Clodfelter and others that seems to be executed by a different hand, Sowers's engraving, in a freer, more spontaneous style, was probably his own work.

The headstone of Caderina Sauer, who died in 1816 at the age of one month, is one of the first examples (and indeed one of the finest) of Sowers's new Gothic style.[47] Sowers channeled his grief over his little sister's death into the creation of a touchingly beautiful memorial. He covered the entire rear of the ogee-shaped headstone with a tree-of-life containing two upside-down blossoms and three separate evergreen trees (Fig. 4.41). On the front of Caderina's footstone, he repeated her name and date and, on the rear, he carved another tree-of-life, flanked by six-pointed compass stars.

In the mid-1820s, probably influenced by the three or four dramatic pierced gravestones cut by Joseph Clodfelter, Sowers added piercing to his own stock of techniques for decorating stones. The earliest stone that Sowers pierced is the headstone of Susanna Conrad (d. 1823), at Pilgrim Church. A fylfot cross pierces the standard semicircular tympanum of the stone. One of Sowers's finest pierced stones is the headstone for Peter Lopp (Lapp) (d. 1827), at Pilgrim Churchyard. Lopp's estate, settled in 1830, contains an explicit reference to "David Sowers's recp. for Tombstones 5.00."[48] Sowers energized Peter Lopp's tall head and footstone of dark-gray soapstone by piercing the traditional German symbols of love and resurrection through the stones rather than merely incising them into the surface (Figs. 4.42, 4.43). Instead of leaving squared shoulders, he cut deeply indented foils (the leaf-shaped curve of a Gothic stone window design) into the squared shoulders. The German inscription is engraved in elaborate German Gothic lettering, and a bracket below the fylfot contains Lopp's initials and date of birth. The footstone, a rare survival, has Sowers's trademark pointed arch shape.[49]

Figure 4.41.
Rear of
headstone
of Caderina
Sauer, d. 1816,
Pilgrim
Lutheran and
Reformed
Churchyard,
Davidson
County.
Attributed to
David Sowers.

(opposite)
Figure 4.42.
Headstone of
Peter Lopp,
d. 1827,
Pilgrim
Lutheran and
Reformed
Churchyard,
Davidson
County.
Probated to
David Sowers.

Figure 4.43.
Footstone of Peter Lopp.

Sowers received $20 and $2.41 in interest from the estate of Philip Sink (Cink) in 1831, in payment for an unspecified item or service.[50] Although it might have been for tombstones, the sum is large; in comparison, Peter Lopp's tombstone payment was $5. Payment aside, the appearance of the stone allows an attribution to Sowers. He used the same gray soapstone and cut a semicircular tympanum with foiled shoulders, a molded border, and an English inscription in a neat uppercase Roman-lettering style. The first two lines of text are circular, echoing the shape of the tympanum:

HERE LISE THE CORPS
OF PHELIP CINK
HE
WARS BORN ON THE 2 DAY OF
FEBRUARY IN THE YEARS
OF OUR LORD 17 55 AND HE
DIED ON THE 24 OF MAY
IN THE YEARS OF 1829 AND

IS CED HE WARS 74 YEARS

3 MONTHS AND 22 DAYS

1755 PZ 1829

163

Backcountry
Stonecutters

On the rear, he incised a tall evergreen tree with delicate branches. The foot-stone repeats the shape of the headstone and is inscribed

"1755 IN MEMORY OF PHILIP CINK 1829."

For the symbolic hearts, six-pointed compass stars, and trees-of-life etched into the surfaces of his gravestones, Sowers needed to look no further than German *Fraktur*. Whether handmade or printed, these certificates with ornately decorated symbols commemorating birth, baptism, marriage, and death in the lives of German Americans flourished in the United States from the late eighteenth century to about 1830. There were two major types: the birth and baptismal certificates popular in Lutheran and Reformed communities, and *Vorschrift*, practiced and taught primarily by itinerant schoolmasters who often belonged to Anabaptist sects. These schools stressed penmanship, both cursive script and the decorative *Zierschrift*, or Schwabach-type Gothic lettering, often called *Fraktur* because of its association with these documents.[51]

The tombstone is a form of death certificate, and, given such parallel functions, it is highly likely that David Sowers and other German carvers drew on *Fraktur* for use as visual models. *Fraktur* artists used a delicate drawing style that Sowers translated closely into the densely grained but soft surface of his soapstone headstones. A number of talented *Fraktur* artists worked in western Virginia as late as the 1830s, and at least one itinerant *Fraktur* artist worked in the Moravian community of Friedburg, in north Davidson County, in the first decade of the nineteenth century.[52]

Church records and family genealogies provide the bare outline of Sowers's life. He was a second-generation German American, born in 1794 in the Pilgrim Church community to Valentine and Ann Maria Eva Sowers. Valentine, a carpenter, was a son of Philip Sauer, who had emigrated from Palatinate Germany to Pennsylvania in 1749 and moved to central Davidson County four years later.[53] David Sowers married Sarah Long in 1818, and by 1830 they had four children. In 1835 Sowers and his family joined a group of twenty-five relatives and neighbors, including the Grimes, Myers, and Long families, and moved to Fountain County, Indiana, where they remained the rest of their lives.[54]

The dates when David would have been active as a craftsman, from the age of twenty-one in 1815 to his departure in 1835, dovetail exactly with the death dates on the gravestones attributed to him. The fact that the largest number of the stones, including the most ornamental examples, are at his own Pilgrim Churchyard is also to be expected. The small number of stones that have survived indicate, however, that he was not occupied in gravestone carving full-time. Like the Clodfelters, Sowers probably farmed and did part-time cabinetwork.

Both before and after Sowers left Davidson County in 1835, his distinctive style of gravestones inspired some imitators, for a number of pierced Gothic-style head-stones at Pilgrim, Bethany, and Emanuel Churchyards, as well as two other Lutheran churchyards—Beck's and St. Luke's—and Abbott's Creek Primitive Baptist Churchyard and Spring Hill Methodist Churchyard, relate stylistically to the Sowers stones. These other craftsmen combined the overall forms and symbolism of Sowers's gravestones but could not duplicate the strength and harmony of his shapes.

LEGACY OF THE PIERCED STONES

The richness and complexity of the pierced gravestones are unprecedented in American grave statuary. The only sculptural art recalled by the pierced stones are carved wooden altar pieces in Rococo churches in Germany and Austria. Contrary to popular conception, the Reformation ban on images did not prevent the decoration of European Lutheran churches with extremely ornate altar pieces. These were the products of local craftsmen and featured exuberant sunbursts, elaborate pediments, and extremely sculptural details, often painted in bright, gay color schemes. Because many of the Germans who settled Davidson County emigrated from the Palatinate in southwest Germany, it is possible that these artisans brought this design tradition which flowered into the pierced gravestone style. In North Carolina, the outlet for this sculptural tradition lay in carved, inlaid, and painted furniture, and, in Davidson County, in gravestones carved by these cabinetmakers.

The pierced fylfot crosses, symbols of eternal life, the pedimented sunbursts, symbols of renewal, the trees-of-life, emblems of the cycle of life and death and rebirth, and the heart and lover's knot, promises of true love, assert boldly that life does not end with death. The bird perched on top of Joseph Williams's stone symbolizes the soul of the little boy, poised to fly to heaven. The upright tulip through the center of the stone of Elisabeth Bodenhamer, who died at the age of twenty-two, exemplifies the tradition of carving flower blossoms on the monuments of women who died in their prime.

Visitors to these Davidson County churchyards, regardless of the freshness of their grief over lost family or friends, could not help but be cheered by these dynamic gravestones. When the sun sparkles on the stones and on the grass and flowers around them, the fylfots seem to start turning like pinwheels, accentuating the message of eternity, of the cycle of birth and renewal.

Late German Gravestones, Davidson County, ca. 1830–1860

During Davidson County's late phase of stonecutting activity from about 1830 to 1860, a number of other local artisans cut German gravestones, some derivative of the pierced style and some in original styles. Approximately fifty gravestones fit the general characteristics of the pierced style as cut by imitators, with simpler piercing in abstract decorative shapes rather than in the shapes of specific symbols. These stand at all of the churchyards where the finest pierced-style stones occur, and at a number of additional Lutheran, Methodist, and Baptist churches, a Quaker

Figure 4.44.
Rear of headstone of John Zimmerman, d. 1843, Good Hope Methodist Churchyard, Davidson County. Swisegood School tradition.

Figure 4.45.
Headstone of Peter Clodfelter, d. 1842, Bethany Lutheran and Reformed Churchyard, Davidson County. Swisegood School tradition.

meetinghouse, and a family graveyard. Typical of the group is the headstone of John Zimmerman, whose molded arch and spandrels support a large, ungainly lobed tympanum (Fig. 4.44). Most eccentric is the stone of Peter Clodfelter (Fig. 4.45). The unknown stonecutter carved three tympana with vestigial sunbursts, the top two with misshapen lobed finials, star-flowers in circles on the rear, and horizontal fluting on the sides. The stone's busy design represents a piling up of decorative detailing rather than the masterfully united compositions of more talented stonecutters.

Family graveyards are rare in Davidson County, since both life and death revolved around the churches. Images of the human figure are also rare on Davidson gravestones, since German symbolism was abstract rather than anthropomorphic. The Wagoner family graveyard, located on the family farm near Bethany Church, contains the only pierced stone in the county with human imagery. The powerful headstone of infant Lucinda Wagnor is crowned by a tympanum with five finials; the center has a tiny human face in relief, the flanking ones have outlines like paper

dolls (Fig. 4.46). Because it is such a personal and striking departure from tradition, it may have been cut by a family member, perhaps the father or uncle of little Lucinda. Not a single other folk German gravestone in North Carolina contains depictions of the human face or body.

BEULAH CHURCH OF CHRIST STONECUTTER

The most talented late German stonecutter working in Davidson County cut a group of twenty-two distinctive stones with death dates from 1836 to 1862, at Beulah, Good Hope, Beck's, and St. Luke's Churches. He followed a basic design—semicircular tympanum with squared shoulders—but pierced a Germanic heart through the tympanum. His two last headstones have much more elaborate designs that strongly resemble the upper half of corner cupboards made by the Swisegood School in the first half of the nineteenth century. This stonecutter is an important member of the remarkable group of north Davidson cabinetmakers who applied their repertory of decorative furniture forms to the creation of grave sculpture. For Katharine Yonts (1801–1857) and Sarah Fishel Hanes (1813–1862) at Beulah and

Good Hope, respectively, he carved classical colonnettes with bases and capitals framing the inscription and supporting a baroque tympanum with molded sunbursts. On the Yonts marker the carver emphasized the effect of a corner cupboard by recessing the area containing the inscription behind the colonnettes and tympanum (Fig. 4.47).

Neither signatures nor estate receipts identify this stonecutter. His distinctive mixture of upper and lowercase letters distinguishes his work. He always cut the lowercase letter *r* as large as the uppercase letters; his *y* and *g* are almost always lowercase and have very long descenders. Although his lettering is nonstandard, it is never awkward. The sprightly rhythm, deep relief, and consistency of the lettering throughout the entire group indicate that he was a skilled stonecutter. Since the largest number of his stones stand at Beulah Church of Christ, he probably lived nearby.

THE NEOCLASSICAL STONECUTTER

The last manifestation of the cabinetmaker-stonecarver tradition in Davidson County is the work of a stonecutter who blended German and neoclassical gravestone symbolism on the headstone of Jane Park at Jersey Baptist Churchyard in south Davidson County (Fig. 4.48). The narrow, vertical proportions, the professionally cut inscription, and the urn-and-willow tableau in the rectangular tympanum reflect mid-nineteenth-century popular taste for the neoclassical. The truncated pediment, vestigial molded finial, six-pointed compass stars with crimped borders, and the decorated rear face, for which no popular precedent existed, with a tall, boldly abstracted tree-of-life, surmounted by a molded sunburst within a sunburst, are elements held over from Germanic traditions (Fig. 4.49).

This progressive stonecutter cut at least nineteen fashionable stones, some with traces of traditional German motifs, for people who died between 1824 and 1848. He used native Davidson stone but transformed it into stylish baroque shapes and added urns and drapery to create the earliest locally produced neoclassical gravestones in Davidson County. The artisan signed none of these stones and is mentioned in none of the corresponding estate records. He occupied the same position in Davidson County that Scots-Irish carvers Robert and William Crawford occupied in the Catawba Valley, that of commercial craftsmen who bridged traditional and popular cultures. Indeed, he may have been of Scots-Irish rather than Germanic descent, for it was usually the Scots-Irish who combined German decoration and neoclassical features on stones.

The stones of this unknown carver are generally the same color and have a distinctive shape, ornament, and lettering style. Like David Sowers, he preferred a dark-gray, dense, smooth stone that permitted a crispness of detail not possible in the more porous light-gray soapstone used for most baroque pierced gravestones. Like the Swisegood School, he incorporated design elements from furniture in his stones. His basic form was a baroque tympanum, sometimes elaborated by a recession of planes between the main body of the stone and the tympanum, or between the finial and turrets, or by the convex surface of the front side of the stone. Chamfered borders and bosses, sometimes pierced, further link the stones to the cabinet-

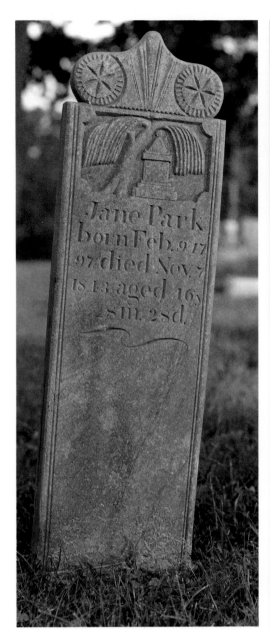

(left)
Figure 4.48.
Headstone
of Jane Park,
d. 1843,
Jersey Baptist
Churchyard,
Davidson
County. The
Neoclassical
Stonecutter.

(right)
Figure 4.49.
Rear of head-
stone of Jane
Park, Jersey
Baptist
Churchyard,
Davidson
County. The
Neoclassical
Stonecutter.

making tradition. A vestigial finial and turrets, derivative of the pierced tradition, top the stone of Louiza E. Grimes (d. 1842), but the overall form is crisp and simple. Molded sunbursts, from the German tradition, decorate headstones dated 1841, 1842, and 1847. A stylized drapery motif of generic classical character outlines the tympanum of Mary M. Brinkle's headstone (d. 1846), yet little German six-pointed compass stars accent the corner bosses (Fig. 4.50). The stone of Daniel Leonard (d. 1848) displays a well-proportioned neoclassical urn in the recessed panel of the tympanum (Fig. 4.51). The upper and lowercase lettering is well proportioned and well spaced, proof of professional training, yet an occasional backward letter, inconsistent capitalization, or awkwardly divided word betrays the provincial heritage of the engraver. The same lettering style appears on a number of the pierced gravestones and several other local headstones, indicating that this engraver inscribed them, too.[55]

IN
MEMORY
of
MARY. M.
BRINKLE
born Jan. 31. 1781.
Died Oct. 14. 1846
Aged 65 yrs. 8 mo.
14 Days

We all do fade
as a lief

(opposite)
Figure 4.50.
Headstone
of Mary M.
Brinkle,
d. 1846,
Pilgrim
Lutheran and
Reformed
Churchyard,
Davidson
County. The
Neoclassical
Stonecutter.

Figure 4.51.
Headstone
of Daniel
Leonard,
d. 1848,
Pilgrim
Lutheran and
Reformed
Churchyard,
Davidson
County. The
Neoclassical
Stonecutter.

These stones could have been cut by Davidson County Scots-Irish cabinetmaker Nathan Parks (Park, Parkes), whose life fits the profile of an artisan bridging the divide between traditional and commercial manufacture. Parks was born in 1813 to a local Scots-Irish farming family. When his father, Joseph, died, young Nathan was apprenticed to cabinetmaker Joseph Conrad of Lexington and thrust into a different world from the Piedmont farm or the traditional artisan's shop.[56] Conrad, born in North Carolina but trained as a cabinetmaker in Philadelphia, had relocated to Davidson County about 1820 and the following year used the *Western Carolinian* to inform "the citizens of Rowan and the adjoining counties, that he has a quantity of prime St. Domingo Mahogany. . . . Persons who may want Furniture of Mahogany, would do well to call and see a specimen. . . ."[57]

Mahogany was a highly desirable imported wood whose strikingly patterned grain accentuated the swelling curves of the Empire-style furniture popular during this period, and none of the traditional furniture attributed to the Swisegood School is made of it. Researchers, however, have not discovered any of Conrad's furniture. Joseph Conrad owned a stone quarry near Lexington, and, in addition to being a skillful cabinetmaker and carpenter, he was an engraver, perhaps engraving a few gravestones. The Lexington legend that Conrad had invented the circular saw in Philadelphia but failed to get a patent indicates that he was held in awe by local tradesmen.[58] In 1825, orphaned twelve-year-old Nathan Parks was apprenticed to Joseph Conrad "until he arrives to full age to learn the cabinet making business or trade, & when free to give him a freedom suit of cloaths worth $30 and $20 in tools. . . ."[59]

Parks learned the trade well, becoming one of Davidson County's most successful cabinetmakers by the 1840s. When Conrad opened a second cabinetmaking shop in nearby Salisbury in 1831, he left Nathan Parks, his eighteen-year-old apprentice, to tend the Lexington shop.[60] In 1833 Parks married Elizabeth Conrad, perhaps a daughter of his teacher. By 1837 he had set up his own cabinetmaking shop, and he took apprentice Jackson Abbarty, another junior craftsman who would learn the "art and mystery of the cabinet business."[61] Parks and Conrad were the two largest coffinmakers in the county from the 1830s to the 1850s.[62] Parks was the only cabinetmaker in the county listed in the 1860 Industrial Schedule of the United States Census. Working with $500 of capital, he and two employees produced a hundred cupboards, coffins, bureaus, and related items in that year. After Parks's death in 1865, his son Albert took over the cabinetmaking business but sold out soon afterward to J. W. McCrary, another local cabinetmaker-undertaker who subsequently credited Parks as being Lexington's first undertaker.[63] Since blanks were sometimes cut by one artisan and engraved by another, Parks might have lettered some of the pierced gravestones cut by other cabinetmakers, as well as cut and shaped some of his own. It is difficult to imagine Philadelphia-trained cabinetmaker Conrad carving traditional gravestones, but easy to imagine his local-born apprentice, Parks, combining traditional forms with professional engraving.

If Parks did cut tombstones, they might have been a mixture of folk and popular elements. Joseph Conrad's cabinetmaker training would have provided Parks with a popular aesthetic quite different from the traditional model of John Swisegood and his school. Parks was the busiest coffin maker in the county and also served as undertaker. That the finest headstone of the group was carved for Jane Park, Parks's sister-in-law, and stands in their churchyard of Jersey Baptist Church, is circumstantial evidence that he may be the Neoclassical Stonecutter.[64]

Rev. Alex Wilson, Appalachian Stonecutter, 1880s–1920s

The most recent examples of traditional soapstone gravestones stand in the mountains of North Carolina. Although competition from commercial marble yards put most backcountry stonecutters out of business when the railroad arrived in the 1850s, local stonecutters in isolated rural Piedmont and mountain areas remained largely unaffected until good highways and railroads were built in the early twentieth century. One of many part-time stonecutters who continued to work in the mountains was Lemuel Alexander Wilson, a Watauga County Baptist preacher and farmer. Preachers had a close connection with gravestones through their official function at funerals, and many preachers acted as agents for marble yards on the side.

Wilson was born in Watauga County in 1861 to parents who had moved there from the Jersey Church community in Davidson County. Perhaps he learned the craft from his father, who grew up in this Scots-Irish settlement where there was a strong tradition of soapstone carving. Wilson was called to the Baptist Church to preach in his early twenties and served twenty-four Baptist congregations in the mountains of North Carolina and Tennessee during a fifty-year career. Until about 1907, he lived in Tamerac community in Watauga County, then purchased a farm on Meat Camp Creek in the county. A large outcropping of soapstone jutting from the bank of the creek immediately in front of his house provided him with the raw material to create gravestones. From 1907 until 1929, he, his four sons, and numerous grandsons cut gravestone blanks.[65] Grandson Raymond Wilson recalled sawing gravestones out of large chunks of soapstone with a crosscut saw in the 1920s, which was a slow process. In the winter and on rainy days when he couldn't farm, Reverend Wilson carved the inscriptions in his tool shed, and granddaughter Georgia Morris recalled that the newly cut soapstone "was so white it looked like snow."[66]

His head and footstones stand in at least two cemeteries in Watauga County, the Jont Brown Graveyard and Meat Camp Baptist Churchyard (Fig. 4.52). His preferred shape was thin and picket-like. He cut inscriptions with a mixture of uppercase printed and cursive lettering that seems to have been written rather than chiseled on the soft stone. Reverend Wilson moved to Meat Camp in 1907 and may have cut the simple soapstone for Thomas Brown (d. 1835) at Jont Brown Graveyard soon afterward. He also cut headstones for other Brown family members who died in 1863, 1871, and 1905, and a stone for Benjamin and Elizabeth Green, who died in 1899 and 1900. Wilson left all his stones unembellished except that for Polly Brown's stone (Fig. 4.53). She died in 1905, and perhaps the family was willing to pay the preacher a little more to personalize her stone than it was for the stones of family members who had died many years ago. Wilson carved a segmen-

tal arched top and ornate side moldings, incised three stars across the tympanum, and cut an epitaph. At Meat Camp Baptist Churchyard, where he was pastor, he probably carved the plain soapstone headstones for members of the Norris family who died in 1880, 1882, and 1902.

Gravestones were not a lucrative business. Reverend Wilson never charged more than $5 per stone and often made them as a favor to members of his churches.[67] (People who wanted a commercial monument paid between $40 and $200 for marble tombstones from Carolina Marble & Granite Company over the Blue Ridge Mountains in North Wilkesboro, then paid a $10 hauling fee.)[68] In 1929, Wilson remarried at the age of sixty-eight and reportedly stopped cutting gravestones because his new wife did not approve of it; however, other factors were surely involved—his advancing age and the changing taste of the community, for soapstone headstones would have been old-fashioned by the 1920s. When two church members died in 1915 and 1918, they were buried at Meat Camp Church-yard beneath an identical pair of marble headstones with the clasped-hands motif. Their grandson claims that Preacher Wilson carved these marble stones, but this is unlikely.[69] Wilson had neither the tools nor the specialized training necessary to work marble, and the commercial design indicates that the stones were the work of a marble yard, perhaps which Reverend Wilson served as agent. Wilson died in 1935 and is buried at Meat Camp Church beneath a commercial marble headstone.

Figure 4.53.
Headstone of
Polly Brown,
d. 1905,
Jont Brown
Graveyard,
Watauga
County.
Attributed
to Rev. Alex
Wilson.
(Photo by
M. Ruth Little)

Scots-Irish, German, and Appalachian Craftsmanship

Two distinctive backcountry regions, the mixed German and Scots-Irish Catawba
Valley in the western Piedmont and the strongly German county of Davidson in
the central Piedmont, had ethnic gravestone traditions during the antebellum period. In the last quarter of the eighteenth century, the Piedmont-based Scots-Irish
workshop of Samuel Bigham Sr. and his family, working with local stone, their own

Scottish symbolism, and the backdrop of English and German traditions, created headstones that are at the same time the finest Scots-Irish gravestones in North Carolina and distinctively American. In the early nineteenth century John Caveny and James Crawford brought the neoclassical style to the region and swept away the old-fashioned ethnic symbols from graveyards. Farther east, in the second decade of the nineteenth century, a number of talented German artisans, including Joseph Clodfelter and David Sowers, emerged.

Throughout Davidson County, the masterful soapstone headstones with fylfot crosses pierced through the stone and elaborate engraved and molded decoration are the finest German stones in North Carolina. These were labors of love for family and community members, and are suffused with deep emotion that only artisans working in traditional communities could convey. The presence of malleable soapstone in the county allowed the carvers to create dramatic open-work grave decoration that was perhaps closer to the baroque and rococo sculptural tradition of southwest Germany than that of any other region settled by the Germans in America. In Davidson County the artisans created German gravestones for some thirty years after the tradition had died out in German communities in Pennsylvania and for ten years longer than in Virginia. The German decorative idiom so pervaded the county that even an unknown artisan who tried to evolve a stylish neoclassical gravestone style in the 1830s combined German sunbursts and trees-of-life with his urns and swags.

By contrast, in the early 1800s, the large German communities in the Catawba Valley counties of Lincoln and Catawba no longer preserved their culture in their cemeteries, for the major sources of gravestones were the Scots-Irish stonecutting shops of the Bighams and the Caveny-Crawfords from the nearby counties of Mecklenburg and York. Even German stonecutter Peter Harman, in Catawba County, cut plain baroque stones with no symbolism. Perhaps cultural intermingling in the Catawba Valley caused German carvers to abandon the German symbolic style. Yet the continuing need of German communities for ethnically distinctive monuments resulted in a late antebellum efflorescence of German symbolism in Catawba Valley cemeteries. From the 1830s until the 1870s, the Caveny-Crawford Shop supplied headstones with German sunbursts and trees-of-life for Lutheran and Reformed families. It's strange that the last trees-of-life and compass stars on gravestones were carved by Scots-Irish rather than German stonecarvers, but Scots-Irish artisans were more culturally diverse and commercially oriented than their German counterparts. Not all folk art is the naive, unselfconscious expression of an isolated community.

Fifty years later, local gravestone production survived only in the Appalachian Mountains, in the work of men like Alex Wilson in Watauga County. This itinerant mountain preacher made soapstone headstones as a service to his congregations, and in the 1920s competition from commercial monument companies finally ended the long western North Carolina tradition of cutting gravestones from native stone.

5 Marble Yards and Marble Cutters

DUNCAN McNEILL,

The son of Neill McNeill,

of Kintyre, Scotland,

The Pioneer and Friend of the Scottish

Emigration to the Cape Fear region

was born in Kintyre, Scotland,

in 1728,

and died near the Bluff,

Oct.r 2nd. 1791,

Leaving to his Children the legacy

of an honest upright Character,

North Carolina's commercial funerary monument industry began with the influx of British-trained stonecutters who worked on the new state capitol in Raleigh and two major masonry projects, the U.S. Arsenal in Fayetteville and the U.S. Mint in Charlotte, all in the 1830s. The construction of bridges for the emerging railroad network from the 1830s to the 1850s also brought in stonecutters. The first resident funerary monument firm in the state was established in Raleigh in 1837 by William Stronach, a capitol building stonecutter. By 1845 George Lauder, another stonecutter from the capitol project, had established a shop in Fayetteville. Prior to the late 1830s, with the exception of Moravian stonecutter Traugott Leinbach in Salem, all of the stonecutters working in the state had been either itinerant professionals or backcountry artisans. Once the rail lines were complete, commercial stonecutters could set up marble yards along the rails, ship in blocks of marble, and turn out monuments that competed directly with the itinerants and the country artisans.

Most commercial stonecutters in North Carolina were European-trained artisans who came to the United States to find work. Their European training gave them a higher status than the native artisan.[1] Stonecutters generally followed the apprenticeship system which developed in Europe during the Renaissance and continued in colonial America. Master craftsmen working in Boston, New York, Philadelphia, Baltimore, and other eastern seaboard centers formulated standards that were disseminated by apprentices, patternbooks, and various publications. In the nineteenth century these artisans reached a national market through newspaper advertisements. A stonecutter who specialized in monuments, generally known as a marble cutter, nearly always practiced his trade full-time, often signed his work, and usually worked in a large metropolitan center near shipping or rail lines that provided transport of monuments to clients. Such a commercial stone industry operated in the industrialized Northeast, but in North Carolina the general lack of a masonry building tradition and of building stone in the eastern, developed section initially retarded the emergence of a skilled stonecutting tradition.

During the late eighteenth and early nineteenth centuries, the academic model for gravestone design, as for the decorative arts in general, was the neoclassical revival style popularized by the Adam brothers and others in England. The "urn-and-willow" style, so called because of the popularity of this stereotypical image of mourning on gravestones, emerged from this movement. By 1820, the urn-and-willow image had become the most popular image on gravestones from Maine to Georgia. Later in the nineteenth century, various Victorian revival styles, such as the Gothic Revival and the Renaissance Revival, influenced gravestone design. Stones carved by marble cutters are similar in design within each stylistic period, since these men drew their designs from mass-produced media (such as books) as well as from each other. Their imagery tends to be naturalistic and representational, often with literary allusions.

The preferred material for funerary monuments throughout the nineteenth and early twentieth centuries was marble, obtained either domestically or imported

Figure 5.1.
Advertisement of Martin Stevenson,
undertaker and tombstone agent, *Newbern
Spectator*, 1835.

MARTIN STEVENSON,

TO whose care the interment of the dead in the town of Newbern and vicinity, has been confided for the last ten or fifteen years, who still has charge of the burying ground, and who has taken great pains and incurred considerable expense, to give satisfaction to all,—still assures the publick that every necessary attention will be given, and charges made satisfactory, in all instances in which his services may be required. He should have deemed this notice wholly unnecessary, but for a recent advertisement in the Sentinel, headed "John M'Donald undertaker," conveying the idea that he, the said M'Donald, is in charge of our burying place —which is not the fact. In the mean time it is hoped that those of our citizens, who wish to preserve order in the burying-ground, and to guard against the disturbing of the remains of the dead, the trespassing on lots, &c. &c. will take such measures as may prevent the painful consequences which must necessarily result from the officious interference of a person, who, from the shortness of his residence in the place, must be wholly unacquainted with the details of the burying ground ; and who cannot be supposed capable of that sensitiveness on the subject, peculiar to those to whom the place has been made sacred by the remains of kindred and friends.

N. B. M. Stevenson would at the same time inform the people of Newbern, and the publick generally, that Head and Foot Stones and Monuments of white marble, of any description, can be had according to order, at the shortest notice, and at moderate prices—he being an agent for an extensive factory in New-Haven, Con. Samples of workmanship, &c. may be seen by calling at the store of the above, two doors south of the Bank of the State.

from Europe. In North Carolina, marble was not a native stone (though a small amount is found in the extreme west). North Carolinians turned to marble quarries in Pennsylvania and Vermont in the late eighteenth century, and, additionally, to quarries in New York, Maryland, Kentucky, Tennessee, and Georgia in the first half of the nineteenth century.[2] Although the gravestones produced by marble cutters were a considerable expense for North Carolina clients, their beauty and permanence gave dignity and status to a grave.

A marble grave monument reflected the wealth and fashionable taste of the client, but seldom offered clues to his ethnic background. The spread of marble funerary monuments in North Carolina from the upper classes who could afford to import them in the eighteenth century to the middle-class client in the late nineteenth century parallels the state's transition from an agricultural barter economy to an industrialized cash economy. In the eastern towns during the first half of the nineteenth century, local cabinetmaker-undertakers served as agents from whom clients could order marble monuments. Farther inland, itinerant marble cutters filled this function. A few marble yards opened in larger inland towns in the 1830s and 1840s; some urban artisans in such trades as contracting and engraving also made monuments as a sideline. After 1850, the railroads brought the marble and the marble cutters to towns across North Carolina, enabling clients to order stones from the local marble yard. All three sources of commercial monument producers—out-of-state marble cutters, itinerant and part-time marble cutters, and resident marble cutters—were important to the change in gravemarkers that occurred in this hundred-year period.

Out-of-State Marble Cutters

Before 1850, numerous marble cutters in metropolitan centers along the East Coast sold their stones through local agents in North Carolina towns. The Coastal Plain had access to the work of New England, mid-Atlantic, and Charleston stone-cutters via sailing vessels; the northern Piedmont to Petersburg, Virginia, and Philadelphia via overland and water transportation; and the southern Piedmont with Columbia and Charleston, South Carolina, via overland and river transportation. Undertakers in North Carolina's ports advertised that they were "tombstone agents" for New England stonecutters and their connections to Northeast export-ers were extensive. New Bern undertaker and house-carpenter Martin Stevenson advertised in the *Newbern Spectator* in 1835 that he was agent for a New Haven gravestone firm and could provide marble monuments cheaply and on short notice (Fig. 5.1).[3] The firm was probably D. Ritter and Son, later J. Ritter, who signed stones with death dates in the 1820s, 1830s, and 1840s in New Bern, Wilmington, Fayetteville, and Edenton.

Connecticut marble cutter C. T. Duncomb served an extensive network of agents in North Carolina, including cabinetmaker-undertaker Matthew Lawton of Wilmington, who informed readers of the *Wilmington Advertiser* in 1838:

> Marble Monuments
> and Tombstones of Every
> Description
> Manufactured at Norwalk, Connecticutt
> by C. T. Duncomb
>
> Matthew Lawton, Wilmington
> Calebb Bell, Newbern   agents
> Wm. O'Cain, Washington, N.C.
>
> Orders are solicited and received at
> the Cabinet Wareroom of Mr. Lawton, where
> SPECIMENS may be seen, and all necessary
> information given.
>
> Wilmington, June 21st, 1838

Lawton operated his Wilmington business from the 1830s to the 1860s.[4] His dual role in Wilmington was duplicated by men in towns throughout North Carolina until the late nineteenth century, when a tendency to specialize forced the combination of careers apart.[5]

Duncomb's "specimens" were probably full-size blanks, as may still be seen at mortuary firms, and his long-running advertisement produced results. Several marble stones in the St. James Churchyard in Wilmington with death dates of 1837 are signed by him. Out in the county, Henrietta Foy, who had survived her husband and two daughters, requested in her will that stones for herself and her family be purchased.[6] Henrietta died in 1840, and her executor ordered four stones from Duncomb in the early 1840s. The four tall urn-and-willow-style headstones stand in the family graveyard in northern New Hanover County, but only that of husband

Figure 5.2.
Headstone of Fanny Foy,
d. 1826, Nixon-Foy Graveyard,
New Hanover County. Attributed
to C. T. Duncomb, Newark, N.J.

James Foy (d. 1825) is signed "C. T. Duncomb, Newark, N.J." (Apparently Duncomb had moved to New Jersey by this time.) Each stone has a different tableau: James's stone has a prominent obelisk flanked by willows, Henrietta's has a tall urn shaded by a single willow, daughter Eliza's has a smaller obelisk with a single willow, and daughter Fanny's has a simpler version of the scene on Henrietta's stone (Fig. 5.2).

Another out-of-state marble shop patronized by North Carolina's gentry during the period was John Struthers & Son of Philadelphia. Stylish neoclassical head-stones, obelisks, and ledgers for wealthy individuals who died from the 1820s to the 1840s, usually signed simply "Struthers," adorn cemeteries in the Coastal Plain and Piedmont, including the Raleigh City Cemetery and the Old Lutheran Ceme-tery, Salisbury. Planter Bennehan Cameron of Orange County ordered ledger stones from Struthers for four of his daughters who died in the late 1830s and are buried in the graveyard of Fairntosh Plantation. Cameron, who served on the state capitol building committee in the 1830s, no doubt learned of Struthers's work through his supplying the marble mantels for the new building. Thomas Bennehan, Cameron's brother-in-law, who lived at nearby Stagville Plantation, died in 1847 and is buried beneath a Struther tomb-table in the family graveyard.[7]

Importing a monument often involved an intricate network of middlemen who added to the already considerable expense, thus only the wealthiest estate could afford such a memorial. When well-to-do Fayetteville merchant John Kelly died in 1842, his will stipulated that an "elegant marble stone supported by pillars together with a base stone of marble" was to be ordered from New York. A letter postmarked 28 January 1845 from Sackett Belcher & Co. of New York (probably the import merchants), to Kelly's executor Jonathan Evans, reports that "one Italian Marble Tomb with Balusters," already engraved, had been shipped to Hector McKellar in Wilmington. Sackett Belcher paid "Bird and Fisher," either the stonecutters or an-other import firm, $88.54 for the tombstone, then added a commission fee and in-surance fee and requested $91.75 payment from Evans. Wharfage to Wilmington for the three boxes containing the tomb was $1.42. It arrived on 1 February 1845 in Wilmington.[8]

Itinerant and Part-Time Marble Cutters

Until the railroad era, there was insufficient demand for monuments in most of North Carolina to support full-time marble cutters in a single community. Accord-ingly, locally based artisans worked either as itinerants or combined stonecutting with another trade. Indeed, the itinerant rhythm was a fact of life for the full-time American artist and artisan in the eighteenth and first half of the nineteenth centu-ries. Population was widely dispersed, and the percentage of citizens with the means and aesthetic education to patronize the "fine arts" was very small. Portrait painters, silversmiths, architects, sculptors, and other craftsmen who produced luxuries rather than necessities had to create a wide variety of related, practical goods, or else accept an itinerant life. Portraitists earned their bread and butter painting signs, houses, coaches, and even graveboards. Silversmiths made and re-paired clocks and watches, ran printing presses, made guns, and even engraved gravestones. Cabinetmakers were also carpenters and undertakers, and stonecutters worked in the building trades, doing stone masonry and supplying mantels, trim work for buildings, and even curbstones.

Since itinerant stonecutters found greater demand for their products in inland towns than in ports, which had ready access to imported monuments, trading centers such as Fayetteville, Salisbury, and Charlotte were probably the chief destinations of these roving artisans. Fayetteville, the second largest town in North Carolina after Wilmington, was served by itinerant marble cutters almost continuously during the 1820s, 1830s, and 1840s. The earliest identified itinerant stonecutter in the state was Apollos Sweetland, for whom newspaper advertisements track a southerly progress through Virginia, North Carolina, and South Carolina from 1818 to 1827. Richmond, Virginia, was, like Fayetteville, at the head of the major navigable river in the state. On 8 August 1818 in the *Richmond Commercial Compiler*, Sweetland offered a

Notice to Builders.

THE Subscriber respectfully informs the inhabitants of Richmond, that he has now landing from the sloop Driver, capt. Waterman, a quantity of Connecticut river

STONE,

suitable for Building. The Stone is of an excellent quality and handsome color, and is in general use throughout most of the principal cities in the United States.—The subscriber solicits employment. Work will be done on short notice and in good style. Any favors will be gratefully received. Apply at the Indian Queen Tavern, to

APOLLOS SWEETLAND.

He cut monuments in Richmond for two years, then moved to Fayetteville, where in 1821 Sweetland advised readers of the Wilmington newspaper, *The Cape-Fear Recorder*,

Stone Cutting.

The subscriber keeps constantly on hand, a
supply of WHITE MARBLE and FREE STONE, and
will furnish those who want, with
    Plain Tomb Tables,
    Box Tombs, or
    Tables with Balusters,
    Head Stones, & c.
On the most reasonable terms.

November 24   A. SWEETLAND
    Hay street, Fayetteville

From January through August 1823, his announcement ran continuously in the Fayetteville paper, the *Carolina Observer and Fayetteville Gazette.*

In August 1823 Sweetland gave up his Fayetteville shop to David Anderson Jr., a Scottish stonecutter, and moved on. By 1825 Sweetland (probably the son of Isaac Sweetland, a stonecutter listed in the 1799 directory of Hartford, Connecticut) had returned to Hartford and gone into business with Waterman Roberts. The next year both marble cutters came south, and in 1826 again advertised in the Fayetteville newspaper:

Cheraw Marble Yard

The Subscribers have commenced business two doors east of the Brick Store on Church Street, where they will supply those who may wish to call on them with MARBLE TOMB STONES, TABLETS and MONUMENTS, at the shortest notice, and the work will be executed in the neatest manner. All orders from the country will be promptly attended to.

The Subscribers will furnish Marble or Free Stone for steps, underpinning, Door and Window Sills, Caps &c. for buildings.

Cheraw, Dec. 21   ROBERTS & SWEETLAND[9]

Cheraw, located in upland South Carolina just south of the North Carolina border, on the Pee Dee River, was a busy trading center somewhat smaller than Fayetteville. This location, like the previous ones, had enough accumulated demand for gravestones to keep Sweetland busy for about two to three years, and as he moved farther south, he continued to advertise in his former locations in order to keep his old clients. Like Duncomb, he may have left blanks with local undertakers.

The contrast between the two men's business is telling. Duncomb's coastal location enabled him to remain at his factory and export his work. Sweetland was an inland Connecticut craftsman who traveled down through the western edge of the southern Coastal Plain to the towns where Duncomb's stones could not cheaply be shipped. Sweetland could not work without a dependable supply of suitable stone. He brought his own Connecticut sandstone via the James River to Richmond; marble and "freestone" (stone such as sandstone or limestone that could be cut easily without splitting) that he used in Fayetteville was probably brought up the Cape Fear River in the same way. Although the Pee Dee was not as navigable as the Cape Fear, it may have been the route for his Cheraw marble, or it may have been brought overland from Fayetteville.

Sweetland's work gained wide distribution from his Fayetteville center, identified by his decorative signature of "A. Sweetland, Fayetteville" entwined in a feather design. For two monuments at St. James Churchyard, Wilmington, dated 1819 and 1820, Sweetland cut plain marble slabs with long epitaphs and molded borders. For John Maccoll (Fig. 5.3), he cut a typical Adamesque headstone, featuring an urn in a baroque tympanum and corner fan motifs. Sweetland engraved his decorative signature in the lower right corner of the plain baroque headstone of Mary Munn (d. 1820), at Philippi Presbyterian Church, Hoke County (see Figure 1.13). Although no stones signed by Sweetland appear in Fayetteville's largest cemetery, Cross

Creek Cemetery, he probably cut a number of the marble ledgers there that have death dates in the early nineteenth century, such as the 1803 Angus Campbell stone. Campbell would have been dead eighteen years by 1821 when Sweetland arrived, but, as the first stonecutter known to have worked in Fayetteville, most of Sweetland's first orders were probably for old graves.

David Anderson Jr., Sweetland's successor in Fayetteville, immediately placed his own notice in the Fayetteville *Carolina Observer*, reusing Sweetland's engraving of a female mourning beside a monument (Fig. 5.4).

The advertisement ran from August 1823 to January 1824. No further advertisements nor any Anderson-signed gravestones have been located. Anderson, apparently in his early twenties when he opened up shop, may have moved elsewhere in search of work.[10] The unique headstone for one David Anderson in Cross Creek Cemetery may commemorate the stonecutter himself or perhaps his father, David Anderson Sr.:

> David Anderson
> Born at
> Stirling No. Britain
> 1767.
> Died 9th April 1844.

The shape of the stone is severe, and the lettering is in a raised sans serif style, characteristic of Scottish (North Britain) lettering rather than the usual relief Roman lettering of English monuments.[11] If this is typical of David Jr.'s work, it is certain that he executed few gravestones in Cumberland County.

By 1839 a new stonecutter, James Foster, had come to Fayetteville. He ran the following notice, with the usual mourning scene, in the local newspaper, *The North-Carolinian*, from at least March 1839 to the end of 1840 (see Figure 1.18):

> Dress the Grave of thy Friend.
> MARBLE FACTORY, by
> JAMES FOSTER,
> Liberty Point-Fayetteville, opposite THE
>   JACKSON HOTEL.
> May 4.

Foster, a middle-aged artisan with a wife, small children, and three slaves, was an itinerant.[12] He was still in Fayetteville in 1843, but must have moved on by about 1845 when George Lauder established his marble yard. Nothing is known of Foster's background, but three James Fosters—father, son, and grandson—were stonecutters in Dorchester, Massachusetts, in the eighteenth century, and this James Foster may be their descendant.[13]

Foster's two known signed stones indicate that he worked in the same neoclassical style as his predecessors. Both the headstone of the Reverend Angus McDiarmid (d. 1827), at Longstreet Presbyterian Churchyard in Moore County, and the headstone of Jane Munroe (d. 1826), in the McIntyre Graveyard in Cumberland County, are neoclassical marble stones of commercial quality, signed "J." and "Jas.

Figure 5.3.
Headstone
of John
Maccoll,
d. 1819,
Longstreet
Presbyterian
Churchyard,
Hoke County.
Signed by
Apollos
Sweetland,
Fayetteville.

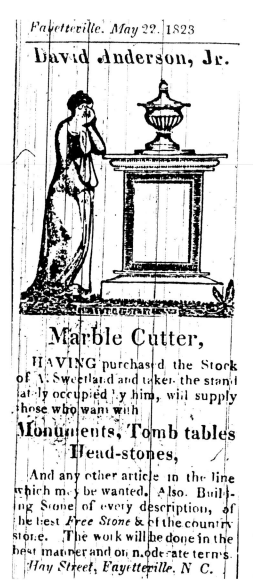

Fayetteville. May 22. 1823

David Anderson, Jr.

Marble Cutter,

HAVING purchased the Stock
of A. Sweetland and taken the stand
lately occupied by him, will supply
those who want with

Monuments, Tomb tables

Head-stones,

And any other article in the line
which may be wanted. Also. Building Stone of every description, of
the best *Free Stone* & of the country
stone.   The work will be done in the
best manner and on moderate terms.
Hay Street, Fayetteville. N C.

Figure 5.4.
Advertisement of
David Anderson Jr.,
marble cutter, *Carolina
Observer*, 1823–24.

Foster, Fayetteville." The McDiarmid stone is plain, but the Munroe stone is a
standard urn-and-willow design (Fig. 5.5). Foster was a natural choice to execute
the tomb-table that Fayetteville merchant John Kelly, who died in 1842, requested
in his will, but Foster's talents were apparently sufficient only for a minor role. The
executor commissioned Foster to make a marble cross for the arched entrance gate
of Kelly's tomb, and paid him $8 for it in late 1843. Kelly's monument, a tomb-table
of Italian marble, was ordered from New York.

The itinerant marble cutter was the final agent in the spread of the neoclassical
gravestone style throughout the eastern seaboard in the early nineteenth century.
While Isaac Sweetland's stones probably reflected his Connecticut environment,
either in technique, form, or choice of ornament, his son Apollos' marble urn-and-
willow stones carved all over the upper South were interchangeable with those of
Foster, Duncomb, or any of the marble cutters in the eastern United States. All
used the same patternbooks, and the popularity of the delicate weeping willow
trees sheltering urns or obelisks on which a female mourner leaned was universal.
Yet this standardized model was not easily produced. The long apprenticeship nec-

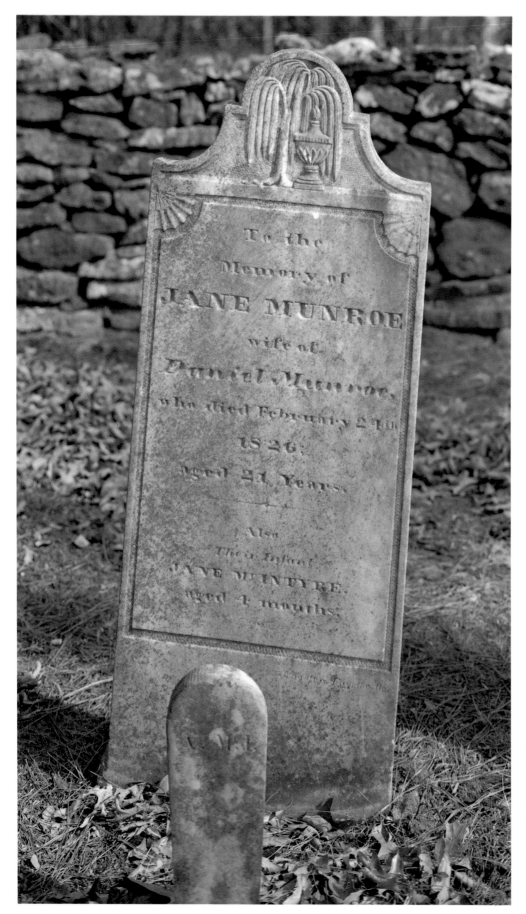

Figure 5.5.
Headstone
of Jane
Munroe,
d. 1826,
McIntyre
Graveyard,
Cumberland
County.
Signed by
James Foster,
Fayetteville.

essary to carve these refined classical monuments is made glaringly apparent by the gawky imitations carved by part-time stonecutters in the Piedmont. A finite number of marble cutters worked in the United States during the first half of the nineteenth century, and Fayetteville was perhaps unique in North Carolina in having had four of them.

Traugott Leinbach, Salem, ca. 1831–1850

Traugott Leinbach (1798–1881), a Moravian silversmith who worked in Salem throughout his long career, is the earliest-known resident marble cutter in North Carolina, though his monument business was merely a sideline to silversmithing. Leinbach was born in Salem in 1798, was apprenticed to master silversmith John Vogler between 1811 and 1818 to learn silversmithing and watchmaking, took additional training in Pennsylvania in 1818, and in 1821 opened his own shop in Salem, where he worked for sixty years. His goblets, knives, spoons, ladles, and other silverware follow the restrained Federal style he learned from John Vogler. Like most Moravian craftsmen, Leinbach also took on numerous sidelines, including silhouettes, daguerrotype photography, and gravestones.[14] He was apparently quite a successful businessman, building a large brick residence on Salem's main street about 1830.[15]

The earliest mention of his gravestone work is in a Moravian document from 1831: the Moravian Elders forbade him to erect a gravestone, cut for a gentleman from South Carolina, in the Moravian cemetery.[16] Leinbach probably usually cut standard flat Moravian plaques, the only gravemarkers allowed in Moravian cemeteries, but produced fashionable neoclassical style monuments for non-Moravian clients. Numerous clients in the adjacent county of Davidson ordered gravestones from Leinbach in the 1830s and 1840s, at an average cost of $6.50 each.[17] For William Ledford (d. 1842), Leinbach cut a marble plaque, the only Moravian marker in the Midway United Methodist Churchyard, but it is mounted vertically like a headstone rather than set flush in the ground as in a Moravian cemetery. For Juliana Mock he cut an elegant marble urn-and-willow headstone with deep relief lettering (Fig. 5.6). The adjacent headstones of Juliana's husband, Jacob (d. 1844), with an urn-and-willow tympanum, and of Margaret (d. 1843), probably their child, with a baroque tympanum with a large urn, Adamesque fans, and an oval frame surrounding the inscription, resemble Juliana's stone and were probably cut by Leinbach. The headstone for the "gentleman from South Carolina" probably resembled the fashionable Mock stones, and would certainly have introduced a jarring note into the austerely egalitarian atmosphere of Salem's God's Acre.

The geographic range of Leinbach's gravestones beyond Salem and Davidson County is unknown, but his stylishly up-to-date monuments would have appealed to customers throughout the central Piedmont. Residents of adjacent Davidson County who wanted marble gravestones during the 1830s and 1840s had little choice but to patronize Leinbach. One "Davidson, Petersburg" carver signed two stylish marble headstones with death dates of 1817 and 1828 in the Bethany Church-

Figure 5.6.
Headstone
of Juliana
Mock, d. 1843,
Bethany
Lutheran and
Reformed
Churchyard,
Davidson
County.
Probated
to Traugott
Leinbach,
Salem.

yard, but the earliest-known marble cutter in Salisbury, the nearest sizable town, did not appear until about 1852. Leinbach does not fit the general definition of a marble cutter since he worked part-time within a limited geographic range, but his gravestones are equal in technique and aesthetic appeal to the work of full-time marble cutters.

Architects Who Designed Monuments: A. J. Davis and William Nichols

A number of nineteenth-century architects throughout the United States designed monuments in addition to their usual architectural work. The pedestal-tomb and the obelisk became popular in the early nineteenth century as a result of the national vogue for commemorating the heroes of the American Revolution with classical monuments and Egyptian obelisks in city squares in the Northeast. One of the best known is the Washington Monument, erected by Robert Mills in Baltimore from 1815 to 1829. The obelisk (a tall, slender, tapering pillar) and pedestal-tomb (a thick column or pillar surmounted by an urn) were handy small-scale exercises in classical design for struggling young architects such as Thomas Tefft of Rhode Island, who designed scores of these tombstones in the 1840s for New England cemeteries.

Some of the earliest-known examples of architect-designed monuments in North Carolina were the work of William Nichols, the English-born architect for the state of North Carolina, who stylishly redesigned the old State House in Raleigh in the early 1820s. After the death of prominent jurist and statesman Archibald Henderson of Salisbury in 1822, his legal colleagues formed a "Monument Association" and commissioned Nichols to design a monument for him. Henderson's tall marble and brownstone neoclassical pedestal-tomb bears the first monument signature known in North Carolina that represents the designer rather than the stonecutter (Fig. 5.7). Although Nichols was "in superintendence" of the monument in October 1825, he was not the stonecutter. Nichols's design services were much in demand in the 1820s, and it is highly unlikely that he had either the technical ability or the time to actually execute these monuments. The association probably sent Nichols's design drawing to Philadelphia or New York where a marble cutter fashioned the urn and tablet and engraved Nichols's signature as designer. They then probably hired a local artisan to cut the pedestal, perhaps of local brownstone. They paid Charles Fisher, probably a local quarryman, for hauling the rock and sand for the monument.[18] Nichols designed and signed a similar monument for Francis Locke, a Revolutionary War hero who died in 1823, at Thyatira Presbyterian Church in Rowan County.

Prominent New York architect A. J. Davis designed the tomb of statesman William G. Gaston (d. 1844). Gaston's daughter Susan and her husband, Robert Donaldson, one of A. J. Davis's major New York City patrons, probably commissioned the tomb.[19] Davis commemorated Gaston with a striking bold Roman sarcophagus monument, of white marble, with swelling sides and a gabled lid (Fig. 5.8). The identity of the stonecutter is unknown, but because of Davis's New York connections he was likely from New York.

Resident Marble Cutters: The First Generation

WILLIAM STRONACH, RALEIGH, CA. 1837–1857

North Carolina's resident commercial monument industry began in the early to mid-1830s, when British stonecutters recruited from the Northeast poured into Raleigh to cut and lay up the stone walls and classical finish of the new state capitol. One of these was William Stronach, who was born in northern Scotland, at Stoneveach in the Shire of Elgin, in 1803, and apparently trained as a stonecutter in Leith, Scotland, before immigrating to America. By 1833 he was in North Carolina.[20] According to family tradition, he and a number of other Scottish stonecut-

Figure 5.7.
Pedestal-tomb of
Archibald Henderson,
d. 1822.
Old Lutheran Cemetery,
Salisbury.
Signed "Wm. Nichols, Archt."

Figure 5.8.
Monument
of William G.
Gaston,
d. 1844,
Cedar Grove
Cemetery,
New Bern.
Designed
by architect
Alexander
Jackson Davis
of New York.

ters came directly to Raleigh to work on the capitol (Fig. 5.9), but it is more likely that he was recruited in a northeastern city.

Construction of that stone building, which lasted from 1833 to 1840, brought talented professionals to Raleigh. At the height of construction (1835–36), some seventy stonecutters were employed under David Paton, a young Scot hired in 1834 by Ithiel Town in New York to superintend the capitol stonework.[21] Paton had learned architecture and stone construction under his father in Edinburgh and had worked in London as an assistant to John Soane, the great English neoclassicist architect. Because North Carolina had few stonecutters, Paton recruited the majority of his skilled workers from New York, Boston, and Philadelphia.

The stonecutters brought with them a highly developed sense of status as artisans. An 1836 letter from a group of New York stonecutters accepting Paton's offer of employment to come to Raleigh and work on the capitol states that "We are First Rate Tradesmen having regularly served our apprenticeship to the Trade of Stone Cutting and can execute all the Entablature according to patterns in a tradesmanlike manner. . . ."[22] Once in Raleigh, the capitol stonecutters organized themselves in order to negotiate wages equal to those paid stonecutters in northern cities. And according to contemporary reports in the Raleigh newspapers, the stonecutters marched in full artisan regalia in civic parades, flying banners with such mottoes as "Industry, the sure source of Independence," topped by an American eagle.[23]

The naturalization papers of the stonecutters who gained U.S. citizenship during their employment in Raleigh reveal that most of them were born in Scotland,

Figure 5.9. North Carolina State Capitol, Raleigh, 1833–40. William Nichols Jr., Ithiel Town, A. J. Davis, and David Paton, architects.

Ireland, or England and came to the United States in their twenties and thirties by way of Liverpool, England, Greenock, Scotland, or Quebec. Most of them moved on following completion of the capitol, for stone construction was almost nonexistent in North Carolina for all but the most monumental civic projects, which were few and far between during the antebellum period. William Stronach was one of about a half dozen who remained in Raleigh.[24]

According to tradition, Stronach supervised the construction of the capitol foundation. Like the other skilled stonecutters, he was paid $2 a day. In 1837 he purchased a two-acre lot on Hargett Street opposite Raleigh City Cemetery, where he must have established a marble yard almost immediately. He began to advertise that his marble yard was "at his house, SE corner of the Burying ground" in the local newspaper in 1838, even though he was still working on the capitol.[25] George Lauder, a fellow capitol stonecutter and fellow Scot, seven years younger than Stronach, worked as his assistant for several years prior to moving to Fayetteville and establishing his own marble yard.[26] By 1838 Stronach had married and by 1850 had five children (Fig. 5.10).[27]

Figure 5.10. Miniature portrait of William Stronach, ca. 1850, by an anonymous artist. (Courtesy Stronach family, Raleigh)

Stronach's first gravestone commissions perhaps mark the graves of fellow stonecutters who died during their stay in Raleigh. The section of City Cemetery known as the "Strangers Section" contains the "Stonecutters' Plot," in which three stonecutters and two of their wives, who died in the 1830s, are buried beneath tall neoclassically curved granite headstones (Fig. 5.11). The granite is almost certainly from the capitol quarry, located about two-thirds of a mile east. Stronach may have carved the impressively scaled headstones, which retain the roughly dressed finish appropriate to granite. In 1839 Stronach purchased a portion of the capitol granite quarry to ensure himself a steady supply of stone.[28]

Stronach probably had some difficulty establishing his business, for Raleigh citizens had been accustomed for many years to importing gravestones from out-of-state suppliers such as Thomas Walker of Charleston, Davidson of Petersburg, and John and William Struthers of Philadelphia.[29] And even Duncan Cameron, the chairman of the capitol building committee in the early years who valued Stronach's stone craftsmanship, still turned to Struthers when ordering fine marblework, such as his own family tombstones and the capitol mantelpieces.[30] To prosper in the small town of Raleigh, Stronach took all manner of masonry jobs, often working in the shadow of other artisans. In 1841 he installed the Gothic marble mantelpieces cut by Struthers into their places in the library of the new capitol building. In 1842 he erected a stone wall around the tombstones cut by the Strutherses for the Cameron family in Fairntosh Cemetery on Duncan Cameron's plantation in Durham County. In 1847 he constructed a granite foundation for the iron fence cast by Raleigh mechanic Silas Burns around Union Square.[31]

Stronach's 1840s stones were virtually indistinguishable from those of his out-of-state competitors. His earliest documented gravestones are the head and footstones he carved in 1844 for Ephraim Mann, a member of the General Assembly

On the gravestones in the image:

SACRED
to the memory of
GEORGE PAGE,
(stone-cutter)
a native of Scotland,
who departed this life
April 24th, 1836,
aged 25 years.

ERECTED
to perpetuate the memory
of
WILLIAM S. COBB,
stone cutter,
native of ENGLAND
... Raleigh, Aug ... 1816,
... Respect by all who knew...
AGED 26 YEARS.

Figure 5.11. "Stonecutters' Plot" at City Cemetery, Raleigh, where stonecutters and their wives who died during construction of the capitol are buried.

who died in 1834 (Fig. 5.12). In 1845 he carved the tombstone of John Rex, who died in 1839 (Fig. 5.13). The 1840s tombstone of wealthy citizen John Devereux (Fig. 5.14) is attributed to him.[32] Stronach gave Mann's marble headstone a baroque-lobed pediment and a simple inscription that resemble the stones of Thomas Walker of Charleston. For Rex he cut a box-tomb with a thick granite base and a marble ledger. Such box-tombs were especially popular among Raleigh's wealthy families during this period. For Devereux he carved a weighty tomb-table with voluptuously curved granite balusters supporting an elegant marble ledger.

During the 1850s Stronach worked hard at providing his Raleigh customers with the most up-to-date funerary designs. In 1853 he announced that he had "been North and purchased a large assortment of Italian and American MARBLE for Monuments, Tombs, and Headstones. . . ." In 1854 he had "a first-rate Northern Carver and Letterer." He also owned several slaves who probably assisted in the business. By 1856 he had added obelisks to the list of funerary monuments that he was prepared to make.[33] Unfortunately for us, because Stronach apparently never signed his gravestones, examples of his work cannot be documented except in written records. The style of his probated gravestones is similar to that of his out-of-state competitors; in the absence of unique characteristics that would link unsigned or unprobated stones to those that were, positive attribution is impossible. A good number of the granite and marble gravestones that crowd City Cemetery with death dates from the 1830s to the 1850s are probably his handiwork. Of special interest are a group of granite ledgers and headstones scattered throughout the cemetery from the years of Stronach's career that were probably cut by him from his granite quarry. The unusual coped bodystone and headstone of granite for Mary Beasle (d. 1831) represent a revival of a medieval British monument type that Stronach might have carved early in his career (Fig. 5.15). Stronach's own tombstone is a thick granite slab set directly on the ground, with a small marble obelisk set on top, and may have come from his own shop. Stronach was buried in City Cemetery, but his and his wife Sarah's graves were later moved to suburban Oakwood Cemetery.[34]

Figure 5.12. Headstone of Ephraim Mann, d. 1834, City Cemetery, Raleigh. Probated to William Stronach, Raleigh.

Figure 5.13.
Box-tomb of John Rex, d. 1839,
City Cemetery, Raleigh.
Probated to William Stronach, Raleigh.

Figure 5.14.
Tomb-table of John Devereux, d. 1846, City Cemetery, Raleigh.
Attributed to William Stronach, Raleigh.

The "Northern Carver" that Stronach hired in 1854 may have been Eleazer Colbourn, a Massachusetts stonecutter who lived in Raleigh by 1838, when he was supervising the quarrying of stone for the capitol at the State Quarry. By 1850 Colbourn lived just four doors from Stronach.[35] Colbourn and another Scottish-born capitol stonecutter, Donald Campbell, witnessed Stronach's will in January 1856 and were his executors after his death in May 1857.[36] Although none of Stronach's sons followed him in the stonecutting business, stonecutter Thomas Grier bought his marble yard, which eventually became known as the Raleigh Marble Works. The Cooper Brothers bought the firm in 1894, and it continued to operate until the Great Depression.[37]

Figure 5.15. Headstone and coped bodystone for Mary Beasle, d. 1831, City Cemetery, Raleigh. Attributed to William Stronach, Raleigh.

Of the remarkable generation of Scottish stonecutters drawn to North Carolina in the 1830s, George Lauder had the most lasting impact on its graveyards. When he set up his marble yard on Hay Street in 1845, the role of the itinerant stonecutter ended in Fayetteville. Lauder's spare Scottish style filled graveyards throughout the Upper Cape Fear for the next forty years. Lauder cut the largest number of gravestones, spread over the widest geographic region (almost two-thirds of the state), of any stonecutter in North Carolina prior to the twentieth century. The size of his total output numbers thousands of gravestones standing in cemeteries from New Hanover County on the coast to Orange, Randolph, Guilford, and Davidson Counties in the Piedmont.

Born in Edinburgh, Scotland, in 1810, Lauder was one of the many stonecutters whom David Paton enticed to Raleigh to work on the state capitol. Lauder left for a time in 1835 to assist in the construction of the U.S. Arsenal in Fayetteville but returned to Raleigh to complete the capitol, then worked in William Stronach's marble yard for a few years.[38] In 1845 he established his own marble yard in Fayetteville. It was an auspicious moment, for between 1849 and 1852 Fayetteville became the focus of five plank roads stretching into the backcountry, the longest of these being the Fayetteville-Salem Plank Road, which traversed Moore and Randolph Counties.[39] Lauder's business experienced phenomenal growth during the 1850s. In 1850 Lauder and three assistants produced about 500 tombstones; in 1860 he and four assistants made 2,500 tombstones.[40] His success is particularly surprising since Fayetteville was not connected to the main rail lines in the state until long after the Civil War, a situation that probably preserved Lauder's Fayetteville market from outside competition but also made it more difficult for him to ship the gravestones to clients in other counties. In 1855 the North Carolina Railroad was laid through Piedmont towns where he had customers. A savvy businessman, Lauder notified readers of the *Lexington and Yadkin Flag*:

Marble Factory

He still operates his Marble Factory, at his yard on Hay St., where he is prepared to execute at short notice and in the best styles all orders for Monuments and Tomb and Grave Stones and other descriptions of stone-work if required. He constantly keeps on hand a large supply of the best and finest Italian and American marble. From his experience in the business he flatters himself that he can give satisfaction to all who may favor him with their patronage. He can also supply painters with Paint-stones and Mullers.

George Lauder
Nov. 23, 1855[41]

Soon after Lauder moved to Fayetteville, he built a frame Greek Revival house, designed, according to local tradition, by David Paton, at 118 Hillside Avenue on Haymount Hill, overlooking the business district along Hay Street (Fig. 5.16).[42] Lauder, a bachelor, adopted Christina and Henrietta Clow, orphaned children of a Scotsman, a close friend, and raised them.[43] He played an active role in Fayetteville's civic affairs. An earnest Mason, Lauder joined Fayetteville's Phoenix Lodge No. 6 in 1850, and from 1862 to 1866 he served as Lodge master.[44] His friendship with Raleigh native Andrew Johnson (U.S. president 1865–68) resulted in his appointment as Fayetteville postmaster, a position he occupied from about 1870 to 1875.[45] During his tenure as postmaster, his son-in-law James B. Smith operated the marble yard, but Lauder may have done some design work and cutting.[46]

Lauder's first marble yard was on Hay Street, perhaps at the same location as Sweetland and Anderson's shop. His daughter's house servant remembered it "on the point of Flat Iron Place," probably the name by which the intersection of Old and Hay Streets was known, where an old triangular-shaped brick store still stands.[47] He used both American and foreign marble, most probably delivered by river boat.[48] About 1870, he moved the yard to Franklin Street, behind the old Hay Street Post Office.[49]

George Lauder retained a strong affection for his native Scotland and his Scottish heritage. During a return visit to Scotland in later life, he is said to have visited the home of Sir Walter Scott, and upon his return carved a copy of a sundial that he saw in Scott's garden. A red sandstone pedestal that now stands on the grounds of the First Presbyterian Church in downtown Fayetteville is said to be the base of this sundial, moved here from Lauder's garden in 1924 (Fig. 5.17).[50] Another non-funerary sculpture that Lauder carved is the marble baptismal font for St. Bartholomew's Episcopal Church in Pittsboro.[51]

Figure 5.16. George Lauder House, 1840s, 118 Hillside Avenue, Fayetteville. (Photo by Dru Haley, 1978; courtesy North Carolina Division of Archives and History)

From the beginning Lauder signed many of his stones with "Lauder, Fayetteville." Yet his style is so distinctive that unsigned stones can be easily attributed to him. Like Apollos Sweetland, Lauder made a number of backdated gravestones for old graves; for example, he signed stones in Cumberland County cemeteries for people who died in 1780, 1786, 1820, and 1828.

During Lauder's forty-three-year career in Fayetteville, the designs of his monuments corresponded decade by decade to national fashion and to his clients' tastes and pocketbooks. In the 1840s and 1850s the gentry often preferred ledgers, whether set flush on the ground, raised on legs as a tomb-table, or on a solid base as a box-tomb, but Lauder cut only a few of these. For infants Duncan Williams (d. 1847) and George Williams (d. 1853), buried at Cross Creek Cemetery, he created an unusual double marble ledger, 47 inches wide and 59 inches long, on a 20-inch-high brick base. Between the inscriptions for the two children, Lauder carved a sinuously curved vine. At Antioch Presbyterian Churchyard in Hoke County, he cut a group of ledgers, set on brick bases, with the unusual addition of head and footstones abutting the ledgers that carry the major portion of the inscriptions. In what seems like duplication, Lauder cut for Mary McBryde (d. 1849) both a decorative headstone with a willow tree and floral spandrels and a ledger that carries additional inscription. He created a similar ensemble for the tomb of Mary C. McCormick (d. 1860) but notched the head and footstones into the ledger (Fig. 5.18). In the same cemetery, for the Reverend John McIntyre (d. 1852), Lauder cut

Figure 5.17.
Base of sundial cut
by George Lauder,
First Presbyterian
Churchyard, Fayette-
ville. (Photo by M.
Ruth Little; Southern
Folklife Collection,
Wilson Library,
University of North
Carolina at Chapel Hill)

an ornate paneled marble base for the marble ledger. The combination of ledgers and head and footstones may be a survival of a Scottish burial tradition.

Taste was shifting away from ledgers to headstones and obelisks by the time Lauder began work. In the 1850s the form of Lauder's headstones changes from relatively small-scale baroque shapes of the 1840s to larger, austere, rectangular Classical Revival silhouettes, terminating in a shallow segmental or pointed arch. Lauder initially embellished these with urn-and-willow ornament and calligraphy, but by the 1860s was generally leaving them undecorated. In the 1870s and 1880s he thickened the slab, made the top round-arched or scalloped, with large beaded or molded borders, and raised the entire stone on a thick base of granite or marble. In contrast to the austere slabs of the 1860s, these late monuments often contain high-relief Gothic Revival ornament of the type made popular by the books of English architect Charles Eastlake.

Most of Lauder's plain stones were probably precut blanks, to be inscribed at the time of purchase. Stones with unusual ornament were most likely special com-

missions, such as one for Henrietta Evans, a child who died in 1848. Her father, James Evans, supposedly designed the stone.[52] Lauder's signed, rectangular headstone bears an eclectic combination of motifs that were more often used separately: a segmental-arched top, a willow tree flanked by floral spandrels, and a decoratively curved inscription in three different lettering styles (Fig. 5.19). Evans probably arrived at his "original" design by leafing through patternbooks, scrutinizing actual gravestone blanks, and combining individual motifs into a rich ensemble.

During the 1840s Lauder continued the neoclassic formula used by Sweetland, Foster, Davidson, and other early-nineteenth-century professional stonecutters, but his strength and breadth of form, perhaps the mark of his Scottish training, sets his stones apart. The headstone of Ann Jenkins characterizes Lauder's use of the old urn-and-willow tableau (Fig. 5.20). A muscular willow tree, with foliage in a distinctive, spiral pattern, fills the baroque tympanum. High-relief carving emphasizes the thick, organic roots, and the background is stippled, a trait characteristic of Scottish stoneworkers. For the headstone of Archibald McDiarmid,

Figure 5.18.
Ledger and
headstone
of Mary C.
McCormick,
d. 1860,
Antioch
Presbyterian
Churchyard,
Hoke County.
Signed by
George
Lauder.

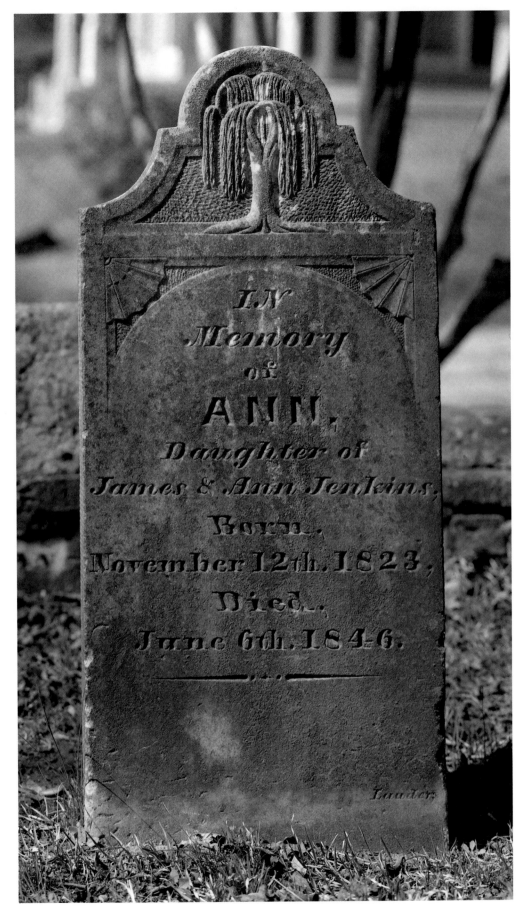

(opposite)
Figure 5.19.
Headstone of
Henrietta
Evans, d. 1848,
Evans Grave-
yard, Cumber-
land County.
Documented
to George
Lauder,
Fayetteville.
(Photo by
M. Ruth Little;
Southern
Folklife
Collection,
Wilson Library,
University of
North Carolina
at Chapel Hill)

Figure 5.20.
Headstone of
Ann Jenkins,
d. 1846,
Cross Creek
Cemetery,
Fayetteville.
Signed by
George Lauder,
Fayetteville.

Figure 5.21.
Headstone of
Archibald
McDiarmid,
d. 1846,
Longstreet
Presbyterian
Churchyard,
Hoke County.
Signed by
George Lauder,
Fayetteville.

Lauder selected the new tall rectangular form and filled the top section with a deeply recessed panel with an unusually complete mourning tableau of urn, mourner, and willows (Fig. 5.21).

A number of Lauder's headstones feature religious symbolism. The open Bible that Lauder cut in bold relief into the top of the tall rectangular headstone of the Reverend James W. Douglass represents an interesting and early example of customized religious decoration (Fig. 5.22). The ornate calligraphic heading, embellished with flourishes that cover the entire upper third of the stone, recalls the delicate engraved headings of such Federal stonecutters as Thomas Walker of Charleston. Two of the prime virtuoso displays of Lauder's stonecutting skill are stones depicting a famous passage from Ecclesiastes exhorting individuals to "Remember your creator in the days of your youth." Both stones commemorate young men who died at the age of twenty-two. When Lewis Bowen Holt, a member of the Dialectic Society of the University of North Carolina in Chapel Hill, died in 1842, his fellow students commissioned a marble ledger for his grave in the Old Chapel Hill Cemetery. In a recessed panel occupying the top third of the ledger, Lauder carved a tableau—containing a fountain, a cistern, and broken objects set in a desert landscape framed by palms—illustrating the two verses from Ecclesiastes that constitute the epitaph:

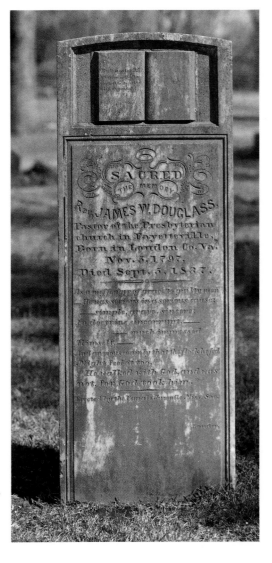

Figure 5.22. Headstone of Rev. James W. Douglass, d. 1837, Cross Creek Cemetery, Fayetteville. Signed by George Lauder, Fayetteville.

> Or ever the silver cord be loosed, or the golden bowl be broken or the pitcher be broken at the fountain, or the wheel broken at the cistern. Then shall the dust return to the earth as it was; and the spirit shall return unto God who gave it.

ECCL XII ver. 6.7

Sixteen years later, Samuel H. Pemberton died at the age of twenty-two. For his grave Lauder cut a tall, rectangular headstone with the identical tableau and biblical reference; this one he signed. The Pemberton stone enables the earlier, unsigned Holt stone to be attributed to Lauder (Fig. 5.23).[53] Four rectangular headstones with crosses in low relief at the top stand at Cross Creek Cemetery: one is for John Bourke, who died in 1856, a native of Galway, Ireland, and thus probably a Catholic; another for Charles T. Haigh (d. 1868), a native of Lambeth, Surry, England, and a leader in the local Episcopal church.[54]

Lauder occasionally carved the Scottish thistle on monuments. The Highland Scottish heritage of the Upper Cape Fear Valley struck a chord in this displaced Scotsman. A century after the Highland

Scot emigration to North Carolina, Lauder carved Scottish Revival monuments for Old Bluff Presbyterian Church, one of the pioneer Highlander churches. In 1858, to commemorate the centennial of Old Bluff's founding, he cut a marble obelisk decorated with a thistle. The headstone of Duncan McNeill, leader of one of the first groups of Highland Scot immigrants in the Valley, is another of his works, albeit unsigned (Fig. 5.24). Lauder probably cut McNeill's stone about the same time as the church obelisk; thus he backdated it by some sixty years.

(opposite)
Figure 5.23. Headstone of Samuel H. Pemberton, d. 1856, Cross Creek Cemetery, Fayetteville. Signed by George Lauder, Fayetteville.

Figure 5.24. Headstone of Duncan McNeill, d. 1791, Old Bluff Presbyterian Churchyard, Cumberland County. Attributed to George Lauder, Fayetteville.

Lauder, a Mason, cut a number of stones with Masonic imagery. Three of these stand in Cumberland County. The lodge members, apparently of Lauder's own lodge, erected a stone for James Hollingsworth (d. 1855) at Cross Creek Cemetery, and Lauder cut a Masonic eye in a triangle on the stone. The lodge members of William H. Strickland (d. 1851) commissioned him to cut a stone with a star in a triangle for the Cumberland Cemetery. On the stone of Mason William H. Haig (d. 1870) at Cross Creek Cemetery, Lauder cut the familiar square-and-compass emblem below the inscription.

For girls and women, Lauder sometimes created personalized floral iconography. During the late 1840s and early 1850s, it was a rose branch in varying stages of bloom. On the stone of the two-year-old daughter of John and Ellen Smith (d. 1847), at Cross Creek Cemetery, he carved a branch with a broken rosebud set in a flat panel at the top. Inside an oval panel at the top of the headstone of twenty-six-year-old Catharine Murchison (d. 1854), at the Murchison Graveyard in Harnett County, he cut a rose branch with two buds, a full bloom, and another full bloom that dangles from a broken stem.

Some of Lauder's headstone designs relied on decorative form rather than symbolism. Although said to have been fond of Sir Walter Scott and his romantic novels, Lauder apparently created few of the Gothic Revival monuments so popular in the mid-nineteenth century. He cut a pair of delicate Gothic-style headstones for the McKay children. The top of each stone features a Gothic arched tympanum flanked by floral spandrels (Fig. 5.25). By the 1870s, in his last decade of stone-carving, Lauder enthusiastically embraced the Eastlake Gothic style. He carved one of his finest, late headstones for W. S. Pemberton (d. 1871), at Cross Creek Cemetery. He created a tall, thick, pointed arch capped by a molded coping, crockets, and finials, standing on a high marble base, with an epitaph from a popular hymn:

"In my hand no price I bring,
Simply to thy Cross I cling."

The voluted headstone represents one of Lauder's most ornate variants of the rectangular form. One of these, the headstone of the Reverend Jacob Grieson (d. 1854), towers over the traditional stones of his congregation at Low's Lutheran Churchyard in Guilford County. His wife is buried under a similar marker beside him. A pair of richly carved classical volutes frames a center finial on top of the shallow pediment of Grieson's stone, and the epitaph, with its reference to Reverend Grieson's vibrating voice, fits a preacher (Fig. 5.26). Lauder cut an even more ornate version of the voluted headstone for Marion Smith, the son of his adopted daughter, Henrietta, who died as a Confederate soldier in 1862. For his fallen grandson, the marble stone, seven inches thick, has deeply carved floral spandrels, and rests on a high marble base at Cross Creek Cemetery.

Lauder's only signed essay in the "bedstead monument," a style popular in England in the mid-nineteenth century and in wealthy Northern suburban cemeteries in the third quarter of the century, is a small marble "bed" for the infant son of John

Figure 5.25.
Headstone
of Flora
Margaret
McKay,
d. 1848,
Summerville
Presbyterian
Churchyard,
Harnett
County.
Signed by
George
Lauder,
Fayetteville.

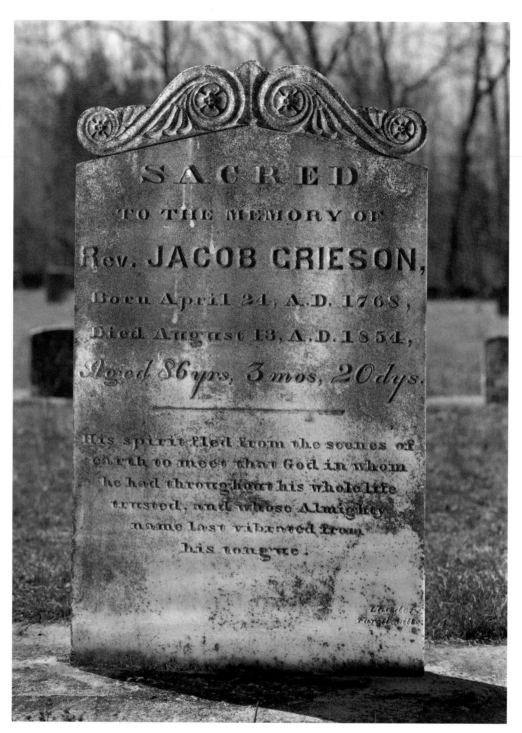

Figure 5.26. Headstone of Rev. Jacob Grieson, d. 1854, Low's Lutheran Churchyard, Guilford County. Signed by George Lauder, Fayetteville.

(opposite) Figure 5.27. Headstone of infant of John and Ellen Smith, d. 1857, Cross Creek Cemetery, Fayetteville. Signed by George Lauder, Fayetteville.

and Ellen Smith. A tall headstone forms the headboard, a smaller footstone forms the footboard, and the side rails have a serpentine border at the top (Fig. 5.27).

Lauder created a sizable number of obelisks throughout his career, although his commissions for these dignified monuments declined after the 1860s.[55] He signed eight obelisks with death dates between 1848 and 1858 in Cross Creek Cemetery, varying in design from the five-foot-high plain tapering shaft for eleven-year-old Owen T. Holmes to the ornate ten-foot-high obelisk of John Crow, who was born in Dundee, Scotland, in 1783 and died in Fayetteville in 1857. In the late 1860s, the

effort to commemorate Civil War casualties brought Lauder a spate of large obelisk commissions. The most famous of these is the approximately ten-foot-high obelisk for the Confederate dead buried at Cross Creek, the first Confederate monument in North Carolina, erected in 1868. (In the fall of 1865, a group of Fayetteville women made a silk quilt, which they raffled at $1 per share to raise the money to pay Lauder's fee.)[56] A pad of red sandstone supports a high marble base and a towering polygonal shaft (Fig. 5.28). Around the four sides of the base are these inscriptions:

ERECTED

Dec. 30, 1868

"Nor shall your glory be forgot

While Fame her record keeps

or honor points the hallowed spot

where valor proudly sleeps."

IN

MEMORY

OF THE

CONFEDERATE

DEAD

WOMAN'S

record

to the

HEROES

in the dust.

"On Fames eternal camping ground

Their silent Tents are spread

Rest on embalmed & sainted dead

Dear as the blood ye gave."

Another postwar obelisk at Cross Creek that appears to be the work of Lauder is a thick shaft with a pyramidal cap, on a high base erected in the late 1860s by John R. Tolar for his father and eight uncles who were killed or disabled in the war.

Lauder signed gravestones until about 1880, but he was blind in his last years and his late stones were probably carved by his apprentices. After Lauder's death, E. L. Remsburg (1860–1946) continued the old marble yard on Franklin Street in Fayetteville, although it became a branch of the Raleigh Marble Works, operated by Charles A. Goodwin, for a few years. Remsburg, a Maryland native, had moved to Fayetteville, probably about 1880, from Danville, Virginia, to apprentice under Lauder.[57] On 8 June 1888, the day following Lauder's death, this advertisement appeared in *The Messenger*, a Fayetteville newspaper:

Raleigh Marble Works

415 and 419 Fayetteville St.

Raleigh, N.C.

—Branch yard—

Lauder's old stand—

Fayetteville, N.C.

Manufacturer of all kinds of monuments,

and tombstones in marbles or Granite,

Also contractor for all kinds of Building

Work, Curbing, Posts, Steps, Sills & c.,

(opposite)
Figure 5.28.
Confederate
Monument,
erected 1868,
Cross Creek
Cemetery,
Fayetteville.
Signed by
George
Lauder,
Fayetteville.

DESIGNS of all descriptions kept on hand and
sent to any address on application,
CHAS. A. GOODWIN.
Proprietor

Railroad Marble Yards

GEORGE VOGLER, SALISBURY, CA. 1852–CA. 1860

In the early 1850s, an artisan in the bustling Piedmont town of Salisbury saw a market for marble monuments sufficient to induce him to change careers. Moravian gunsmith George Vogler (younger brother of Salem silversmith John Vogler) set up shop in Salisbury, forty miles southwest of Salem, in the early 1800s, and by the 1820s he was also operating a linseed oil mill there.[58] By 8 April 1852, the sixty-three-year-old Vogler had established the first marble yard in Salisbury and was advertising his gravestones in the Salisbury newspaper, the *Carolina Watchman*. (Vogler took up stonecutting about the same time that silversmith Traugott Leinbach, with whom he must have been well acquainted, ceased cutting gravestones in Salem, and the careers of both artisans illustrate that stonecutting was not a craft that had to be practiced from youth in order to master.) Vogler located his shop at his Market Street residence, and within two years announced in the Salisbury *Republican Banner* of 3 November 1854:

> JUST RECEIVED on last Saturday, From Baltimore A NEW SUPPLY OF FINE MARBLE. The subscriber would respectfully inform the citizens of Salisbury and the surrounding county that he has opened a MARBLE ESTABLISHMENT in Salisbury, which may be found at his residence on Market Street, where he is prepared to furnish *Grave Stones* of Marble Slabs, Fancy Upright Stones on pedestals, Tombs, Monuments, &c., at a very small profit. Having made the necessary arrangements the subscriber can, at short notice, fill any order from $5 to $500. No pains will be spared to give entire satisfaction. Old Tombstones restored to their pristine whiteness.
>
> GEORGE VOGLER

The extent of work that Vogler was able to accomplish in his decade of marble cutting remains unknown, but the sophistication and complexity of design of his few known monuments suggest he had an extensive knowledge of national monument styles. Perhaps Leinbach gave Vogler basic training, but Vogler's adventurous designs far exceeded Leinbach's own standard neoclassical headstones. Two marble monuments signed "G. Vogler" stand in Davidson County graveyards: a fashionable Gothic Revival headstone for Dr. Tesse F. Pinkston (d. 1846), at the Fitzgerald-Pinkston Graveyard, and a headstone for Robert Bradshaw (Fig. 5.29). For Bradshaw, Vogler carved an elaborate scene depicting Gabriel blowing a trumpet over an urn—a variation on the urn-and-willow theme not found anywhere else in the state—with upside-down torches, symbolic of the extinguishing of life, in the flanking caps. Apart from a slight disproportion in the angel's body, the design and

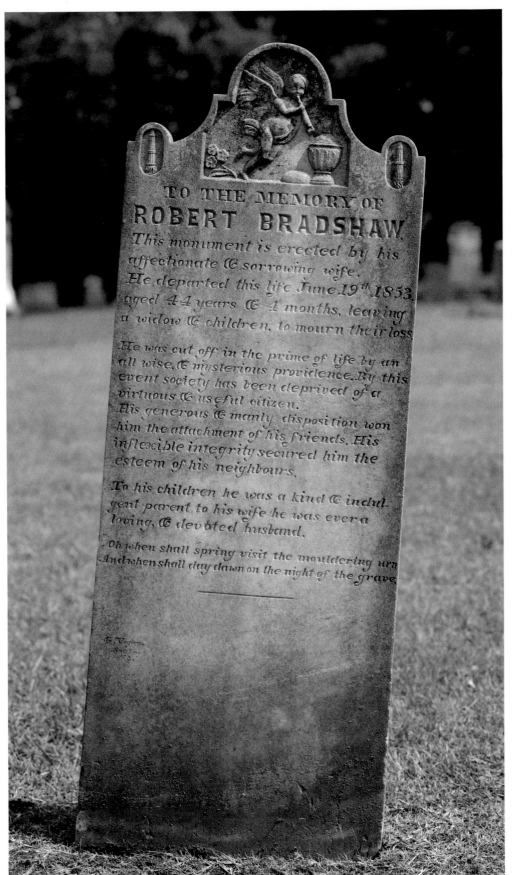

Figure 5.29.
Headstone
of Robert
Bradshaw,
d. 1853,
Jersey Baptist
Churchyard,
Davidson
County.
Signed by
George Vogler,
Salisbury.

execution of both stones are remarkably ambitious for a craftsman who turned to marble cutting in late life.

Vogler probably cut the double marble headstone of simple design for his first wife, Mary Utzman Vogler (d. 1850), and their daughter, Louisa Vogler Randolph (d. 1851), as well as the more ornate stone for Ruth, a daughter by his second wife, in the Old Lutheran Cemetery in Salisbury.[59] For the little girl he cut a diminutive obelisk topped by a resting dog, perhaps representing the family pet watching over her grave, one of the most original and charming monuments of the antebellum period in North Carolina (Fig. 5.30). Vogler signed an elaborate marble headstone for William Shemwell (d. 1852), at the Old Lutheran Cemetery, featuring a classical pediment with bold volutes and a victory wreath. By 1855, when cheaper competition moved into Salisbury on the railroad, George Vogler's skill and ingenuity may not have guaranteed customers. Nonetheless, according to the census records he was still working as a gravestone cutter in 1860 at the age of 71.[60]

Figure 5.30. Monument of Ruth Vogler, d. 1854, Old Lutheran Cemetery, Salisbury. Attributed to George Vogler, Salisbury.

KELLOGG'S MARBLE SHOP, SALISBURY, 1855–CA. 1860

Three months after the railroad came through Salisbury, this advertisement ran in the local paper:

A.A. & M. Kellogg Would respectfully announce to the public that they have opened a MARBLE SHOP at Salisbury, & Letter, Carve and Finish here instead of doing it at the North as we heretofore have done. From our long experience, and from the amount of Business we have been able to do the past year, we are encouraged to locate permanently, hoping to merit the patronage of all who want TOMB-STONES, MONUMENTS, SLABS & c. As to prices we can defy our competition on account of our facility in obtaining Marble. Our workmanship is now generally introduced in some 20 Counties in this State and speaks for itself. Call and see us. Shop opposite the Livery Stable of Bell, Rimer & Co., and near the Railroad Depot.

Salisbury, April 6, 1855[61]

Feeling the competitive pressure, Salisbury's George Vogler ran this notice in the newspaper opposite the Kelloggs' advertisement:

The proprietor of the old Marble Yard in Salisbury still continues to furnish all orders with neatness and dispatch, from the smallest Head Stone to the finest Monument, at the shortest possible notice. Engraving done at the usual prices. He would respectfully solicit a continuance of patronage.

Feb. 24, 1855   GEO VOGLER

The firm had found its niche. Salisbury citizens quickly patronized the new shop. Mary Ferrand Henderson, daughter-in-law of prominent lawyer Archibald Henderson, noted in her diary the fashionable obelisks she had commissioned to be erected in Chestnut Hill Cemetery:

> Monday, July 9 [1855.] Mr. Kellog's marble shop... Called at graveyard to inspect monuments... he does very handsome work... beautiful one for Grandma [Mary N. Steele] $125... one for Pa [Stephen L. Ferrand] plain $100... very pretty little one for Baldy [her son Archibald] (Fig. 5.31)....[62]

In 1857, executors of John Ward's sizable estate (valued at $27,000), paid A. Kellogg $118 for a set of "Tombstones."[63] The Kelloggs' stay was brief. By 1860 they had left Salisbury, perhaps returning to the North.[64]

The Golden Age of Marble Yards, 1880s–1920s

The proliferation of commercial marble yards ended the role of the rural artisan in all but the poorest and most isolated areas of the state. When the railroads arrived in the mid-1850s, they cut the cost of shipping marble in half, and marble yards sprang up in towns and cities throughout the state during the second half of the century.[65] From the three urban marble yards in 1850—Lauder in Fayetteville, Stronach in Raleigh, and English marble-cutter William Tiddy in Charlotte—a dozen marble yards sprang up along the rail lines by 1872—three each in Salisbury and in Charlotte, two in Raleigh, one in New Bern, Wilmington, Fayetteville, and, surprisingly, one in rural Robeson County (see Appendix B). Few families in North Carolina had ordered gravestones during the Civil War, and the new marble yards

Figure 5.31. Monuments for the Ferrand-Henderson family, 1850s, Chestnut Hill Cemetery, Salisbury. Kellogg's Marble Shop, Salisbury, cut the obelisk, second from left, for Mary N. Steele for $125 in 1855.

prospered by supplying fashionable monuments to those North Carolinians who had buried many family members during the tragic years of the Civil War and Reconstruction and had cash to purchase suitable memorials for these loved ones. Successful marble cutters began to establish branch offices in nearby towns. William Tiddy operated a marble yard in Charlotte by 1850, and he and his sons, Richard, James, Josiah, and Thomas, continued to operate it until at least 1870. During the 1850s they apparently opened a branch in Lincolnton, in the adjacent county, and in 1860 produced there some 200 headstones valued at $4,000, 12 "stobs" at $480, 10 monuments at $800, and 50 pieces of "furniture" (probably garden or cemetery benches) at $225.[66]

During the 1880s and 1890s the railroad network crisscrossed the entire state with the exception of the northwestern Blue Ridge (Fig. 5.32). In 1896, thirty marble yards served towns and cities along the lines, with competing yards in the cities of Raleigh, Greensboro, Salisbury, Charlotte, and Gastonia and at least one yard in the eastern towns of Wilmington, New Bern, Fayetteville, Goldsboro, and Sanford, the Piedmont towns of High Point, Lexington, Winston, Statesville, Gastonia, Lincolnton, Huntersville, Reidsville, Newton, and Marion, and the mountain towns of Hendersonville, Asheville, and Sylva (see Appendix B). Large firms, such as the Tucker Brothers Marbleyard in Wilmington, founded around 1890, and the Cooper Brothers Marble and Granite Works in Raleigh, founded by 1894, worked in a multistate region and diversified into building construction and street paving (Fig. 5.33). These firms aggressively expanded by buying up smaller firms to establish branch offices. When George Lauder died in 1888, his firm was bought by Lougee & Goodwin, a Raleigh marble yard in business since at least 1884. Some of the most elaborate monuments in Cross Creek Cemetery and elsewhere in Cumberland County in the late nineteenth century display the signatures of this firm.[67] They produced the splendid Gothic Revival shrine for William Grove Matthews (d. 1884), his wife Isabella, and his four children at Cross Creek Cemetery. By 1896 Lougee & Goodwin were themselves absorbed by W. A. Cooper Brothers of Ra-

Figure 5.32. The North Carolina railroad network in 1900. (Map by Michael T. Southern, North Carolina Division of Archives and History)

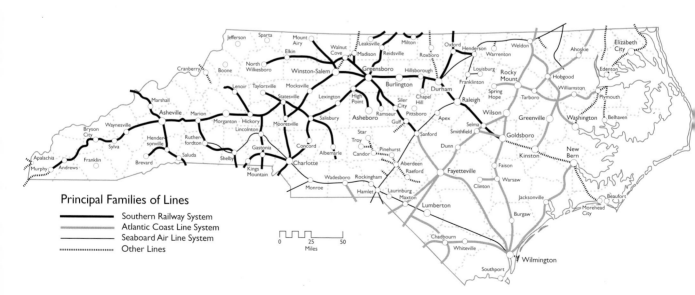

Principal Families of Lines

—— Southern Railway System
—— Atlantic Coast Line System
—— Seaboard Air Line System
·········· Other Lines

0   25   50
Miles

leigh. Cooper Brothers had already taken over William Stronach's old firm, known as the Raleigh Marble Works, in 1894. (Cooper Brothers' Raleigh Marble Works operated in Raleigh until 1930.)[68] Firms such as the Tucker Brothers, R. I. Rogers of Durham, I. W. Durham of Winston (later of Raleigh and Charlotte), and Van Conden & Young of Philadelphia also erected monuments in Fayetteville's Cross Creek Cemetery after Lauder died. The signature of "I. W. Durham, Raleigh, N.C." identifies a large classical obelisk to George D. Baker (d. 1881), adorned with a victory wreath and a three-dimensional urn covered with drapery (Fig. 5.34) and a Gothic-style obelisk to James Kyle (d. 1881), which has a tall spire rising in three stages. Among the most grandiose obelisks in the cemetery are a group of four signed by Van Conden & Young in the Lilly family plot. Similar monuments by this Philadelphia firm stand in Oakdale Cemetery, Wilmington, and Oakwood Cemetery, Raleigh.

Small specialty-monument firms, such as Lauder's successor, Remsburg Marble Works in Fayetteville, Lincoln Marble Works in Lincolnton, and W. O. Wolfe's marble works in Asheville, coexisted with these large firms that operated with branch offices and traveling agents. The careers of John Thomas McLean in Lincolnton and William O. Wolfe in Asheville illustrate the scope of the trade when production was an art created by the marble cutter from raw marble to finished monument. Both men began their careers at the beginning of the golden age of marble yards, in the 1870s and 1880s, when marble monuments became affordable to the middle classes, and both died about 1920 at the end of the marble era.

JOHN THOMAS MCLEAN, LINCOLNTON, CA. 1885–1920

John Thomas McLean, born in 1864 to a clerk of the court in Lincoln County, took an early interest in stonecutting. In 1876, at the age of twelve, perhaps inspired by his father's beautiful penmanship on court documents, young McLean was apprenticed to R. H. Templeton, operator of a Lincoln County marble works.

Figure 5.33. H. A. Tucker & Brother Marble and Granite Works, 310 North Front St., Wilmington (from *Wilmington, North Carolina Up-to-Date*, 1902). Some of the twenty employees stand in front of the office, sheds, and yard of the marble and granite firm, which sold monuments and building stone work throughout North and South Carolina through branch offices and traveling agents. (North Carolina Collection, University of North Carolina at Chapel Hill)

Figure 5.34.
Obelisk of
George D.
Baker, d. 1881,
Cross Creek
Cemetery,
Fayetteville.
Signed "I. W.
Durham,
Raleigh, N.C."

Soon after reaching the age of twenty-one, in 1885, he opened his own marble yard, known variously as the Lincoln Marble Works and McLean & Company, in Lincolnton, in the 400 block of Main Street several blocks east of the courthouse. Templeton continued in business until the mid-1880s, but by 1890 McLean's firm was the only county marble yard listed in the state business directory.

McLean's son, John Thomas McLean Jr., known as "Mac," who carried on his father's business until about 1930, was one of the last generation of marble cutters who cut monuments from start to finish. Interviewed in his eighties in the old McLean marble shop on Main Street which he had converted to his residence, Mac recalled his father's business and his own experiences carrying on the marble yard. These reminiscences provide a uniquely human dimension to the facts gathered from business directories and newspapers about stonecutting in North Carolina at the turn of the century.[69]

Until World War I, his father carved monuments using the same hand technology that had been used for centuries. He worked with marble and small amounts of granite, purchased primarily from Vermont. Mac stated admiringly that his father "raised seven children with just a mallet and chisel." Mac still had some of his father's lignum vitae and hickory mallets that he used to drive the points of the metal chisels to cut the marble. The elder McLean could lay off and cut five inscriptions in a day. Mac recalled that his father cut out a marble tree trunk for a "Woodman of the World" gravestone by drilling a hole in each end of a round block of marble, inserting dowels into the holes, and supporting it on two sawhorses. As he chiseled, he turned it around on the horses. The elder McLean was always in search of new and more attractive lettering styles. "Everytime he'd see a bunch of letters in a magazine or a catalog or anything that appealed to him," Mac said, "he'd tear it out and then he would stick it up" in the shop. Although the signature "McLean & Co." appears regularly in Lincoln County cemeteries, McLean also had a hidden signature. His "Born" always sloped to the left, his "Died" to the right, distinguishing his work from other stonecutters' work.

Typical of McLean's signed headstones are the stones of Henry Whitener (1861–1875), at Salem Lutheran Church, and of Henry P. Heavner (1840–1886), at Old White Zion Methodist Church (Fig. 5.35). McLean cut granite bases and shaped tall, thin marble slabs with segmental-arched tops that fit into the bases. Instead of indulging in the naturalistic floral imagery or romantic architectural forms that characterize many late-nineteenth-century gravestones, McLean gave focus to the composition by cutting the name in large uppercase letters. Whitener's name is inscribed in a rectangular panel, Heavner's name in a semicircular panel. Like most small-town marble cutters of this era, McLean produced a professional-quality, plain headstone that has no additional decoration.

McLean's market was relatively limited, for several large marble yards in nearby Charlotte offered stiff competition. John Jr. was born in 1899 while McLean and his wife were keeping the Old North State Hotel in Lincolnton as a sideline to the stonecutting business. While Mac was stationed in France during World War I, his father bought a pneumatic air hammer to ease his labor. The hammer was placed against the chisel and provided the striking force to cut the stone, speeding up the carving process considerably and lowering the price of the finished stone. This was an enormous investment, for it cost $500 at the same time that a Ford automobile was selling for $350, but was a necessity to compete with the large Charlotte marble firms. The labor-saving power of the air hammer was the motivation that drew Mac into the business when he returned home from the war.

During Mac's apprenticeship, he learned all the tricks of the marble-cutting trade. He recalled his father's advice concerning lettering during a training session: "Now son, you've not only got to work the lines, but you've got to take optical illusion into consideration. Now a letter that is round at the top and the bottom, you've got to go slightly below and above the line. If you don't, it looks too short. And the "V" is one bar wider than a normal letter. A "W" is practically square." Concerning the carving of decorative images, his father's main advice was, "Son, don't try to carve human figures. If you get the human body out of proportion a little bit, it looks conspicuous." Mac followed this counsel, carving lambs and doves, but no human bodies. Both father and son used design books furnished by Vermont monument firms, Georgia Marble Company, and Georgia Marble Finishing Works. (Some of the big marble works had draftsmen who would execute a special design for $10, and if the stonecutter then bought the raw stone from the marble works, the design would be included at no charge.)

Occasionally he and his father copied a design from a gravestone in a cemetery by using pieces of harness leather with black dressing on them in the same way that carbon paper is used today. They placed the leather on the gravestone and rubbed, then laid it on the surface of the stone to be cut and rubbed again, thereby transferring the image to the smooth stone.

In Memory of

HENRY R. WEATHER

BORN

March 1, 1810

DIED

February 1, 1886

Aged 75 years

McLean & W.
Lincolnton

After his father suffered a stroke and died in 1920 at the age of fifty-six, Mac carried on the business and for some years did very well. Sometimes he cut blanks from design books furnished by the stone companies where he purchased his marble and granite and displayed them in front of the Main Street shop, but generally the client chose a design from the books and Mac executed it. He never signed his gravestones, but like his father sloped some of his letters in a certain way to distinguish his work.

Mac's method of laying out the design on the stone was probably the same as his father's. After polishing the surface, which he first did by hand but later with a carborundum wheel, he put a final finish on the stone with oxalic acid and putty. Then he coated the stone with a mixture of gum arabic and plaster of paris powder. He drew the design into this coating with a "penny pencil." A rectangular walnut lettering block, a T-square, and various triangles were used to establish the horizontals, verticals, and diagonal lines of the letters. The letters were always ruled off upside down in order to judge the proportions more objectively.

Mac cut many of his monuments from raw stone. Most of his marble came from Georgia, but a small amount was from Vermont. He very occasionally used "Regal blue" marble from a quarry in the Blue Ridge Mountains of North Carolina, near Murphy, because its beautiful dark blue coloration contrasted strikingly with the gray coloration of the interior of the stone where it had been inscribed. Because the deposits were small, however, it was quite difficult to obtain.

Sometimes Mac ordered blank monuments from the big stone companies. For his biggest commission, a tomb for a Dr. Summers of Winston-Salem, at Salem City Cemetery located adjacent to God's Acre, he collaborated with Scoggins Memorial Art Company of Charlotte. In order to convince the family to give him the $1,000 commission, he had the Scoggins Company do an artistic drawing of the tomb with the name and inscription on it. This tipped the balance and Mac got the job. He subcontracted the shaping of the monument to Scoggins, and did the decorative work and inscription himself.

Like any other small-town stonecutter, Mac had to have other products besides gravestones. Using a portable air hammer, he did all of the trimming and fitting of the Indiana limestone blocks for the Lincoln County Courthouse, erected in the 1920s, and carved the cornerstone. He cut hearths and hearth linings for fireplaces out of soapstone from a quarry in east Lincoln County.

By the late 1920s, competition from big marble companies reached the point that:

(opposite)
Figure 5.35.
Headstone
of Henry P.
Heavner,
d. 1886,
Old White Zion
Methodist
Churchyard,
Lincoln
County.
Signed
"McLean &Co.,
Lincolnton."

> Every little jackleg preacher in the country had a design book and was selling tombstones. He didn't make them—he was agent for some marble firm in Charlotte or Salisbury. . . . It got to the place a small man couldn't start up in Gastonia at all. Charlotte and Spartanburg and those folks would come in there and sell the work cheaper than he could buy it, until they choked him out, and then they would go up on the other customers. . . . I saw fairly early in the game . . . you've got to get big, or get out, or work for someone else.[70]

And when the Great Depression hit, tombstones were one of the first luxuries people began to forego. Mac said of his craft, "This is the first thing that feels a depression and the last thing that feels a recovery." Mac took a civil service exam and became a postman. He continued for a few years to cut gravestones in the afternoons, then decided to get out of the stonecutting business altogether.

THE ANGEL ON THE STONECUTTER'S PORCH: WILLIAM OLIVER WOLFE, RALEIGH AND ASHEVILLE, CA. 1872–1921

Thanks to the title of Thomas Wolfe's well-known novel, *Look Homeward, Angel*, his father William Oliver Wolfe is the best-known marble cutter to work in North Carolina. Wolfe named the book for the marble angels that stood as business advertisements on the porch of his father's shop on the square in Asheville. One of these now stands atop a monument at Oakdale Cemetery in Hendersonville, cut by Wolfe to commemorate Margaret Johnson, who died in 1905 (Fig. 5.36).

William O. Wolfe was a skilled marble cutter with a cosmopolitan training. Born in Pennsylvania in 1851, he apprenticed in Baltimore for Sisson & King's Monument Works in the 1860s, then worked for about a year in Columbia, South Carolina, carving the friezes of the stone capitol building. About 1870 he came to Raleigh to work, along with a large number of other stonecutters, on the state penitentiary and in 1872, at the age of twenty-one, began a six-year partnership with marble cutter John Cayton. A number of handsome marble monuments in Wake County have the "Cayton & Wolfe" signature. They cut ledgers, headstones, and obelisks with stylish forms (Fig. 5.37).

In 1880, in hope of curing his wife Cynthia's consumption, Wolfe moved to Asheville, a resort city in the Blue Ridge Mountains, but she died soon after the move. Wolfe remarried, and he and his new wife, Julia Westall, raised a large family, including novelist Thomas Wolfe. Wolfe's stonecutting shop stood in the same spot from 1886 until 1921 (Fig. 5.38). Thomas's first short story, *The Angel on the Porch*, recounts his childhood memories, and in his novella, *The Lost Boy*, he describes the shop as seen through his brother Grover's eyes on a day in 1904:

He saw it all—the iron columns on his father's porch . . . two angels, fly-specked, and the waiting stones. . . . Beyond and all around, in the stonecutter's shop, cold shapes of white and marble, rounded stone, the base, the languid angel with strong marble hands of love.

The partition of his father's office was behind his shop. He went on down the aisle, the white shapes stood around him . . . upon the shelves the chisels of all sizes and a layer of stone dust; an emery wheel with pump tread, and a door that let out on the alleyway. . . . Here in the room, two trestles of this coarse spiked wood upon which rested gravestones, and at one, a man at work.

. . . The man looked up. He was a man of fifty-three, gaunt-visaged, mustache cropped, immensely long and tall and gaunt. . . . He worked in shirt sleeves with his vest on. . . . a striped apron going up around his shoulder, and starched cuffs. And in his hand, the wooden mallet, not a hammer, but a tremendous rounded wooden mallet like a butcher's bole; and in his other hand, a strong cold chisel tool. . . . He worked upon the chisel and the wooden mallet, as a jeweler might

SACRED
to the memory of
LUCY SAVAGE,
BORN IN
Caroline Co. Va.
Jan. 27th. 1784,
DIED IN
Raleigh,
Sep. 10th. 1859.

work on your watch, except that in the man and in the wooden mallet there was power too.[71]

The young boy's fascination and awe with his father and his work was shared by all of the Wolfe children. Mabel Wolfe Wheaton wrote a biography about her family in which she described her father:

> He could carve anything he wished—the most wonderful entrances to the heavenly land-gates of heaven, they were called—clasped hands, garlands of roses, lilies of the valley, as Tom described them in *Look Homeward, Angel*, "letters fair and fine, and doves and lambs, and hands joined in death."
>
> I used to go down to the shop and watch Papa lay out his work. First he would draw his design, freehand entirely, and then, working from this design, he would transfer it to the marble. Usually he did his carving in marble, because granite was too hard. . . . I would say that almost all of Papa's work was done on marble—white or varicolored, like Georgia silver gray or white from Rutland, Vermont.
>
> . . . Papa displayed his tombstones and kept his marble and granite stock in the front section, which included his office and Mr. Jeanneret's cubbyhole [watch] repair shop. Back of this, beyond the partition and extending from it to the rear wall of the building, a distance of some twenty feet, was the workshop. Here the stock of marble or granite, usually marble, was transformed into tombstones. The shop equipment included two large benches and many carving tools—dozens of various-size steel chisels, some with solid sharp edges for cutting, others with saw-tooth edges for roughing surfaces, hammers, mallets, among them wooden mallets with heads hollowed out so as to drive the chisel more gently, Papa would explain. In one corner stood a foot-pedal-propelled emery wheel . . . used in sharpening his cutting tools. All smooth carving, the carving of his laid-out designs, and all lettering was done with chisels driven by the wooden-headed mallets, never with steel hammers.
>
> . . . There were actually several angels on the shop front porch. I remember how we children sometimes would sit on the bases of those angels. Papa loved them. But sometimes when he was feeling his whisky, he would come out on the porch, stamp his feet, and shake his fist at them. "You damned angels!" he would

(opposite)
Figure 5.37.
Ledger and headstone of Lucy Savage, d. 1859, Oakwood Cemetery, Raleigh, signed "Cayton & Wolfe" of Raleigh. Lucy Savage was stonecutter William Stronach's mother-in-law.

storm at the winged creatures in stone. "Damn your stony souls to hell! Little did I reckon that one day you would be my ruination!"

The angels that Papa sold were not his handiwork, however. Though I'm quite sure that he always wanted to do it and perhaps looked forward to accomplishing the task, Papa never carved an angel, not in his entire life, as far as I have been able to learn. The angels on the porch on Pack Square were of genuine Carrara white marble, imported from Italy, the finest marble in the world. Papa ordered them from Cameron and Company of New York, who were distributors for the Italian quarries. Sometimes there might be three angels on the porch, and Papa had a considerable amount of money tied up in them. That's why in his moments of alcoholic depression, no doubt, he would come out on the porch and curse them. But he adored his angels nevertheless.[72]

Even after moving to Asheville, W. O. Wolfe continued to receive commissions from Raleigh for monuments, and probably shipped these back on the railroad.[73] By the 1910s, agents for mail-order monument companies were competing with him for Asheville business, but he persevered until failing health forced him out of business in 1921. He died the next year.

William O. Wolfe's Italian angels, which figured so prominently in son Thomas's writings, served both real and symbolic functions in the marble cutter's life and work. Wolfe kept them for a number of reasons—as shop advertisements, to sell as the crowning element of a particularly grand monument, and because he admired their craftsmanship. But the angels also represented the pinnacle of stone-carving skill to which Wolfe aspired but never reached, and were thus a symbol of lifelong frustration. Wolfe was as skilled as any stonecutter in the state during this period, but none of the North Carolina stonecutters were capable of carving angels. John Thomas McLean, Wolfe's contemporary in Lincolnton, accepted the limitation of his skill and never attempted to carve the human body. But McLean had apprenticed in Lincoln County, while W. O. Wolfe's apprenticeship in Baltimore, and his first job carving figurative frieze work on the South Carolina state capitol, brought him into contact with a higher standard of sculptural skill. Perhaps alone of all the stonecutters in North Carolina during the golden age of marble yards, William O. Wolfe measured his achievement to a higher standard, the lifesize, three-dimensional figural sculpture of Italy. The power of his angels as symbols of beauty and frustration deeply influenced the writings of his famous son, novelist Thomas Wolfe.[74]

Consolidation, Mechanization, and the End of the Marble Era

The railroad was the agent that caused the proliferation of small marble yards, and of their demise. Consolidation and mass production inevitably forced shops like Mac McLean's Lincolnton marble yard out of business by undercutting their prices. Small marble yards all over the state were absorbed by larger marble yards during the turbulent turn-of-the-century consolidation era. The ease of shipping monuments by rail led to the rise of the mail-order monument business. By the

1910s, competition from mail-order monument works affected William O. Wolfe's monument business in Asheville. By the 1920s, as Mac McLean in Lincolnton recalled, "Every little jackleg preacher in the country had a design book and was selling tombstones." One of these preachers was Rev. Alex Wilson in Watauga County, who served as agent for a monument company when he got too old to cut his own soapstone headstones.

The final blow to marble cutters was dealt by the introduction of new stone-cutting technology that transformed the potential of an old material. Most granite was too hard to be worked with hand tools and thus it had been used primarily for bases. Granite is a metamorphic rock composed of feldspar, quartz, and biotite, or mica grains, and is extremely durable and capable of being polished to a glossy surface sheen. Marble, a sedimentary limestone that has been compressed, is a soft stone that weathers easily. The challenge was that granite's durability made it a superior material for mortuary monuments. In 1898, the first monument was carved out of granite from the Elberton granite deposit in Elbert County, in northeast Georgia, adjacent to North Carolina. Within a few years, new power tools—including large diamond saws, polishing machinery, grinding machines, and pneumatic hammers—enabled entire monuments to be made out of granite, rather than just bases, as had been the case. Large granite quarries began to produce finished monuments and ship them to local agents. Some of these agents were merely retailers; sometimes, like Mac McLean, they sandblasted the inscriptions and decorative work themselves. Gradually, the indestructibility of granite monuments eliminated the market for marble monuments, and the technology of granite carving standardized monument shape and decoration. Granite replaced marble as the stone of choice for grave monuments because of its superior weathering qualities, but it is such a hard stone that only large firms generally had machinery capable of shaping it.

In the early 1900s John Thomas McLean relied on Vermont marble; two decades later when his son Mac took over the business, most of the stone was Georgia granite. In North Carolina graveyards, granite monuments began to outnumber marble monuments by the 1930s. Granite has become more and more popular in recent decades, and marble monuments have been relatively unusual since the mid-twentieth century. Because of the huge scale of quarrying and finishing operations in the Elberton area, Elberton granite could be purchased by North Carolina monument companies more cheaply than granite from other parts of the United States, and Elberton granite became the largest supplier of monument stone to North Carolina.

With the rise of the Elberton granite industry, the artistic role of the local stonecutter changed from sculptor of the overall monument to mere engraver of the inscription. Marble yards that had formerly purchased rough slabs of marble from which to cut individual gravestones now purchased ready-made granite monuments in a variety of stock shapes from Elberton granite plants. Beginning in the 1920s, the plants supplied booklets of designs that functioned both as catalogs and as design guides (Fig. 5.39).[75]

Designs have changed little since the 1930s, when forms and motifs began to become fixed. Monuments are generally thick, rectangular slabs set on shallow bases, with floral or religious motifs placed around the centralized inscription.[76] Although most North Carolina towns still have a local monument works, these artisans cut few original designs. Cain Memorials, the monument firm that is the direct successor to Lauder's Fayetteville marble yard, inscribes precut blanks shipped from the memorial companies in Elberton, Georgia. (Lauder's successor Remsburg purchased the business back from the Goodwin company, and in 1925 Troy Cain purchased the business, then known as Fayetteville Monument Works.) Cain's son Vincent succeeded him, and now grandsons Bruce and Keith Cain operate the firm. The Cains are accomplished stonecutters and have occasionally created custom designs on monumental blanks or even sculpted monuments from raw stone. Vincent Cain designed and cut a marble headstone for Albert Stewart that was based on the headstone of noted Fayetteville painter Elliott Daingerfield (1859–1932), perhaps designed by the artist himself. Both monuments are in Cross Creek Cemetery Number Three (Figs. 5.40, 5.41).[77]

A Lost Art

History is said to repeat itself, and the story of commercial gravestones in North Carolina from the eighteenth to the twentieth centuries certainly goes full circle, from imported marble monuments to locally made monuments and back to im-

Figure 5.39.
This granite monument for
Frank Parker Drane, d. 1918,
at St. Paul's Episcopal Churchyard,
Edenton, was probably cut in the
1920s and represents the first decade
of the widespread appearance of
granite in North Carolina cemeteries.

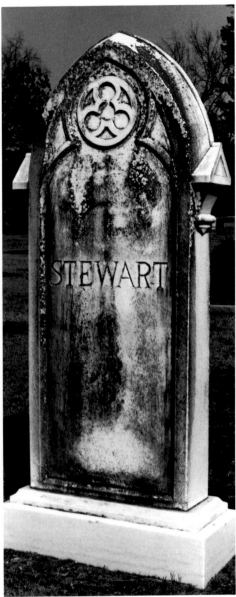

(left)
Figure 5.40.
Marble
monument
of Elliott
Daingerfield,
d. 1932, Cross
Creek
Cemetery No.
3, Fayetteville.
Daingerfield,
a well-known
Romantic
painter, may
have designed
this stone
himself.
(Photo by
M. Ruth Little)

(right)
Figure 5.41.
Marble
monument
of Albert
Stewart,
d. 1970, Cross
Creek Ceme-
tery No. 3,
Fayetteville.
Stonecutter
Vincent Cain
of Fayetteville
designed and
cut this stone
as a reproduc-
tion of the
earlier
Daingerfield
monument.
Custom monu-
ments were
created rarely
after the
1920s. (Photo
by M. Ruth
Little)

ports, of granite rather than marble. Before the 1840s, any North Carolinian who desired a fashionable marble gravestone had few choices but to order it from out of state. With the exception of a few itinerant stonecutters, there were no resident marble cutters. Out-of-state urban marble yards sold stones through local agents, usually the local undertakers. Construction of monumental public-works projects in the 1830s initiated the era of local monument manufacture that lasted from the 1840s to the 1920s. Scottish-trained stonecutters William Stronach and George Lauder came to work on the state capitol in the 1830s and stayed to open the first permanent marble yards in North Carolina. In the Piedmont, Salem Moravian silversmith Traugott Leinbach carved gravestones as a sideline in the 1830s and 1840s, and Moravian gunsmith George Vogler took it up in Salisbury in the 1850s, late in life. Thanks to railroads, marble yards operated by commercial stonecutters sprang up in more than thirty towns by the end of the century. John Thomas McLean in Lincolnton and William O. Wolfe in Asheville typify these railroad-era stonecutters who operated in North Carolina from the 1870s to about 1920, the golden age of the marble yard. Since the 1920s, small marble yards have been forced out of business, and most monuments now are imported from large granite monument factories, primarily in Elberton, Georgia. Stonecutters still work in North Carolina, but most of their business is sandblasting inscriptions onto blanks. Little regional or cultural character remains in North Carolina graveyards, and, with a few exceptions, gravestone carving is a lost art.

The Living Vernacular

North Carolina's agricultural economy and rural population dispersal has preserved the traditional nature of many communities up to the present, and in family graveyards and country churchyards, sometimes by necessity, sometimes by choice, people still create their own gravemarkers. Just as whites and free African Americans chose between commercial and traditional markers throughout the eighteenth and nineteenth centuries, both whites and African Americans have continued to make this choice in the twentieth century. The choice depends more on socioeconomic status than on race. In large urban cemeteries, middle-class families select commercial monuments; a monument for an urban African American is indistinguishable from one for an urban white. In rural community graveyards, both white and black families often chose traditional markers.

There are fundamental distinctions between white and African American graveyards in rural communities.[1] The McMillan Presbyterian Churchyard in Cumberland County exhibits the features typical of rural white graveyards (Fig. 6.1). The cemetery occupies a cleared area, landscaped with a few shrubs and trees. The ground is left in its natural, sandy state, with no grass planted. Sometimes the ground is actually scraped clean so that only bare dirt or sand remains. Graves are oriented head to west, feet to east, and arranged in rows by family groups. If walls or fences are constructed, the unit of enclosure is the family plot rather than the individual grave.

The Cumberland Union Free Will Baptist Churchyard, Cumberland County, is characteristic of rural African American graveyards (Fig. 6.2). It is sited in a wooded area; high grass, undergrowth, and trees prevent the observer from gaining a clear vista of the entire graveyard. Individual graves are generally oriented east-west, but they are not placed in even rows. Families are loosely grouped, and the placement of individual graves within the family grouping has no established order, so that the rhythm of the overall design is irregular and strongly individualistic. The unit of enclosure is the individual grave rather than the family plot.

Fundamental visual distinctions also separate black and white traditional gravemarkers in North Carolina. White graveyards contain grave mounds, shell graves, wooden head and footboards, concrete monuments, grave fencing, and customized granite monuments. Traditional white artisans attempt to follow commercial monument design in their handcrafted concrete monuments. African American graveyards have the types of traditional markers found in white graveyards, but also have distinctive grave enclosures and grave sculpture. Traditional African American artisans create original gravemarker designs and are less influenced by commercial norms. They appropriate various building materials and actual objects that have symbolic meaning or aesthetic appeal and incorporate them to create often startlingly original gravemarkers. They use ephemeral materials such as shells and bric-a-brac, commercial metal and plastic items intended for functional household use, concrete, or perishable materials such as sculpted earth and wood.

Figure 6.1. McMillan Presbyterian Churchyard, Cumberland County. Typical traditional white graveyard. In recent years this graveyard has been grassed. (Photo by M. Ruth Little; Southern Folklife Collection, Wilson Library, University of North Carolina at Chapel Hill)

Figure 6.2. Cumberland Union FWB Churchyard, Cumberland County. Typical traditional African American graveyard. In recent years this graveyard was cleared of its undergrowth and the railings removed. (Photo by M. Ruth Little; Southern Folklife Collection, Wilson Library, University of North Carolina at Chapel Hill)

White Traditions

GRAVE MOUNDS AND SHELL GRAVES

A dirt mound, the minimal gravemarker, covers many white graves in the Coastal Plain. Usually a monument identifies the grave, but in particularly poor areas the mound alone signifies the grave. In the Piedmont, mounds are rarer. In Davidson County, the rural white cemetery of Goodwill Baptist Church contains grave mounds covered with concrete stucco and gravel. At Macedonia Baptist

Church, a white church in Lincoln County, sand or gravel covers many of the graves and concrete block or granite borders outline family plots.

Shell graves, the decoration of dirt grave mounds with arrangements of sea-shells, occur uniquely in the sandy, rural terrain of the southeastern Coastal Plain in the twentieth century, and perhaps earlier. Various types of seashells, most often conch and large mollusk shells, are arranged decoratively, sometimes covering the dirt mound completely, sometimes forming a central spine. In addition to the shell decoration, head and footstones mark most of the graves. The shells hold no sym-bolic significance to local residents questioned about the practice, who explained them simply as grave ornament. People in the Coastal Plain use shells for other decorative purposes as well, such as borders for flower beds and sidewalks. Mere proximity to the ocean is not sufficient explanation—more shell graves exist in Cumberland County, one hundred miles from the ocean, than in coastal New Hanover County.

Found in both white and African American graveyards, shell graves have both English and African precedent. Seashells have been found in prehistoric burials in England, apparently used as fertility or life symbols. Until recently in England shells were used for grave decoration in ways that suggest a remarkable persis-tence of folk memory. In Anglesey, for example, seashells and white pebbles deco-rate modern graves.[2] Shells are also among numerous objects with decorative and spiritual significance placed on graves in West Africa. The connection is strong in southeastern North Carolina, where we find one of the highest percentages of black population in the state.[3]

Shell decoration is ephemeral; shells tend to become scattered with time and are discarded during graveyard maintenance. Judging from the freshness of shells at recorded shell graves, family members had recently decorated the graves. In a few cases the shells had weathered to a dull gray color and had obviously been in place for some time. Rains erode the mound and scatter and discolor the shells, and loved ones must periodically rework them. The Martin and Sauls family plots at a white church in Cumberland County consist of ten graves dating from the 1920s to the 1990s, each covered with clam shells (Fig. 6.3). A white cemetery in Brunswick County contains an elaborately designed example of the clam and conch shell grave, with a single row of conch shells along the spine and a double row arranged as a border (Fig. 6.4). The shell graves that form the Beard Graveyard, a white cemetery in east Cumberland County, harmonize perfectly with the blindingly white sand dune where they are located. The only recorded shell grave in which the shells can be dated is for white infant Jennings Leslie Horne (d. 1918), aged two, in the family graveyard. Enoch L. Horne, the baby's father, created a stuccoed con-crete grave mound with seashells embedded in the concrete and placed a cast concrete head and footstone at each end (Fig. 6.5).[4] Many years later the family added a granite plaque in front of the headstone to better identify the grave.

An even more ephemeral material used to decorate grave mounds is eggshells, visible in a cemetery photograph taken in the 1920s (Fig. 6.6). Beulah Churchyard, located in the Coastal Plain, contains bare sand, flowering shrubs planted around the graves, and a fence separating it from the flat farm fields beyond. Each grave is

Figure 6.3. Martin and Sauls family plots with shell graves, Big Rockfish Presbyterian Churchyard, Cumberland County.

Figure 6.4.
Shell grave in cemetery in Grissettown vicinity, Brunswick County. (Photo by Michael T. Southern, 1985, North Carolina Division of Archives and History)

(top)
Figure 6.5.
Shell grave of Jennings Leslie Horne, d. 1918, Hall-Horne Graveyard, Cumberland County.
(Photo by M. Ruth Little; Southern Folklife Collection, Wilson Library, University of North Carolina at Chapel Hill)
(bottom)
Figure 6.6.
Three grave mounds decorated with eggshells, Beulah Churchyard, Sampson County, 1920s.
(Dr. George Marion Cooper Photograph Collection, North Carolina Division of Archives and History)

marked by a wooden head and footboard, but the eggshell decorations overshadow the humble boards. On two small graves, probably for children, the eggs are arranged in diagonal rows, and on the larger grave eggshells cover the entire mound. The absence of this type of decoration in surveys taken since the 1920s suggests that, if this was a regional tradition, it has since died out. In some areas of rural North Carolina, "decoration day" was held at the family graveyard just prior to Easter. Families converged on the cemetery to clean it up after the ravages of winter and to honor their ancestors for the coming of spring and of the resurrection of Jesus Christ. This Sampson County family might have used eggshells as a symbol of rebirth for their Easter grave decoration.

WOODEN HEADBOARDS AND FOOTBOARDS

Head and footboards continued to be used until at least the 1940s. Several generations of the Horne and Hair families in east Cumberland County near Autryville made coffins and head and footboards. Enoch Arthur Horne, active in the early twentieth century, made coffins. His son, Enoch Leslie Horne, made head and footboards for the M. Lee Funeral Home in Fayetteville until the 1940s. William Streeter Hair, an early-twentieth-century cooper, made "fat lightwood" graveboards from the stumps and roots of longleaf pine trees of the area.[5] A simple squared-off headboard in Cumberland County is probably typical of early-twentieth-century headboards, although its inscription, in neat lettering that appears to be burned into the wood, is atypical (Fig. 6.7).

CAST CONCRETE MONUMENTS

Concrete, introduced in the late nineteenth century, quickly became popular among those individuals who could not afford a marble monument. They made markers for family members by casting concrete onto an armature of scrap metal.[6] Commercial mass-produced concrete markers, markers made in limited quantities by a local artisan using commercial molds, and folk markers made from homemade molds appear in large numbers in rural areas. Most of these imitate popular marble or granite monuments, with little ornament, and cast inscriptions. Yet concrete is a

plastic medium that encourages deviation from the rigid stylistic norms governing gravestone design in stone, and creative concrete headstones form the largest body of twentieth-century traditional gravemarkers in North Carolina. A parallel in the building industry of the period was the widespread adoption of "cast stone," actually concrete, for architectural trim in lieu of real stone.

The earliest type of concrete gravemarker in large-scale use was a mass-produced concrete headstone with neat, uppercase Roman lettering cast into the front face and popular decorative motifs cast into the shallow-arched tympanum. These have death dates from the 1890s to the 1920s, and are in both white and African American graveyards throughout the Coastal Plain and Piedmont regions. These concrete headstones have the same tall, thin vertical proportions as marble headstones, but are of smaller height and width, and include a short epitaph (Fig. 6.8). They are so standardized that they seem to be the product of a single firm.[7]

Widespread poverty in the rural South allowed few families to purchase marble gravestones at the turn of the century, and a large pent-up demand for grave-markers would have existed. Families probably bought many of these markers in the 1920s to mark old graves. Often these concrete headstones have the earliest death dates in the graveyard because fieldstones or uninscribed headboards mark older graves. Ironically, many of the concrete markers have survived better than contemporaneous marble headstones because marble is susceptible to damage by air pollution.

In the 1930s concrete gravestone production became more localized. Continuing in that type of business in the 1970s, Joseph Bass operated the South River Monuments Company (one of two such firms in his area) at his home on Highway 13 in east Cumberland County. Like many small cast-concrete gravestone manufacturers in North Carolina, he made monuments in small quantities, for a one- or two-county region. He worked in a small utility shed in his backyard and had an array of blank monuments on display in the front yard.[8] Although Bass was a local, small-scale artisan, his product was not folk art because his designs imitated the marble and granite monuments that had been popular nationally since the 1940s. Bass used commercial molds and both white- and pink-tinted concrete to cast thick, rectangular monuments with smooth front and rear surfaces and rusticated sides, top, and base, in imitation of rough-hewn granite. A decorative motif in low

(opposite)
Figure 6.8.
Headstone of Wm. Isaac Langley, d. 1908, Mount Ararat AME Zion Churchyard, New Hanover County.

Figure 6.9.
Headstone of Richard Pone, d. 1959, Willis Creek Churchyard, Cumberland County. Made by Joseph Bass, Cumberland County. (Photo by M. Ruth Little; Southern Folklife Collection, Wilson Library, University of North Carolina at Chapel Hill)

Figure 6.10.
Concrete marker for unidentified grave,
Spring Hill Methodist Protestant Churchyard,
Davidson County.

relief enlivens the center of the segmentally shaped front surface. The headstone of Richard Pone is typical of Bass's high-quality concrete work (Fig. 6.9). Willis Creek Church is an African American congregation, but Bass, who is white, sold his monuments to both African American and white clients throughout east Cumberland County. Many of his markers, like the concrete headstones of the 1920s, were backdated, and most of his original orders marked old graves.

Artisans often made their own molds, and the imagery chosen reflected local traditions. A group of small, thick concrete headstones with unusual abstract geometric designs stands at Spring Hill Methodist Protestant Churchyard in northeast Davidson County. Their maker impressed a variety of circular, triangular, and linear shapes, perhaps parts of old machinery, into the front of each marker, but included no dates or inscriptions. Judging by the extent of weathering, the markers appear to have been cast no earlier than the 1950s. A typical one of the group is decorated with a geometric design reminiscent of the tree-of-life motif popular in early-nineteenth-century Davidson County gravestones. If so, it is a remarkable continuation of folk German tradition (Fig. 6.10).

Another mid-twentieth-century evocation in concrete of Davidson's German gravestone tradition stands at Lick Creek Baptist Church, an isolated rural church in the south of the county. The cast concrete headstone mimics granite monuments in form but above the inscription is a large heart cast in low relief. The maker engraved the inscription in blockish lettering on a plaque of local slate that he recessed into the concrete, and, like his nineteenth-century counterparts, separated words and dates with the Gothic dots:

LELA. V. OWEN

AUGUST. 13. 1913

JANUARY. 30. 1944

CUSTOMIZED GRANITE MONUMENTS

In recent years customized designs have been returning to cemeteries in reaction to monument standardization. The North Carolina Marble and Granite Company in Clinton, which has been operated by the Edgerton family since about 1900, has created a number of designs that make a personal statement about the deceased. Symbols that the firm has designed and cut on gravestones are a motorcycle, two large tractor-trailer trucks, a dog treeing a raccoon, a house, a large motor grader, and a souped-up 1955 Chevrolet.[9] Other customized monuments, probably by different firms, occur all over the state. The headstone of Billy Everett Jr. (1955–1972), at Bethany Lutheran Churchyard in Davidson County, sports a perspective view of a Ford Mustang automobile above the inscription. That for Albert Lucas Jr. (1968–1980), at the Williams Graveyard in Cumberland County, has a basketball goal and the epitaph "gone to play ball with Jesus" on the headstone and an image of a tractor on the footstone. The family of Mack and Nannie Pendergrass, an Orange County couple (d. 1918, 1942), commemorated them with a double monument decorated with an engraving of the family homestead, complete with log house, well, and trees (Fig. 6.11).

Figure 6.11. Monument of Mack and Nannie Pendergrass, d. 1918 and 1942, Pendergrass Graveyard, Orange County.

African American Traditions

Although slave and free black cemeteries were discussed in Chapter 1, the twentieth century is almost the only opportunity to study African American cemeteries and markers, for few of the earlier gravemarkers survive. One of the earliest handcrafted African American gravestones known in North Carolina stands in Flemington Cemetery, New Hanover County. It is a fragment of a marble grave ledger, with one molded edge, and an inscription in an artistic but unskilled lettering style:

> Earhbow Hainelt
> BORNE 1814
> died aug. 1st, 1888
>   The
> Mother of [illegible]
> Armstrong and John James.

Little written information exists on the general subject of African American gravemarkers, and the books and articles that have been published are not widely available.[10] Gravemarkers made in the African American folk tradition of homemade, inexpensive materials are ephemeral and susceptible to weathering. Their independence from the aesthetic norms of commercial monuments is characteristic of the work of African American artisans. Family members decorate graves with shells and objects used by the deceased, such as lamps, bowls, vases, and mirrors, which may have more than decorative function. Some explain that they place broken household objects on graves to appease the spirit of the deceased and to prevent the spirit from returning to the home.

GRAVE MOUNDS

Mounding the dirt over a grave is as common a method of grave finish in African American graveyards as in white graveyards. Because of sinking and erosion, grave mounds must be reworked periodically to maintain their shape, a practice that is not always followed. At an African American family graveyard in east Cumberland County, Lisa Burns, an eighty-year-old member of the family, asked a relative about a row of four fresh grave mounds. When told that one was a new grave and that the other three were reworked when the new grave was dug, she exclaimed, "It's bad luck to rework a grave. Supposed to just let 'em sink on down."[11] One relatively permanent method of finishing grave mounds is to cover them with concrete stucco. Large groups of such stuccoed mounds occur at Swans Creek Baptist Church and Willis Creek Church, African American congregations in Cumberland County, most with headstones and footstones that carry the inscriptions, but on M. B. McNair's (d. 1959) grave mound, the inscription was scratched in the side of the mound while the concrete was still wet.

WOODEN HEADBOARDS

Wooden gravemarkers occur as commonly in African American graveyards as in white graveyards, and generally follow the same symmetrical forms. But the bold wavy-sided contour of this headboard for an unknown black person in the piney backwoods of Lee County represents the African American delight in asymmetrical, flowing form (Fig. 6.12). The unknown artisan who sawed out this headboard created a remarkable deviation from the traditional form..

Figure 6.12.
Headboard, Green Grove AME Zion Churchyard, Lee County.
(Photo by J. Daniel Pezzoni, 1991; North Carolina Division of Archives and History)

Cast concrete monuments make up the majority of gravemarkers in traditional

African American graveyards in North Carolina. William Isaac Langley's concrete headstone, a typical example of the mass-produced concrete markers distributed in the early twentieth century, is decorated with an anchor, symbolic of God, intertwined with ivy, symbolizing immortality (see Figure 6.8).

In the 1960s African American funeral homes began providing concrete markers in some eastern North Carolina regions. Shaw Funeral Home, the oldest black undertaking company in Wilmington, made concrete headstones with a rectangular recess fitted with a cardboard plaque containing a stamped inscription with the name of the interred individual, the date of death, and the name of the funeral home.[12] The company abandoned this short-lived but very popular experiment in the late 1960s, and many of these markers stand throughout the county.

In the 1970s a number of African American funeral homes began leaving the concrete slab which forms the top of the concrete burial vault flush with the ground level. This slab then served as a gravemarker. To it they attached a small tablet, usually of marble or bronze, to the head end of the slab and a small plaque identifying the funeral home at the foot end of the slab.[13] Sometimes the funeral home provided a decorative plaster or bronze relief plaque, such as Christ kneeling at the Mount of Olives or a pair of praying hands or a feather, in the center or lower end of the slab. Most slabs have a smooth finish covered with white paint, but a few have a rusticated finish and even a covering of reflective silver paint (Fig. 6.13). The silver paint may create the impression of reflective water, an American version of a West African tradition in which the grave symbolizes the bottom of a river bed where the soul rests.[14]

Most concrete headstones are handcrafted rather than purchased from commercial concrete monument makers or supplied by the funeral home. Throughout North Carolina African American artisans make concrete headstones which vary from plain slabs to imitations of commercially manufactured markers to creative improvisations. Perhaps typical of these artisans are Renial Culbreth, a blacksmith, and Issiah McEachin, a brickmason. Both men lived in the coastal region and both served as community undertaker by making coffins, digging graves, and fashioning gravemarkers.

RENIAL CULBRETH

> Sleep on Mother
> We Love You But God
> Loves U Best

(opposite)
Figure 6.13.
Silver-painted
concrete grave
slab for Frances
G. Gainey, d.
1980, Mount
Zion AMEZ
Churchyard,
Cumberland
County.

This epitaph for Irene McLaurin, which Renial Culbreth made with store-bought letters that he pressed into wet concrete, as well as the monument itself, express the essential qualities of African American folk gravemarkers in North Carolina. Culbreth made the marker of inexpensive materials with emotionally direct words and symbols—a large dove in flight with rays of light beaming toward it, a cross, and a vase of flowers (Fig. 6.14).

Renial Culbreth (1892–1974) made customized gravestones as a sideline from the 1940s to the 1960s (Fig. 6.15). Born near Vander in east Cumberland County, Culbreth left his family farm and worked as a mechanic and blacksmith in the small town of Vander and later in Roseboro, in adjacent Sampson County. Before the advent of professional undertakers in the rural African American community, which occurred after World War II, he also made wooden coffins and carried bodies to the graveyard in his horse-drawn wagon. In later years he cast concrete gravestones, working out of his shop in Roseboro and, in his last years, in a shed behind his house in the 600 block of West Railroad Street, Roseboro.[15]

About twenty of Culbreth's markers stand in nine African American graveyards within a twenty-mile radius of Vander in Cumberland County, and others are in cemeteries in adjacent Bladen and Sampson Counties.[16] Culbreth made four wooden headstone molds of distinctly different shapes: a dove and cross, a scroll, a tablet, and a double headstone with urn. He poured concrete into the wooden mold to produce the basic form, then pressed commercially produced letters and numbers into the wet concrete to incise the inscription and used small wooden press molds and scraps of metal to achieve additional relief decoration. Finally, he painted each marker white (on most the paint has worn off). The dove and cross is the dominant motif on Charlie Fuller's headstone at Lock's Creek AME Zion Church, on which the epitaph reads:

Figure 6.15. Renial Culbreth at home in Roseboro in the 1960s. (Courtesy Culbreth family)

HE IS GONE

SLEEP ON

TAKE YOUR

REST

The headstone of Clinnie M. Owens, typical of Culbreth's scroll design, is a thick concrete headstone on a concrete base, with a segmental-arched top (Fig. 6.16). Strips of wood in the mold created the effect of a molded pediment. He placed Owens's name into an arched recessed panel beneath the pediment and put his birth and death dates at the bottom, below a large scroll inscribed, "THE LORD IS MY SHEPHERD." Culbreth apparently made the molds for the scroll and the abstract curvilinear corner decoration by bending metal strips to the desired shapes.

Culbreth's basic tablet resting on a stand design is reminiscent of a recognition plaque set on a display stand (Fig. 6.17). A concrete base supports the rectangular face of the stone at a 45-degree angle, and the inscription and optional decorations are set within a recessed frame.

The fourth form, an urn and cross flanked by two headstones, is based on a popular granite monument design. For the Geddies' (Fig. 6.18), he placed one inscription on each flanking headstone, placed abstract curvilinear designs in the corners, and inscribed on the central cross:

(opposite) Figure 6.14. Monument of Irene McLaurin, d. 1968, Mount Zion AMEZ Churchyard, Cumberland County. Made by Renial Culbreth.

Figure 6.16. Monument of Clinnie M. Owens, d. 1966, First Baptist Church, Stedman vic., Sampson County. Made by Renial Culbreth.

Figure 6.17.
Tablet-style
monument
for Dixon
McLaurin,
d. 1949,
Mount Zion
AMEZ
Churchyard,
Cumberland
County.
Made by
Renial
Culbreth.

Figure 6.18.
Monument
of John and
Laura Geddie,
d. 1941 and
1942, Kelly-
McLaurin
Graveyard,
Cumberland
County.
Made by
Renial
Culbreth.
(Photo by
M. Ruth Little;
Southern
Folklife
Collection, Wil-
son Library,
University of
North Carolina
at Chapel Hill)

All four of Culbreth's basic shapes correspond closely to commercial granite monument designs. His originality emerges in the handcrafted decorations that he pressed into the wet concrete—doves, scrolls, vases of flowers, crosses, and floral ornament. Although he probably drew much of this imagery from commercial monuments as well, he simplified and used it in combinations meaningful to his own community—the AME Zion congregations of Cumberland, Sampson, and Bladen Counties. As part of a tradition of homemade concrete gravemarker production in African American settlements of North Carolina, Culbreth's work easily fits the definition of traditional art, produced outside the mainstream of rapidly changing fashions.

Figure 6.19.
Issiah
McEachin
at home in
Eastover,
Cumberland
County, 1982.
(Photo by
M. Ruth Little;
Southern
Folklife
Collection,
Wilson Library,
University of
North Carolina
at Chapel Hill)

ISSIAH MCEACHIN

Issiah McEachin lives and works in Cumberland County. Ten of his markers stand within a fifteen-mile radius of his home in Eastover, a small community east of Fayetteville.[17] McEachin (pronounced McAhern) was born on 15 June 1922, near Red Springs in Robeson County. Following World War II, he trained as a brick mason with Player Construction Company in Fayetteville. McEachin is a self-employed man who lives with his wife in a one-story frame house on a sandy dirt road surrounded by tobacco and cornfields (Fig. 6.19). His ingenuity and creativity are evident in the semicircular brick steps he added to his front porch and in the turn-of-the-century brackets and spindlework he recycled and installed on his porch in an unorthodox, upside-down position.

McEachin began making gravestones about 1970 as a result of another part-time occupation—gravedigging. Having too often dug into inadequately marked existing graves, he recognized the need for good, inexpensive gravemarkers in his community. He has made about eighteen markers: each of them took about two-and-one-half hours and for each he has charged about $50. He casts the markers on a framework of steel rods, like those used in concrete footings, and leaves portions exposed at the base to bury in the ground when the marker is put in place. Like Culbreth, he built his own wooden mold and uses commercially produced metal letters and numbers for the inscriptions. His decorations, however, are glass marbles that he presses into the wet concrete at the borders. The idea of using marbles occurred to him as a substitute for the shiny quality of granite, which he wanted to duplicate but could not achieve with the rough surfaces of concrete. McEachin noted proudly that the marbles are impossible to chisel out because he buried them in the concrete by about three-fourths of their diameter. For the future he dreams of making brick gravemarkers with inscriptions fashioned of metal letters attached to the brick or cast into a concrete panel set into the brick.

McEachin's marble-studded markers sparkle in the sharp Coastal Plain sunlight and give off colored reflections that enliven the family and church graveyards in east Cumberland County. The headstone of Ernest L. Barkin is typical of his work (Fig. 6.20). McEachin's multicolored marbles form a triangular pediment. He inscribed the concrete plaque footstone with Barkin's name and decorated it with a

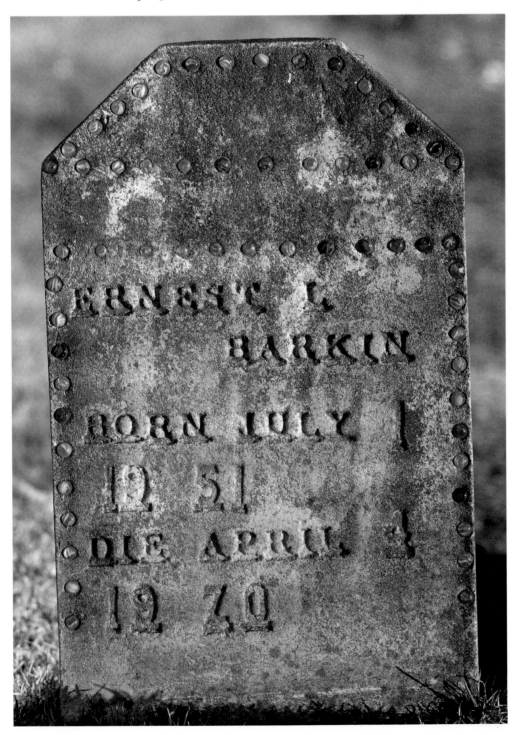

Figure 6.20. Monument of Ernest L. Barkin, d. 1970, Flea Hill Church, Cumberland County. Made by Issiah McEachin.

border of embedded marbles. For an unspecified reason, he used exclusively green marbles in the borders of the headstone for Edith Whitted (d. 1971) at Mount Zion Church.

Unlike Renial Culbreth, Issiah McEachin does not imitate commercial grave monuments in the form of his concrete markers nor in decoration. The strong, simple shapes and creative recycling of marbles qualify these markers as African American folk art.

Anonymous Concrete Artisans

Handcrafted concrete headstones, most of them painted white when new, are found in African American graveyards throughout North Carolina, but their makers are nearly always anonymous. Many of them, probably members of the Masonic order

Figure 6.21. Monument of Jannie McAlister, d. 1943, Snow Hill AME Zion Churchyard, Cumberland County.

themselves, used fraternal symbols for the monuments of deceased Masons. Into the top of the headstone of D. D. Dixon (d. 1907) at Spring Hill Church near Hope Mills, Cumberland County, are a metal compass and a square. Another artisan, working in the 1930s and 1940s in south Cumberland County, used a press mold, probably of metal, to inscribe symbols at the top of round-topped headstones, wrote inscriptions in the wet concrete, and set them on concrete bases. On one of these (Fig. 6.21), he embedded a piece of cast iron, perhaps recycled hardware, beneath the symbol, and inscribed the letters "MEMBR EY" and "K P" and a heart around them. "K P" may stand for the Knights of Pythias, a fraternal order.

A group of five distinctive handcrafted concrete markers at Flemington Cemetery, used by a large black community in rural New Hanover County since the late nineteenth century, stand out as the work of one artisan.[18] His trademarks are bold, undulating forms and abstract floral decoration. He cast headstones of unconventional shapes into which he impressed molds; his inscriptions were made with homemade letters, and he painted them white. The monuments have death dates from 1937 to 1951. In the marker for Lazurs Underwood (d. 1943), this artisan impressed a single large flower in relief at the top. For Georgie Spicer (d. 1946), he made a little marker with an unevenly scalloped top. For Richard T. Nixon (d. 1951), he created an even more unresolved shape—a wavy top that gives the impression that the concrete is still flowing. His boldest designs, the stately monuments of Mrs. Irene Dry (d. 1937) and Mrs. Flora Spears (d. 1950), feature three impressed or cast semicircular floral rondels at the top (Fig. 6.22).

Flemington Cemetery also contains several commercial marble monuments with epitaphs revealing that some of the members of the community were born into slavery, had a deep spiritual faith, and had achieved some financial success. One marble headstone is inscribed:

> EMALINE
> WIGGINS
> African Slave
> Freewoman,
> Christian
> Died
> May 21, 1927

That for Mary E. Johnson (d. 1926) has a remarkably powerful epitaph similar to the lyrics of black gospel hymns:

> We loved her, Yes we loved her,
> But Jesus loved her more, and
> He has sweetly called her, to yonder
> Shining shore, The Golden Gate
> Was open, A gentle Voice said, come
> With a fairwell unspoken she calmly
> entered home

Such lyrical epitaphs could not be included on the concrete headstones that dominate rural African American cemeteries, but the variants in concrete form from one cemetery to another are endless. When Carolin Williams died in 1964 at the advanced age of 101, she was buried in the Oak Grove Community Graveyard in Cumberland County. Someone, probably a family member, made a concrete headstone and purchased metal letters and numerals at a hardware store and glued them to the surface to create an inscription. When O. A. Melvin died in 1961, someone cast for him a tall, strikingly shaped monument that resembles a keyhole, on a high concrete base. The maker arranged letters and numerals on two metal tracks like the name and address on a rural mailbox (Fig. 6.23).

African American artisans in the Piedmont created concrete markers of equally striking form and detailing to those in eastern North Carolina. Someone drew a bird in the wet concrete of each arm of the cross-shaped headstone for Marvin Sims (d. 1926) at Mount Gilead Churchyard in rural Orange County. He outlined the birds with blue paint and painted a scene of bushes or trees near the base of the cross. A person close to the Browder family obviously crafted the small concrete headstone for Albert Browder (d. 1945) and his wife, Lela (d. 1958), since he embedded an actual pocket watch, probably Albert's, into the concrete (Fig. 6.24). Although the hands are now missing, rust marks show that their position was at 5:30, probably the time of death. He also placed corrugated metal strips into the concrete to form stars and other decorative patterns in the tympanum. Other examples of decorative objects inset in concrete occur in a rural black community graveyard near Hillsborough. For Gery Morgan (d. 1939), someone embedded a large seashell into each arm of a concrete cross. This same artisan decorated another concrete cross for Dilroy and Samuel Harrison (both d. 1944) with an embedded sea-

Figure 6.22. Headstone of Mrs. Flora Spears, d. 1950, Flemington Community Cemetery, New Hanover County.

Figure 6.23. Monument of O. A. Melvin, d. 1961, China Grove Baptist Churchyard, Cumberland County.

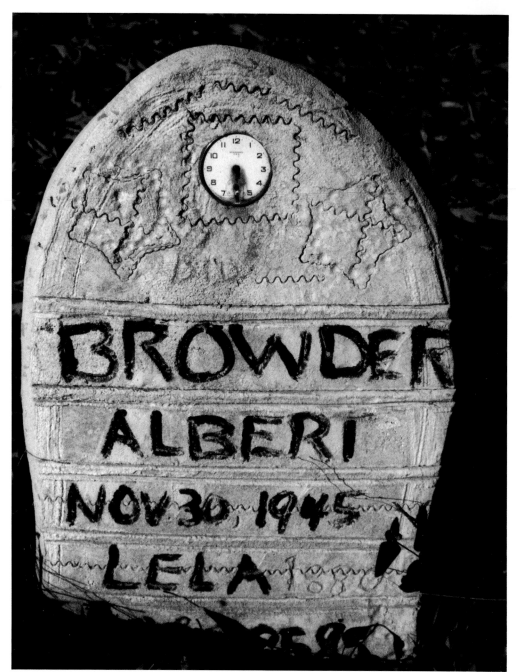

Figure 6.24.
Headstone
of Albert and
Lela Browder,
d. 1945 and
1958, Mount
Bright Baptist
Churchyard,
Hillsborough.
(Photo by
M. Ruth Little;
Southern
Folklife
Collection,
Wilson Library,
University of
North Carolina
at Chapel Hill)

(opposite)
Figure 6.25.
Headstone of
Emma Verdell,
d. 1937,
Buncombe
Baptist
Churchyard,
Petersville,
Davidson
County.

shell and three stars cast in relief and painted yellow—the seashell and a star on the cross's vertical post and a star on each arm.

In Davidson County the marker made by an unidentified artisan from Georgia for Emma Verdell (d. 1937), a Georgia native, has a powerful suggestion of immortality yet includes no name, dates, or any inscription.[19] The Georgia man cast the slender, picket-shaped headstone with a molded border, and pressed fragments of a mirror, cut in the shapes of a quarter-moon and stars, into the front surface (Fig. 6.25). The mirror both symbolizes and reflects the sky. The Verdell marker uses mirror fragments in a manner similar to an evocative concrete headstone in Georgia, perhaps contemporaneous, containing the actual imprint of a human hand with a piece of mirror embedded in its palm.[20]

A headstone of stained glass is located in the African American cemetery of Old Smith Grove Baptist Church in Davidson County. An unidentified artisan cast a segmental-arched headstone and set panels of translucent-blue stained glass in lead muntins into the top third of the monument (Fig. 6.26). The marker has a coat of white paint but no inscription.

Figure 6.26. Head- and footstones of unidentified grave, mid-twentieth century, Old Smith Grove Baptist Churchyard, Davidson County.

African Americans in the Coastal Plain employ a wide variety of materials to fence individual graves: low cinder-block walls, low metal or plastic fencing, bricks, wooden stakes, shells, and rocks. Beginning in the 1950s, decorative concrete blocks became popular. A solid concrete-block border encloses the grave of James F. Little. On the west end of the border, three large pierced concrete blocks form a headpiece, and two identical blocks on the east end form the footpiece (Fig. 6.27). The funeral home supplied a metal identification plaque, centered in front of the headpiece, which is the only identification. A number of similar grave borders, also painted white, are located in Hank's Chapel AME Churchyard and the Freeman Community Graveyard in New Hanover County. Commercial concrete coping blocks surround the double grave of Mamie and James Franks (d. 1958 and 1956), in Zion Chapel Cemetery, New Hanover County, and the inscription on the home-made concrete headstone is lettered with white chalk or tile grout.

Figure 6.27. Grave enclosure of James F. Little, d. 1964, Maides Cemetery, Wilmington.

Grave Sculpture

African Americans have long decorated graves with domestic bric-a-brac, and occasionally these recycled objects become "found sculpture." The objects seem to relate personally to the deceased and represent a spontaneous moment of inspiration. Like the other means of marking graves, grave sculpture testifies to a tradition of freedom in grave decoration among African Americans not evident among whites.

A government-issue marble headstone noting his service in World War II as a technician with a trucking company marks the grave of William Rudolph Coachman. Not content with the "official" monument, family or friends added a sculptural "footstone," an automobile wheel rim topped with a decorative arrangement of socket wrenches and plastic flowers (Fig. 6.28). Occupational symbols serve as traditional grave decoration in West Africa; this American equivalent graphically conveys Coachman's vocation as an automotive mechanic.[21]

In north New Hanover County, a styrofoam chair decorated with greenery and flowers sits at the head of an otherwise unidentified grave (Fig. 6.29). Although its commercial construction suggests that the chair may have been made by a funeral

Figure 6.28.
Grave sculpture of
William Rudolph Coachman,
d. 1966, Swans Creek Baptist
Churchyard, Cumberland County.
(Photo by M. Ruth Little;
Southern Folklife Collection,
Wilson Library, University of
North Carolina at Chapel Hill)

(opposite)
Figure 6.29.
Unidentified grave with
chair sculpture, 1982, private
cemetery, New Hanover County.
(Photo by M. Ruth Little;
Southern Folklife Collection,
Wilson Library, University of
North Carolina at Chapel Hill)

home as a temporary stand for funeral flowers, perhaps as a custom order, it is an unorthodox grave decoration. Its presence gives the grave a domestic security, as if the chair is a symbolic resting place for the deceased.

One African American grave is said to contain a symbolic escape route for the departing soul. People in Hertford County, in the Albemarle region, report a grave in the Menola community, in the west section of the county, containing a wooden ladder that projects up into the air, apparently representing a ladder to heaven.[22] Jacob, one of the biblical patriarchs of the Old Testament, had a dream in which a ladder came down from heaven and God blessed him and promised to be with him wherever he went. An old black spiritual contains the refrain, "We are climbing Jacob's ladder," a metaphor for going to heaven.

Fragile Black and White Traditions

The gravemarkers of rural white and black people, created out of available, inexpensive materials—wood, concrete, building scraps, seashells, and recycled objects—are highly perishable, lasting for a few years or perhaps a generation. Sometimes they are replaced by more permanent and proper grave monuments in later years; often they weather away leaving the grave unmarked. The eighteenth- and nineteenth-century equivalents of these found and handcrafted gravemarkers vanished long ago.

These traditional grave mounds, headstones, grave enclosures, and grave sculptures stand out starkly from commercially produced marble and granite monuments in twentieth-century graveyards, both white and black. Even so, it is generally impossible to distinguish a black grave mound or concrete monument from a white one. The parallel use of homemade concrete markers, shell graves, and decoration with household objects in both African American and white graveyards blurs racial distinctions. The primary distinction is that white gravemarkers adhere more tightly to popular aesthetic norms than the African American ones. In many instances this may be the result of poverty, since African Americans, more frequently than whites, make creative, symbolic use of inexpensive, often recycled materials, and sometimes even fabricate grave sculpture. Black gravemarkers exhibit the animated style and uninhibited handling of materials that characterizes much of the African American material culture, including quilts and paintings.[23] Blacks were generally not drawn into the social posturing of white society in the erection of a fashionable monument, and black artisans remain freer of the preconceptions of a fitting and proper grave monument that guide white artisans. The black and white pattern of vernacular grave art across North Carolina is a continuing chapter in the study of gravemarkers.

Conclusion : Remember as You Pass Me By

Remember as you pass me by
As you are now so once was I
As I am now so you will be
Prepare for death and follow me

Early gravestones, speaking in many different dialects, call us to put our spiritual and worldly affairs in order. Many early North Carolina graveyards express the material culture of the English, Scottish, German, and African settlers more strongly than any other part of the landscape. The old houses of the Highland Scots in the upper Cape Fear, the Germans and Scots-Irish in the Piedmont, or the Africans in the Coastal Plain often speak of the mainstream economy, but the graveyards speak with the accents of the homeland. The grim skulls of New England stones, the exuberant hopefulness of the German stones, with their joyful suns and pinwheels symbolizing resurrection and eternal life, the patriotic coats-of-arms of Scots-Irish stones, and the startling originality of African gravemarkers are fragile signposts of the state's cultural heritage.

Like the Scottish gravestone whose disappearance inspired this book, all early gravemarkers and all traditional gravemarkers are endangered. This sculptural heritage is outdoors and accessible, but much of it will not survive much longer. One measure of a civilization is its reverence for its dead, and North Carolinians, rich and poor, black and white, have found civilized and creative signals by which to convey this reverence during the past three centuries. We must now honor this heritage by protecting these fragile sculptures. Not only must we preserve them through photographs, but we should consider the next preservation step—placing the oldest and most endangered markers in museum collections. In New England, certain historic gravestones have been placed in museums where they are protected and available for future generations, and carefully produced casts replace the original stones in the graveyards.

From the coast to the mountains, graveyards reveal volumes about ordinary people and the gentry. The constant tension between self-sufficient subsistence and the commercial economy has affected gravemarkers since early settlement. Eighteenth-century gravemarkers in North Carolina came from England, New England, and New York, and from the nearby field or forest. Nineteenth-century gravemarkers came from New York, Philadelphia, Baltimore, Petersburg, Charleston, and Columbia, itinerant stonecutters, and, beginning in the 1830s, resident marble cutters. A cross-section through the state in the mid-nineteenth century contrasts the stylish marbles cut by Scottish stonecutters in affluent Raleigh and Fayetteville and the intricately decorated soapstones cut by local artisans in the Scots-Irish and German communities of the Piedmont with the plain wooden slabs and fieldstone markers made by most everyone else.

Gravemarkers tell ethnic stories and recount the saga of vast regional populations. Both geography and culture have influenced the choice of gravemarkers. The markers are a jigsaw puzzle of North Carolina culture, but many pieces are missing from the Coastal Plain. Our perception of life and death in this region during the eighteenth and nineteenth centuries is skewed by the predominant upper-class material culture that has survived—the fine plantation and town houses, the stylish headstones and monuments in family, church, and municipal cemeteries. What stands out most vividly in coastal North Carolina graveyards is economic status. Many families had the funds to order stone monuments from faraway places, but these were the planters and merchants, not the ordinary people. The vast majority of families had only the plentiful timber with which to mark the graves of their loved ones. These humble wooden markers, like their small frame dwellings, farm buildings, stores, and churches, are gone. The first two hundred years of ordinary gravemarkers in eastern North Carolina have disappeared. Likewise, numerous graveyards throughout the state have been destroyed by redevelopment of the land or for reservoir projects.

Piedmont and mountain gravemarkers tell a much more complete story about eighteenth- and nineteenth-century culture. Poverty did not keep Upland North Carolina people from honoring graves with permanent monuments, because the plentiful native stone could be used in its natural form, as field rocks, or shaped by unskilled or skilled hands into dignified head and footstones. Sometimes even the humblest uncarved fieldstone that marks the grave of the poorest farm dweller remains in the cemetery. Most Scots-Irish and German settlers in the backcountry did not aspire to stylish marble monuments, thus what stands out most vividly in Upland graveyards is ethnic or community affiliation. The egalitarianism in the graveyards mirrors a society of yeoman farming families in which kinship was more important than class. Rich and poor Scottish settlers bartered with such local Scots-Irish and German stonecutters as Samuel Bigham, Joseph Clodfelter, or William Crawford for head and footstones decorated with the birds-of-promise, thistles, hopeful sunbursts, and fylfot crosses that represented their beliefs.

By the 1830s, growing numbers of affluent citizens in the towns brought the earliest resident commercial stonecutters, William Stronach and George Lauder. These Scottish-born and trained professionals, using marble imported from Northeast quarries, carved a rich assortment of ledgers, tomb-tables, obelisks, headstones, and pedestal-tombs, some with complex religious, fraternal, and other symbolism that personalized the graves. By the 1840s their tall white marbles towered over the smaller traditional markers of native stone and introduced inequality into the ethnic graveyards of the Piedmont.

Following the Civil War, as railroads connected the various parts of the state, more marble yards were established and the price of monuments came within the reach of a greater percentage of the population. With the advent of the twentieth century, cheap rail shipping and a network of catalog salesmen turned the monument industry into a centralized factory enterprise with mass-produced marble, and later granite gravestones, that in retrospect have a monotonous sameness. In order to compete, local marble cutters switched from hand tools to mechanical carving equipment, but since the 1930s they have largely been reduced to stenciling inscriptions onto monuments shipped from large monument companies.

Yet, even now, late in the twentieth century, the work of traditional artisans enlivens cemeteries that are mostly filled with commercial granite monuments. In the Coastal Plain, twentieth-century rural cemeteries offer almost the only glimpses into traditional white and African American gravemarker practices, since earlier gravemarkers, fashioned of perishable materials, have largely disappeared. In these white and African American cemeteries, creative concrete markers, shell graves, and other types of grave decoration and enclosures represent living traditions.

For much of the twentieth century, gravestone carving was a lost art, but in more recent years the standardized granite blanks that have robbed local stonecutters of their craft have given way to more individualized monuments. Perhaps the artistic renaissance in contemporary gravestone carving will spawn renewed interest in the preservation of historic gravestones as well. Gravemarkers continue to be the largest collection of sculpture in the state and a unique record of culture and ethnicity. The sticks and stones in North Carolina graveyards tell many stories, not all of which are told here. Let us remember as we pass by, and let us also record and preserve.

APPENDIX A

Stonecutters and Gravemarker Artisans
Represented in North Carolina Cemeteries

This list includes both individuals whose signatures appear on gravestones and those documented through other sources. Names are listed exactly as they appear in their sources, such as signatures on stones or directories. Birth and death dates, where known, are given in brackets.

KEY TO SOURCE OF INFORMATION

[Signature]: Information from signature engraved on gravestone.

[Estates]: Information from estate records at the North Carolina Division of Archives and History.

[Fieldwork]: Information from fieldwork conducted primarily in 1980–82, with additional work 1983–96.

[Interview]: Interview by M. Ruth Little during fieldwork.

[Published works]: These sources are listed in the notes and bibliography.

[Newspapers]: Information from newspaper advertisements, etc.

[Personal communication]: Information obtained through others' fieldwork.

[*Branson's*]: Information from *Branson's North Carolina Business Directories*, published in 1866, 1869, 1872, 1877–78, 1884, and 1896.

[U.S. Census]: Information from population or industrial schedules of 1850, 1860, 1870, and 1880 censuses.

[MESDA Index]: Index to artisans working in the South, Museum of Early Southern Decorative Arts, Salem, N.C.

[Patterson]: Unpublished work of Daniel W. Patterson on Scots-Irish stonecutters in North Carolina.

[Combs]: Information from *Early Gravestone Art in Georgia and South Carolina*, by Diana Williams Combs.

[National Register Nomination]: Archaeology and Historic Preservation Section, North Carolina Division of Archives and History.

[Capitol Papers]: Archives and Records Section, North Carolina Division of Archives and History.

A. Allison, Trenton, N.J. Signed obelisk of Dr. William Montgomery, d. 1843, Old Brick Reformed Churchyard, Guilford County. [Signature]

David Anderson Jr. Itinerant stonecutter who worked in Fayetteville in 1823. [Newspapers]

J. Baird. Marble cutter in Philadelphia who signed a gravestone for Rebecca Guion (d. ?), St. Luke's Episcopal Church, Lincolnton. [Personal communication]

Joseph Bass. Concrete gravestone artisan in east Cumberland County who operated the South River Monuments Company in the 1970s. [Fieldwork]

A. E. Baum. Marble dealer in Sylva in 1896. [1896 *Branson's*]

J. B. Beards. Marble dealer in Gastonia in 1896. [1896 *Branson's*]

J. A. Bennett, Winston, N.C. Marble works in Winston in 1896. He signed a number of headstones decorated with the clasped-hands motif, including those for Sirene Fine (d. 1888), Holloway's Baptist Church, and for Alfred W. Smith (d. 1892), Old Mount Vernon Baptist Church in Davidson County. [1896 *Branson's*, Signatures]

Bennett Bros, Winston N.C. Signature on a headstone with a hand holding a flower in a rondel for Nancy Catherine Sink (d. 1886), Old Mount Vernon Baptist Church, Davidson County. This firm is presumably the predecessor of J. A. Bennett. [Signature]

J. Benton. Signed a headstone for John Smith (d. 1805), Goshen Presbyterian Church, Belmont, Gaston County. Benton's accomplished neoclassical style links him to the stonecarvers of Charleston, S.C. [Signature]

W. G. Berryhill, Charlotte N.C. W. G. Berryhill operated marble and granite works in Charlotte in 1880s. Signed a number of headstones, including one for Mary McCaskill (d. 1881) and an obelisk for Daniel and Mary McCaskill (d. 1882), Sandy Grove Presbyterian Church, Hoke County. [1884 *Branson's*, U.S. Census, Signatures]

Berryhill & Johnston. Signed a number of headstones, including a Masonic headstone for Thomas W. Lowry (d. 1883), Old Lutheran Cemetery, Salisbury. Berryhill is presumably W. G. Berryhill; Johnston may be James A. Johnston. [Signatures]

Botsford & Phillips, N. H. Ct. Marble cutters in New Haven, Conn. Signed a headstone with a rose rondel for Mary Johnson (d. 1849), Cross Creek Cemetery, Fayetteville. [Signature]

J. Bourdoc. Signed headstone for Col. James Holland (d. 1826), Olney Presbyterian Church, Gastonia. [Signature]

Boyne & McKenzie, Columbia. Marble cutters in South Carolina. Signed a headstone with a willow tree for Julia N. Brown (d. 1843), Salem Lutheran Church, Lincoln County. [Signature]

Boyne & Sprowl, Colu. S.C. Signed a pedimented headstone for George Montgomery (d. 1855), Old Lutheran Cemetery, Salisbury. [Signature]

Alexander Brown. Marble cutter in Columbia, S.C. Cut a gravestone for Elizabeth Ferguson of Lincoln County in 1847. [Estates]

G. Brown Columbia S.C. Marble cutter in Columbia, S.C. Signed headstone for John Carruth Henderson (d. 1833), Old White Church, Lincolnton, and headstone with a willow tree for Nancy S. Price (d. 1837), Olney Presbyterian Church, Gastonia. [Signatures]

Brown & Weant. Tombstone dealers in Salisbury. [1872 *Branson's*]

Buie, Monroe. Signed headstone for Mrs. Nancy S. Fitzgerald (d. 1860), Fitzgerald-Pinkston Graveyard, Davidson County. Buie worked in the town of Monroe. [Signature]

Stephen Buie. Marble cutter in Robeson County in 1870. [U.S. Census]

John H. Buis. Operated marble works in Salisbury from late 1860s through 1890s. His signature appears frequently on gravestones in the area, including those for Mary Murphy (d. 1867), Old Lutheran Cemetery, Salisbury, and for Charlie Wheeler (d. 1872), Old English Cemetery, Salisbury. [1869, 1872, 1877–78 *Branson's*, U.S. Census, Signatures]

Troy Cain. Marble cutter in Fayetteville who, in the 1920s, took over the marble yard operated by Robert Remsburg. Cain Memorials is now being operated by his son, Vincent Cain, and grandsons. [Interviews]

Carolina Marble Works, Lincolnton N.C. Signed many stones in the Lincolnton area in 1870s and 1880s, including headstones for Mary Magdalene Finger (d. 1876), Salem Lutheran Church, Lincoln County, and for Susan Warlick (d. 1884), Daniels Lutheran Church, Lincoln County. This may be the same firm listed as R. H. Templeton Marble Works in the 1884 *Branson's*. [1884 *Branson's*, Signatures]

J. Caveny [1778–1853]. Stonecutter in York County, S.C., from ca. 1810 to 1853. Of the hundreds of stones that he cut, only a few are signed, such as a panel in the Brevard family obelisk, dated 1829, Machpelah Presbyterian Church, Lincoln County. [Signatures, Fieldwork, U.S. Census, Published works]

R. C. Caveny [1808–90]. Stonecutter in York County, S.C. Son of John Caveny. Signed gravestones at Bethany ARP Churchyard, York County, including one for Col. Thomas C. Black (d. 1853). [Signatures, U.S. Census, Published works]

John Cayton. Marble cutter in Raleigh in 1870s and 1880s. Born in Scotland. In partnership with W. O. Wolfe in 1872 and with King by 1880. By 1884 he had died and his wife, Mrs. John Cayton, ran the business. Cayton & Wolfe signed the gravestone of Lucy Savage (d. 1859) and the stone of John J. Scales (d. 1872), Oakwood Cemetery, Raleigh. [1872, 1877–78, 1884 *Branson's*, U.S. Census, Signatures]

J. A. Childs. Signed headstone of Capt. Sidney A. Shuford (d. 1862), Old White Church, Lincolnton. [Signature]

G. W. Claypoles Marble Works. Marble works that operated in New Bern in the 1870s. [U.S. Census, 1877–78 *Branson's*]

Jacob Clodfelter [1770–1837]. Cabinetmaker in Davidson County who was the father of Joseph Clodfelter. He apparently cut German-style gravestones in the early nineteenth century. [Fieldwork]

Joseph Clodfelter [1801–1871]. Cabinetmaker and stonecutter in Davidson County who signed only one gravestone, the headstone of Josiah Spurgin (d. 1802), Abbott's Creek Primitive Baptist Church, Davidson County, but a number of headstones from the 1820s, 1830s, and 1840s are attributed to him. [Signature, U.S. Census, Estates, Fieldwork]

William Codner. Stonecutter in Boston, Mass., late eighteenth century. The headstone of Mary Evans (d. 1758), Palmer-Marsh Graveyard, Bath, is attributed to him. [Fieldwork, Combs]

Coggins Shelby. Coggins is an otherwise unknown stonecutter who worked in Shelby. He signed the headstone of Warlick Hoover (d. 1875), at Trinity Lutheran Church, Lincoln County. [Signature]

Eleazer Colbourn [1796–1861]. Massachusetts-born stonecutter who worked in Raleigh in the early 1850s, apparently at William Stronach's marble yard. [U.S. Census, Newspapers]

W. A. Cooper Brothers. Marble and granite works in Raleigh from ca. 1894 to 1930. They purchased William Stronach's old firm, the Raleigh Marble Works, in 1894, and purchased Lougee & Goodwin's marble yard in Raleigh in 1896. The firm operated as the Raleigh Marble Works until 1930. [1896 *Branson's*, city directories]

Geo. E. Coulter. Operated a marble yard in Newton, Catawba County, in the 1880s and 1890s. Signed the headstone of John L. Wright (d. 1892), Old Lutheran Cemetery, Salisbury. [1884, 1896 *Branson's*, Signature]

T. D. Couper, Norfolk. Signed a number of gravestones in northeastern North Carolina, including a ledger with a death date of 1856 at St. Thomas Episcopal Church, Windsor, Bertie County, and a box-tomb for Col. Wilson Reed (d. 1860), Hertford Town Cemetery, Hertford, Perquimans County. [Signatures]

L. J. Crawford [1835–1912]. Stonecutter in York County, S.C., at the turn of the century. Lawson James Crawford, son of stonecutter William N. Crawford, carried on the family business. Signed the headstone of Martha A. C. Bradley (d. 1880), Olney Presbyterian Church, Gastonia. [Signatures, Fieldwork]

Robert M. Crawford [1803–1865]. Stonecutter in York County, S.C., and in Lincoln County, N.C., from the 1830s to his death. Son of stonecutter James Crawford and brother of William M. Crawford. Signed a number of headstones at Bethany ARP Church, York County, S.C., and Olney Presbyterian Church, Gastonia, and carved many unsigned headstones in the Catawba Valley. [U.S. Census, Signatures, Fieldwork, Published work]

R. M. Crawford. Marble workers and dealers in Charlotte in 1877–78. [1877–78 *Branson's*]

William N. Crawford [1808–1894]. Stonecutter in York County, S.C., from the 1830s to the 1870s. Son of stonecutter James Crawford and brother of Robert M. Crawford. Signed a number of gravestones at Bethany ARP Church, York County, S.C., and Olney Presbyterian Church, Gastonia, and carved many unsigned headstones in the Catawba Valley. [U.S. Census, Signatures, Fieldwork, Published work]

Renial Culbreth [1892–1974]. Blacksmith in Roseboro, Sampson County, who made concrete gravestones from the 1950s to 1974. [Fieldwork, Interviews]

R. D. Norfolk. This stonecutter, who apparently worked in Norfolk, Va., signed a headstone for a member of the Foreman family who died in 1840, Calvary Episcopal Church, Tarboro, Edgecombe County. [Signature]

Davidson Fecit Petersburg Virginia. Signature, with several variations, which appears on gravestones with death dates in the 1810s and 1820s in Orange County and Davidson County. Davidson, who worked in Petersburg, Va., cut neoclassical marble gravestones. [Signatures]

Alexander Jackson Davis. Nationally prominent architect who designed the neoclassical tomb of Judge William Gaston (d. 1844), Cedar Grove Cemetery, New Bern. [Cedar Grove Cemetery National Register Nomination, 1972]

G. A. Davis. Operated a marble works in Sanford in 1896. [1896 *Branson's*]

Dawson. Signed the willow-tree headstone of Benjamin Cable (d. 1855), Friedens Lutheran Church, Guilford County. [Signature]

C. T. Duncomb, Norwalk Ct.

C. T. Duncomb, Newark N.J.

C. T. Duncomb, Richmond Va. Itinerant stonecutter. Signed marble headstone for James Foy (d. 1825), Nixon-Foy Graveyard, New Hanover County, ordered about 1840. He was in Norwalk, Conn., when he signed a ledger for Robert Edens (d. 1837), St. James Episcopal Church, Wilmington. He was in Richmond when he signed the ledger for William Norwood (d. 1842), Old Town Cemetery, Hillsborough. [Signatures, Estates]

I. W. Durham, Raleigh N.C.

I. W. Durham, Winston N.C. I. W. Durham operated a marble yard in Winston from at least 1878 to 1884, and in Charlotte in 1896. Signed numerous gravestones, including a headstone for Jesse Hamilton Hargrave (d. 1879), Lexington City Cemetery, Lexington, and an obelisk for James Kyle (d. 1881), Cross Creek Cemetery, Fayetteville. [1877–78, 1884, 1896 *Branson's*, Signatures]

Edgerton family. Operated the North Carolina Marble and Granite Company in Clinton from ca. 1900 to the present. [Newspapers]

T. L. Elliott. Operated a marble works in Charlotte in 1896. [1896 *Branson's*]

H. S. Farr, Phila. (Philadelphia). Signed an obelisk for John Wright Holmes (d. 1858), Oakdale Cemetery, Wilmington. [Signature]

Jas. Foster, Fayetteville [ca. 1800–?]. Itinerant marble cutter who worked in Fayetteville around 1840–43. He may be a descendant of the James Foster stonecutter dynasty who worked in Dorchester, Mass. Signed neoclassical marble stones for Jane Munroe (d. 1826), McIntyre Graveyard, Cumberland County, and Rev. Angus McDiarmid (d. 1827), Longstreet Presbyterian Church, Hoke County. [Newspapers, Signatures]

Gaddess, Baltimore.

A. Gaddess Maker Balt. Signed a number of gravestones in eastern North Carolina, including headstones for Nancy Douglas (d. 1848), St. Mary's Episcopal Church, Orange County; Thomas W. Gorman (d. 1863), Oakdale Cemetery, Wilmington; Charles Bailey Murphy (d. 1863), Big Rockfish Presbyterian Church, Cumberland County; and a ledger for Jahaziel Richards (d. 1851), Old Town Cemetery, Hillsborough. [Signatures]

Gaddess & Benbeen, Balt Md. Signed an obelisk to an unknown individual in the Kirkpatrick
   family (death date 1848), St. James Episcopal Church, Wilmington, and a box-tomb to
   Capt. Peter Summers (d. 1837), Friedens Lutheran Church, Guilford County. Gaddess is
   presumably A. Gaddess. [Signatures]

Thomas Gold. Stonecutter of New Haven, Conn., in late 1700s. The sandstone headstones with
   "soul faces" for Levi Gill (d. 1784) and Euphamia Gillespy (d. 1784), Christ Episcopal
   Churchyard, New Bern, are attributed to him. [Personal communication from Jim
   Blachowicz, Evanston, Ill.]

C. A. Goodwin, Raleigh, N.C. Charles A. Goodwin, marble cutter who worked in Raleigh from
   at least 1884 through the 1890s. Signed a headstone for Neil S. Stewart (d. 1889), Old Bluff
   Presbyterian Church, Cumberland County. See also *Lougee & Goodwin, Goodwin &
   Remsburg.* [Signature, Published works, 1884 *Branson's*]

Goodwin & Remsburg, Fayetteville. Charles A. Goodwin, Raleigh marble cutter, purchased
   George Lauder's marbleworks in Fayetteville in 1888 and worked in partnership with E. L.
   Remsburg, Lauder's assistant, for a short time. Signed a headstone at the Evans Graveyard,
   Cumberland County. [Newspaper, Signatures]

George T. Gosett. Marble-yard operator in Reidsville in 1896. [1896 *Branson's*]

D. A. Grantham. Marble dealer in Goldsboro in 1896. [1896 *Branson's*]

Grier Raleigh

Grier & File. Signed gravestones with death dates of 1856 and 1872 in Davidson County.
   [Signatures]

James Hall. Scottish-born marble cutter who immigrated to Charleston in 1803 and worked
   there until his death in 1823. Signed the ledger for Manne McLelland (d. 1803), Jersey
   Baptist Church, Davidson County, and the headstone for John Foote (d. 1816), St. James
   Episcopal Church, Wilmington. [Signatures, Combs]

Peter Harmon [1786–1876]. Part-time gravestone carver in Catawba County from about 1813
   to about 1848. He cut numerous unsigned headstones in Lincoln and Catawba Counties.
   [Estates, U.S. Census, Fieldwork]

L. H. Harrill. Marble cutter who worked in Shelby. Signed a headstone with a late-nineteenth-
   century death date at Machpelah Presbyterian Churchyard, Lincoln County. [Signature]

Richard Hartshorn Sr. Stonecutter in Rhode Island and New York in the late eighteenth
   century. Signed the sandstone ledger of Dr. Samuel Greene (d. 1771), St. James Episcopal
   Churchyard, Wilmington, and a number of sandstone headstones at this churchyard are
   attributed to him. [Signature, Published works]

John Heagarly. Paid for cutting gravestones for Jesse Northington of Cumberland County in
   1830. [Estates]

H. J. Hege [1855–1920]. Henry Jackson Hege operated a marble yard in Lexington from 1880
   to about 1920. Signed numerous Davidson County gravestones, including headstones and
   obelisks. [Signatures; 1884, 1896 *Branson's*; Betty K. Sowers, article on Hege in *Davidson
   County Genealogical Journal* 16, no. 3 (Summer 1996)]

J. H. Hemphill. Operated a marble yard in Marion in 1896. [1896 *Branson's*]

Zenas S. Hill [1808–1877]. Stonecutter in York County, S.C., who worked with the Caveny-
   Crawford Shop from the 1830s to the 1850s. Hill married Lucinda Crawford, sister of
   Robert and William Crawford. [Estates]

Nathaniel Holmes. Stonecutter in Plymouth and later Barnstable, Mass., in the late 1700s. The
   broken headstone of Swift Thatcher, First Baptist Churchyard, Elizabeth City, is attributed
   to him. [Personal communication from Jim Blachowicz, Evanston, Ill.]

John S. Hutchison. Operated a marble works in Salisbury in 1884. Signed the gravestone of
   Henry Cauble (d. 1881), Old Lutheran Cemetery, Salisbury. [1884 *Branson's*, Signature]

J. Jarden Phila. Philadelphia marble cutter who signed a ledger for a member of the Blount or Skinner family (d. 1829), Old Bethel Baptist Churchyard, Perquimans County. [Signature]

T. James. Signed a headstone for Thomas White (d. 1809), Cross Creek Cemetery, Fayetteville. James's accomplished neoclassical style links him to the stonecarvers of Charleston. [Signature]

R. M. Johnson. Operated a marble yard in Goldsboro in 1877–78. [1877–78 *Branson's*]

James A. Johnston. Operated a marble yard in Charlotte from the late 1870s through the 1890s. [1877–78, 1884, 1896 *Branson's*, U.S. Census]

A. Jordan. Operated a marble yard in Greensboro in 1884. [1884 *Branson's*]

B. F. Jordan. Operated a marble yard in High Point from the 1870s to the 1890s. [1896 *Branson's*]

A. A. & M. Kellogg. Operated a marble yard in Salisbury from 1855 to ca. 1860. They cut a number of marble monuments in Rowan County, including a group for the Ferrand-Henderson family at Chestnut Hill Cemetery. [Newspapers, Signature]

Hugh Kelsey [1754?–1818]. Scots-Irish gravestone carver who worked in Chester County, S.C., from the 1770s to about 1817. Most of his native-stone markers are in his home county, but several headstones at Buffalo and Alamance Presbyterian Churches in Guilford are attributed to him, including the gravestone of Mary Starratt (d. 1793), Buffalo Presbyterian Churchyard, Guilford County. [Patterson]

King & Whitelaw. Marble cutters in Raleigh in the 1860s and 1870s. Signed several gravestones at Oakwood Cemetery, Raleigh, and Old Town Cemetery, Hillsborough. [Signatures; 1866, 1869, 1872 *Branson's*; U.S. Census]

J. W. Knight. Marble dealer in Greensboro in 1896. [1896 *Branson's*]

George Lauder [1810–1888]. Scottish-born marble cutter who immigrated to Raleigh in the early 1830s, worked at the marble yard of William Stronach in Raleigh, then moved to Fayetteville and established a marble yard in 1845 that he continued until his death in 1888. Signed many marble gravestones and cut thousands of unsigned stones for cemeteries throughout the Upper Cape Fear area and the eastern and central Piedmont. [Signatures; Newspapers; U.S. Census; Published works; 1869, 1872, 1877–78, 1884 *Branson's*]

Traugott Leinbach [1798–1881]. Moravian silversmith who carved marble gravestones in Salem from ca. 1831 to ca. 1850. He cut a marble urn-and-willow headstone for Juliana Mock (d. 1843), Bethany Lutheran and German Reformed Church, Davidson County. [Estates, Fieldwork]

A. Leslie, Petersburg. Petersburg, Va., marble cutter who signed marble headstones with death dates in the early nineteenth century at Old Brick Reformed Churchyard, Guilford County. [Signatures]

Lougee & Goodwin. Operated a marble and granite works in Raleigh in the 1880s. Signed gravestones with death dates in the 1870s and 1880s at Cross Creek Cemetery, Fayetteville. See also *C. A. Goodwin, Raleigh, N.C.* [Signatures, 1884 *Branson's*]

Lyman & Barnes. Operated a marble yard in Henderson in 1896. [1896 *Branson's*]

McCoy. Signed a gravestone with a death date of 1857 at Machpelah Presbyterian Church, Lincoln County. By 1869 he was in partnership with William Tiddy in Charlotte. See also *William Tiddy.* [1869 *Branson's*, Signature]

Issiah McEachin [1922–]. Brick mason in east Cumberland County who made concrete monuments for Cumberland County graves in the 1970s and early 1980s. [Interview, Fieldwork]

McIntosh, Wilmington. Stonecutter who signed gravestones with death dates in the 1840s and 1850s in Cumberland County. [Signatures]

John Thomas McLean, Sr. [ca. 1864–1920]. Marble cutter who operated a marble yard in
Lincolnton from the 1880s to his death. His "McLean & Co." signature appears on
numerous Lincoln County stones, such as the headstone of Alice Lenhardt (d. 1877), Old
White Zion Methodist Church, Lincolnton. [Signatures, Interview]

John Thomas "Mac" McLean, Jr. [1899–]. Son of John Thomas McLean. Continued his
father's Lincolnton marble yard from about 1920 until the 1930s. [Interview]

F. A. McNinch. Operated a marble yard in Charlotte during the late 1860s to the early 1870s;
by 1877 S. McNinch, presumably a relative, had apparently taken over the business. For a
short time the firm was apparently known as McNinch & Kendrick and at another time
was known as McNinch & Wilson. A gravestone with a death date of 1876 in Lincoln
County is signed "McNinch Concord," apparently indicating that the firm was located in
Concord at some point in time. [1869, 1872, 1877–78 *Branson's*, Signatures]

H. C. Malcolm [1811–1860]. Pennsylvania-born stonecutter who worked in Salisbury in the
1850s. Signed a gravestone for Harry Reeves (d. 1857), Old Lutheran Cemetery, Salisbury.
[U.S. Census, Estates, Signature]

Josiah Manning. Stonecutter in Windham, Conn., in the late eighteenth century. The
headstones of Sarah Stone (d. 1788) and Mrs. Frances Wilkinson (d. 1788), St. James
Episcopal Churchyard, Wilmington, are attributed to him. [Fieldwork, Published works]

Ed T. Marks. Monuments and tombstone dealer in Raleigh in 1896. [1896 *Branson's*]

Mason, Elizabeth City. Stonecutter of Elizabeth City who signed several gravestones with late-
nineteenth-century death dates in the Albemarle region. [Signature]

Milholland & Bell signed a gravestone at the Old English Cemetery, Salisbury. This may be
N. T. Milholland, who had a marble works in Statesville in 1884 and a marble yard in
Huntersville in 1896. [1884, 1896 *Branson's*, Signatures]

W. G. Milligan. Operated a marble works in Wilmington in 1860–61. Signed a gravestone
with a death date of 1853 at Lebanon Episcopal Chapel Cemetery, Wrightsville, New
Hanover County. [Signature, Wilmington Directory]

Monumental Bronze Company. Metal monument works in Bridgeport, Conn. Signed several
zinc monuments with death dates from the 1860s to the 1880s located in Cumberland and
New Hanover Counties. [Signatures]

R. H. Moore & Son. Operated a marble and granite works in Charlotte in 1896. Signed the
gravestone of Benjamin F. Fraley (d. 1886), Old Lutheran Cemetery, Salisbury. [1896
Branson's, Signature]

J. H. Neese. Marble dealer in Greensboro in 1896. [1896 *Branson's*]

William Nichols. Nineteenth-century English-born architect who worked in North Carolina in
the 1820s. Designed and signed the neoclassical pedestal-tomb for Judge Archibald
Henderson (d. 1822), Old Lutheran Cemetery, Salisbury, and a similar monument for
Francis Locke, Revolutionary War hero (d. 1823), Thyatira Presbyterian Church, Rowan
County. [Signatures, Henderson Estate File]

Thomas Norris, 417 Bowery N.Y. Signed the gravestone of Murdoch and Christian McRae
(d. 1832), Philippi Presbyterian Church, Hoke County. [Signature]

John Pearson. English-born stonecutter who worked in Henderson County in the 1850s. The
gravestone of Thomas Rhodes (d. 1827), Old French Broad Baptist Churchyard near
Hendersonville, has the signature "J.P.," which is apparently that of John Pearson.
[Signature; U.S. Census]

Ebenezer Price. Stonecutter who worked in Elizabeth, N.J., from 1747 to 1788. Signed a
sandstone gravestone for William Hunt (d. 1767), St. James Episcopal Church,
Wilmington. [Signature, Published works]

E. Price & Son, Norwalk, Ct. Marble cutters located in Norwalk, Conn., who signed three gravestones with death dates in the 1830s to 1850s located in New Hanover and Brunswick Counties. They may be a continuation of the firm of Ebenezer Price. [Signatures]

T. J. Rake. Marble dealer in Salisbury in 1896. [1896 *Branson's*]

E. L. Remsburg [1860–1946]. Maryland-born stonecutter who moved to Fayetteville from Danville, Va., to apprentice under George Lauder. He took over Lauder's shop at his death in 1888 and worked until ca. 1920. Signed gravestones with death dates in the 1890s and early 1900s in Cumberland County. [Interview, Newspapers, Signatures, 1896 *Branson's*]

John Rikard [Rickard] [1790–1863?]. Part-time gravestone carver in Davidson County in the 1850s. [Estates]

D. Ritter & Son, New Haven, Ct. Marble cutters in New Haven, Conn., who signed gravestones with death dates of 1829 and 1831 in Wilmington and Fayetteville. [Signatures]

J. Ritter, New Haven, Ct. Marble cutter in New Haven, Conn., who signed gravestones with death dates in the 1830s and 1840s in Edenton, Wilmington, and Fayetteville. J. Ritter may be the son in the firm D. Ritter & Son. [Signatures]

S. C. Robertson. Operated a marble yard in Charlotte in the late 1860s and early 1870s and in Greensboro in the 1880s. [1869, 1872, 1884 *Branson's*]

Thomas Robinson. Operated a marble yard in Charlotte in 1870. [U.S. Census]

Roble, Statesville. Marble cutter who signed the tomb-table of Rebecca A. E. Snead (d. 1880), St. Paul's Episcopal Churchyard, Wilkesboro. [Signature]

R. I. Rogers, Durham. Marble cutter who signed a gravestone for Maude Guthrie (d. 1889), Cross Creek Cemetery, Fayetteville. [Signature]

Rowe & White, C.S.C. Signed a gravestone for William Locke (d. 1785), Thyatira Presbyterian Churchyard, Rowan County. These Charleston stonecarvers worked in an accomplished neoclassical style. [Signature]

J. C. Rudisill. Marble worker in Lincolnton in 1877–78. [1877–78 *Branson's*]

Robert Rudisill. Operated a marble yard in Lincolnton in 1870. [U.S. Census]

Lemuel Savery. Stonecutter in Plymouth, Mass., in the late 1700s. The ledger of Sarah Bonner (d. 1779), St. Peter's Episcopal Churchyard, Washington, N.C., is attributed to him. [Personal communication from Jim Blachowicz, Evanston, Ill.; Combs]

James B. Smith. Operated George Lauder's marble yard in Fayetteville in the early 1870s while Lauder served as Fayetteville postmaster. Smith was the husband of Lauder's adopted daughter. [U.S. Census, Published works]

David Sowers [1794–?]. Cabinetmaker and stone carver in Davidson County from about 1815 until 1835, when he emigrated to Indiana. One head and footstone at Pilgrim Lutheran and Reformed Church in Davidson County is probated to him; a number are attributed to him. [Estates, Published works]

Rud. Strehle. Moravian stonecutter who carved grave plaques in Salem, c. 1790. [Published work]

William Stronach [1803–1857]. Scottish-born and -trained stonecutter who came to Raleigh to work on the state capitol building; he set up a marble yard in Raleigh in 1837 that he operated until his death in 1857. Two marble monuments documented to him stand in the City Cemetery in Raleigh. [Census, Newspapers, Published work]

Struthers, Phila. Marble-cutting firm in Philadelphia during second quarter of the nineteenth century. The firm executed the stone mantels for the new state capitol in the 1830s and signed gravestones with death dates in the 1820s, 1830s, and 1840s in the Raleigh City Cemetery, the Old Lutheran Cemetery, Salisbury, and Fairntosh Graveyard, Durham County. The full name of the firm was John Struthers & Son. The son's name was apparently William Struthers. [Capitol Papers, Signatures, Published works]

G. D. Sugg. Operated a marble and stone works in Asheville in 1880. [U.S. Census]

Apollos Sweetland. Itinerant marble cutter from Hartford, Conn., who worked in various southern cities in the early nineteenth century. He was in Fayetteville ca. 1821–23 and signed a number of gravestones with death dates of 1819 and 1820 located in Hoke County and Wilmington. [Signatures, Newspapers]

R. H. Templeton. Operated a marble yard in Lincolnton in the 1880s. Signed many gravestones in Lincoln County. His firm may have been known as Carolina Marble Works. [1884 *Branson's*, Signatures]

William Tiddy. English-born stonecutter who operated a marble yard in Charlotte by 1850 that continued to operate until at least 1870. In the 1860s operated a branch marble yard in Lincolnton with his sons Richard and James. [U.S. Census, 1866, 1869 *Branson's*, Signatures]

Tiddy & McCoy. Operated a marble yard in Charlotte in the late 1860s and signed many stones in Lincoln County graveyards. [Signatures, 1869 *Branson's*]

Tingley Providence, R.I. Stonecutter who signed the tomb-table of Oliver Pearce (d. 1815), Cross Creek Cemetery, Fayetteville. [Signature]

H. A. Tucker & Bros. Operated a large marble and granite works in Wilmington, with branches in other cities, from ca. 1890 to the early twentieth century. Signed the gravestone of Sallie Powell (d. 1897), Cross Creek Cemetery, Fayetteville. [Signature, 1896 *Branson's*, Published works]

Van Conden & Young, Phila. Operated a marble works in Philadelphia in the late nineteenth century. Signed several ornate gravestones with death dates in the 1870s and 1880s located in Wilmington, Fayetteville, and Hillsborough. The firm's signatures are difficult to decipher. [Signatures]

George Vogler [ca. 1785–ca. 1865]. Salisbury gunsmith who carved gravestones from about 1852 to about 1860. Signed gravestones with death dates in the 1840s and 1850s in Salisbury and in Davidson County cemeteries. [Newspapers, Signatures, Published works]

D. A. Walker. Signed a gravestone for Lydia Montgomery (d. 1883), Old Lutheran Cemetery, Salisbury. [Signature]

James Walker. Operated the Wilmington Marble Works, which dealt in mantels, gravestones, and building contracting in the 1870s. [Wilmington Directories]

Walker & Maunder. Operated a marbleworks in Wilmington in the 1860s. Partner John Maunder continued the business from 1870 to ca. 1896. [1866, 1869, 1896 *Branson's*]

Allen Watson. Part-time gravestone carver in Davidson County who cut gravestones at Beulah Church of Christ Churchyard with death dates in the 1840s. [Estates]

Samuel Watson. Stonecutter who worked in York County, S.C., around 1800 in the style of the Bigham Shop. The gravestone of Elisabeth Davis (d. 1795), Olney Presbyterian Church, Gastonia, is attributed to him. [Patterson]

C. B. Webb. Operated a marble works in Statesville in 1896. He may have been the son in J. T. Webb & Son. [1896 *Branson's*]

J. T. Webb & Son. Operated a marble yard in Newton and a marble works in Statesville in 1884. [1884 *Branson's*]

Weir & Whitelaw. Operated a marble and granite works in Raleigh in the 1880s. See also *Whitelaw & Campbell.* [1877–78, 1884 *Branson's*]

J. White. John White, Charleston marble cutter, signed a number of gravestones with death dates in the 1820s and 1830s in Lincoln County. [Signatures, MESDA Index]

W. M. White. Marble dealer in Gastonia in 1896. [1896 *Branson's*]

W. T. White. Marble cutter in Charleston who signed gravestones with death dates in the 1840s and 1850s in Lincoln and Rowan Counties. [Signatures, MESDA index]

Whitelaw & Campbell. John Whitelaw and Donald Campbell operated a marble and stone works in Raleigh in the late 1870s and early 1880s. Campbell, a Scottish-born stonecutter, had come to Raleigh to work on the state capitol and later worked on the Century Post Office and the state penitentiary. He died in 1885. [1877–78 *Branson's*, Newspapers]

Joseph K. Willis. Marble dealer in New Bern in 1896. [1896 *Branson's*]

Isaac H. Wilson. Marble worker in Charlotte in 1877–78. [1877–78 *Branson's*]

W. E. Wilson. Marble and stone works operator in Durham in 1880. Signed a gravestone for Ralph Henry Graves (d. 1876), Old Town Cemetery, Hillsborough. [U.S. Census, Signature]

Wilson & Leak. Operated a marble yard in Winston in 1877–78. [1877–78 *Branson's*]

Witzell & Cahoon, N.Y. New York marble cutters who signed gravestones with death dates of 1815 and 1816 in Wilmington and Fayetteville. [Signatures]

William O. Wolfe [1851–1922]. Pennsylvania-born marble cutter who apprenticed in Baltimore and set up a marble yard in Raleigh in 1872; moved the marble yard to Asheville and operated it there from 1883 to his death in 1922. Cut a number of gravestones at Oakwood Cemetery, Raleigh, and in Watauga and Henderson Counties, some of which are signed. He was the father of noted novelist Thomas Wolfe. [Signature; Newspapers; Published work; 1872, 1877–78, 1884, 1896 *Branson's*]

J. T. S. Young. Operated a "General Store & Monuments & Gravestones" in Wilson in 1877–78, and may have been an agent rather than a stonecutter. [1877–78 *Branson's*]

Zell & Stert Feen, Phila. Philadelphia marble cutters who signed a headstone for Mrs. Jane Keith Sloan (d. 1853), Red House Presbyterian Church, Duplin County. [Signature]

APPENDIX B
Marble Cutters and Stonecutters in North Carolina, 1850–1896

Sources: U.S. Censuses, Population and Industrial Schedules, 1850–80, and *Branson's North Carolina Business Directory*, 1866–96

1850 Census
George Lauder, marble cutter, Fayetteville

1860 Census
George Lauder, marble yard, Fayetteville
Wm. & R. Tiddy, marble yard, Lincolnton

1866 *Branson's Directory*
King & Whitelaw, marble cutters, Morgan Street, Raleigh
James Rigert & Sons, stone mason, Charlotte
Wm. Tiddy & Son, marble cutters, Charlotte
Walker & Maunder, marble and stone works, Wilmington

1869 *Branson's Directory*
John H. Buis, tombstones etc., Salisbury
King & Whitelaw, marble cutters, Raleigh
George Lauder, marble, Fayetteville
Tiddy & McCoy, marble cutting and marble dealers, Charlotte
F. A. McNinch, marble cutting and marble dealer, Charlotte
S. C. Robertson, marble cutting and marble dealer, Charlotte
Walker & Maunder, marble works, Wilmington

1870 Census
Stephen Buie, marble cutter, Robeson County
John H. Buis, marble cutter, Salisbury
Claypooles Marble Works, New Bern
F. A. McNinch, marble cutter, Charlotte
John Maunder, marble yard, Wilmington
Thomas Robinson, marble yard, Charlotte
James B. Smith, marble yard, Fayetteville
Wm. Tiddy, marble yard, Charlotte
Whitelaw & King, stonecutters, Raleigh

1872 *Branson's Directory*
Brown & Weant, tombstones, Salisbury
Jno. H. Buis, tombstones, Salisbury
Cayton & Wolfe, marble cutters, Raleigh
King & Whitelaw, marble cutters, Raleigh
Geo. Lauder, marble, Fayetteville

F. A. McNinch, marble yard, Charlotte

McNinch & Wilson, tombstones, Salisbury

S. C. Robinson, marble yard, Charlotte

1877–78 *Branson's Directory*

John H. Buis, tombstones etc., Salisbury

John Cayton, marble and stone works, Raleigh

G. W. Claypool, marble, New Bern

R. M. Crawford, marble workers and dealers, Charlotte

J. W. Durham, marble yard, Winston

R. M. Johnson, marble yard, Goldsboro

James A. Johnston, marble yard, Charlotte

R. F. Jordan, marble worker, High Point

Geo. Lauder, marble, Fayetteville

S. McNinch, marble worker and dealer, Charlotte

J. Maunder, marble cutter, Wilmington

J. C. Rudisill, marble working, Lincolnton

Whitelaw & Campbell, marble and stone works, Raleigh

Isaac H. Wilson, marble worker, Charlotte

Wilson & Leak, marble yard, Winston

W. O. Wolfe, marble and stone works, Raleigh

J. T. S. Young, general store and monuments and gravestones, Wilson

1880 Census

William G. Berryhill, marble yard and stone works, Charlotte

Cayton & King, marble and stone works, Raleigh

Jas. A. Johnston, marble yard and stone works, Charlotte

John Maunder, marble and stone work, Wilmington

G. D. Sugg, marble and stone works, Asheville

John Whitelaw, marble and stone works, Raleigh

W. E. Wilson, marble and stone works, Durham

1884 *Branson's Directory*

W. G. Berryhill, marble and granite works, Charlotte

Mrs. John Cayton, marble and granite works, Raleigh

Geo. E. Coulter, marble yard, Newton

I. W. Durham, marble works, Winston

H. J. Hege, marble yard, Lexington

J. S. Hutchison, marble works, Salisbury

J. A. Johnson, marble and granite works, Charlotte

A. Jordan, marble yard, Greensboro

B. F. Jordan, marble yard, High Point

George Lauder, marble, Fayetteville

Lougee & Goodwin, marble and granite works, Raleigh

N. T. Milholland, marble works, Statesville

Jno. Munder, marble and granite works, Charlotte

S. C. Robertson, marble yard, Greensboro

J. W. Stanley, agent, Baltimore Stone & Marble Works, Goldsboro

R. H. Templeton, marble works, Lincolnton
J. T. Webb & Son, marble yard, Newton
J. T. Webb & Son, marble works, Statesville
Weir & Whitelaw, marble and granite works, Raleigh
W. O. Wolfe Marble Works, Asheville

1896 *Branson's Directory*

A. E. Baum, marble, Sylva
J. A. Bennett, marble works, Winston
J. B. Beards, marble, Gastonia
John Buis, marble works, Salisbury
Cooper Bros., marble and granite works, Raleigh
G. E. Coulter, marble, Newton
G. A. Davis, marble works, Sanford
I. W. Durham & Co., marble, Charlotte
T. L. Elliott, marble yard, Charlotte
Geo. T. Gosett, marble yard, Reidsville
D. A. Grantham, marble, Goldsboro
H. J. Hege, tombstones, Lexington
J. H. Hemphill, marble yard, Marion
Jas. A. Johnson, marble, Charlotte
B. F. Jordan, marble, High Point
J. W. Knight, marble, Greensboro
Lyman & Barnes, marble yard, Henderson
J. Thomas McLean, marble works, Lincolnton
Ed. T. Marks, monuments and tombstones, Raleigh
John Maunder, marble yard, Wilmington
N. T. Milholland, marble, Huntersville
R. H. Moore & Son, marble and granite works, Charlotte
J. H. Neese, marble, Greensboro
T. J. Rake, marble, Salisbury
E. L. Remsburg, marble works, Fayetteville
H. A. Tucker & Bros., marble and granite, Wilmington
C. B. Webb, marble works, Statesville
W. M. White, marble, Gastonia
Jos. K. Willis, marble, New Bern
W. O. Wolfe, marble works, Asheville

GLOSSARY

Adamesque: *See* Federal style.

attribution: The act of placing a particular object or work of art into the production of a particular craftsman or artist based on the visual similarity of undocumented work to documented work.

backcountry: Refers to the Piedmont region of North Carolina in the eighteenth and first half of the nineteenth centuries when it was remote and isolated from the more thickly settled Coastal Plain.

backdating: The practice of making a marker for an individual who died a number of years earlier. This generally occurred either because of a delay in ordering a gravemarker, because a replacement of the original marker was made, or because of the arrival of a gravemarker artisan in an area that formerly had no such craftsman.

ballast stone: A large rounded rock used in the holds of sailing vessels to stabilize lightweight loads. These were sometimes reused to mark graves in northeastern North Carolina.

baroque: Refers to a European style of architecture and decorative arts popular from about 1600 to 1750, characterized by flamboyant classical forms and grandly sized spaces. The curvilinear pediments and sculptural moldings of the style influenced German American gravestone design in the late eighteenth and early nineteenth centuries.

blank gravestone: A gravestone that has not been inscribed to a particular person. Stonecutters often cut blanks and kept them on inventory.

bodystone: A body-shaped stone mound.

boss: An ornamental knob or projection.

box-tomb: A ledger resting on a high, solid base of brick or stone.

bull's-eye corner blocks: Square decorative accents placed at the corner of a door or other flat surface, containing a circular pattern.

burial mound: A high, man-made mound of earth created by Native Americans as a sacred burial site.

cairn: A pile of stones that cover a grave or other significant site. This type of monument occurred in Highland Scot graveyards in North Carolina.

cemetery: Any type of burial plot, but generally the term is used to refer to a larger, public burial plot owned by a community, town, or city.

chamfered borders: A traditional method of finishing an edge by beveling the square corners, usually at a 45-degree angle to the other two surfaces.

chevron: A zigzag-patterned molding.

Classical Revival: A general term for the styles that reuse the forms of ancient Greek and Roman architecture.

coat-of-arms: A family crest containing images representing family history.

colonnette: A small decorative column placed against a vertical surface.

comb grave: A grave cover composed of two slabs of stone laid in a gabled shape, utilized in east Tennessee in the nineteenth century.

compass saw: A saw with a narrow tapering blade that can cut in a circular manner, like a keyhole saw. Such a saw was used to cut the pierced shapes into soapstone headstones.

compass star: A star, drawn with the use of a compass, that always has points in even multiples, usually six or twelve.

crosscut saw: A saw for cutting wood or other soft materials, such as soapstone, across the grain.

cyma border: A border of double-curved leaf shapes pierced into the soapstone gravestones of Davidson County.

death's head: Grim image of a skull.

discoid: A head- or footstone or head- or footboard with a circular tympanum and square shoulders that resembled a schematized human head and torso.

dove-of-promise: An image of a bird bearing a branch in its mouth, symbolic of God's fulfillment of his promise to Noah to bring back dry land after the flood.

Eastlake Gothic style: A style characterized by heavy, carved, and turned woodwork, named after British interior designer Charles Eastlake and popular during the late nineteenth century.

Empire style: An architectural style popular during the mid-nineteenth century, characterized by the use of Mansard roofs, dormer windows, and ornate classical features.

Federal style: A neoclassical style popular in America in the late eighteenth and early nineteenth centuries, reflecting the influence of the Adamesque style popularized by the Adam brothers in England.

finial: A vertical ornament situated at the apex of an architectural feature, especially the tympanum of a headstone.

fleur-de-lis form: An emblem representing a lily or iris.

foil: The leaf-shaped curve of a Gothic stone window design.

footboard: A wooden gravemarker with the proportions of a footstone.

footstone: A rectangular stone gravemarker, smaller than the headstone, that marks the foot of a grave.

Fraktur: Ornately decorated and lettered certificates commemorating births, deaths, marriages, and other important occasions in German American culture of the eighteenth and nineteenth centuries.

freestone: Stone such as sandstone or limestone that could be cut easily without splitting.

fylfot: A pinwheel shape that symbolizes variously a cross, a sun, or eternity.

Gothic dot: Usage of a dot or colon to separate words, common in late medieval writing and continued on gravestone inscriptions in North Carolina in the eighteenth and nineteenth centuries.

Gothic Revival: Revival of the pointed arch form and religious ornament of medieval Gothic architecture during the mid- to late nineteenth century.

granite: Extremely hard igneous rock that was rarely shaped into monuments in the nineteenth century, but came to be the dominant monument material by the mid-twentieth century as machine-powered tools were adopted by stonecarvers.

graveboard: A post-and-rail gravemarker, constructed of wood, whose shape often resembled the headboard of a bed. Common in Great Britain and England from the seventeenth into the nineteenth centuries.

gravehouse: A gable-roofed, wood-framed structure that shelters and protects the grave. Common in eighteenth- and nineteenth-century North Carolina.

grave shelter: A wooden structure consisting of a roof supported on four posts that shelters one or several graves. Usually enclosed with fencing or latticework.

grave slab: The term for a ledger in medieval England.

gravestone: A funerary monument made of stone.

graveyard: A small private cemetery.

Greek Revival: A revival of Greek classical forms in America in the mid-nineteenth century.

headboard: A wooden gravemarker with the shape and proportions of a headstone.

headstone: A rectangular stone gravemarker that marks the head of a grave.

heart: A symbol that stands for human affection and love. On German American gravestones it has a distinctive two-lobed turnip shape.

hogback (coped stone): Stone mound constructed of two slabs that curve at the ends and meet in a single seam down the spine.

igneous rocks: Rocks that solidified from molten material. Granite is a common example.

ledger: Thin horizontal stone slab covering the entire grave and supported on a low masonry base.

Lowland: The coastal area of North Carolina and other southern seaboard states.

lozenge: A diamond shape.

marble: A sedimentary limestone that has been compressed. Marble is a soft stone that weathers easily.

marble cutter: Term used in the nineteenth century for a stonecutter who specialized in monuments.

marble works: A shop where funerary monuments were cut.

marble yard: A place of business where blocks of marble were stored and carved into monuments.

marl (also known as "shell rock"): A seashell conglomerate quarried for building blocks in eighteenth- and nineteenth-century coastal North Carolina.

mason: An artisan whose work is building with stone and brick.

mausoleum: A family tomb constructed of masonry, usually standing above ground.

metamorphic rocks: Rocks originally of igneous or sedimentary origin that are altered deep in the earth's crust by pressure, heat, and/or chemical changes. Common examples are marble, quartzite, gneiss, schist, and soapstone.

monument: Any type of gravemarker.

negative fylfot: The design of the fylfot cross, cut into the stone.

neoclassical: An approach to design that draws inspiration from ancient Greek and Roman precedents. The Federal style of the late eighteenth and early nineteenth centuries was a revival of Roman classical forms. The Greek Revival style of the mid-nineteenth century was a revival of Greek classical forms. The renewed interest in classicism around the turn of the twentieth century is often called Neoclassical Revival.

obelisk: A stone column or shaft set upon a base.

ogee: A distinctive S-shaped curve.

paling (pailing; *see also* railing): A wooden fence made of individual pales (vertical pieces of wood) and rails (horizontal pieces of wood). Often used to enclose graves in eighteenth- and nineteenth-century North Carolina.

patternbook: A practical guide to architecture featuring detailed plans and measurements, popular in America in the nineteenth century.

pedestal-tomb: A high stone base, often topped with an urn.

pediment: A triangular shape used as a decorative termination for a headstone.

petroglyph: Any inscription cut into the face of a cliff or rock, especially a prehistoric carving of this kind.

pierced headstone: A gravestone made of soapstone, into which the artisan has perforated symbolic shapes.

plaque: A type of gravemarker favored by the Moravians in North Carolina. The small thin stone, with a short inscription, is laid flat on the grave.

plinth: The projecting base of a wall or column pedestal, usually chamfered or molded at the top.

positive fylfot: A fylfot cross created by cutting away the stone around the cross.

press mold: An object used to impress a shape of itself into a pliant surface, such as concrete.

probate record: A record of payment contained in the estate, or probate papers, of a deceased individual. These records were required by county courts to document the dispersal of money from the estate. This sometimes itemized a payment to a particular artisan for a gravemarker.

quarter sunburst: A decorative pattern resembling the sun's rays that occupies one-quarter of a circle, often used to adorn the corners of a gravestone.

quartz: An igneous rock formed when sandstone is metamorphosed. The rock is hard, light colored, and has a flinty sheen. It occurs as intrusions within granite beds under North Carolina's Piedmont region.

railing (*see also* paling): A wooden fence made of individual pales (vertical pieces of wood) and rails (horizontal pieces of wood). Often used to enclose graves in eighteenth- and nineteenth-century North Carolina.

rear face: The surface of the gravemarker opposite the surface bearing the inscription.

Renaissance Revival: The renewed interest in architecture and decorative arts of the Italian Renaissance in mid-nineteenth-century America.

rococo: The last phase of the baroque style, popular in the early eighteenth century, characterized by spatial complexity, lightness, and an abundance of playful, elegant, naturalistic decoration.

Romanesque shrine-tomb: A gabled stone enclosure for a single burial, similar to the wooden gravehouse.

sans serif letters: Letters that do not contain the fine cross lines at the top or bottom that are decorative elements in the Roman alphabet.

sarcophagus: A stone coffin, often elaborately ornamented, utilized by ancient Greeks and Romans.

schist: A metamorphic rock that is easily split into layers.

sedimentary rock: Rock formed by the deposit of sediment in layers. Sandstone and shale are common examples.

skull-and-crossbones: An image consisting of a skull with crossed bones often found on early gravestones.

slate: A metamorphic rock formed when shale is subjected to heat and pressure. Slate is easily split into layers.

soapstone: A soft rock such as steatite or talcose slate containing a large percentage of talc, common in the Piedmont and mountain regions of North Carolina.

spandrel: The triangular space between the side of an arch, the horizontal drawn from the level of its apex, and the vertical of its springing.

star-flower: A geometric symbol that could be interpreted variously as a sun or a flower.

stonecutter: A professional artisan who had apprenticed in the stonecutting trade and generally worked full time at his craft.

sunburst: A geometric symbol representing the sun.

sunstar: A geometric symbol that could be interpreted either as a sun or a star.

thistle: A flower, the national symbol of Scotland.

tooled border: A decorative border of double, alternating squares.

tripartite: A form consisting of three distinct parts.

tomb: A vault large enough to contain multiple burials. It is often submerged wholly or partly in the earth, with walls and a roof.

tomb-table: Elegant variation of the box-tomb in which the ledger rests on stone corner posts.

tree-of-life: An image of a tree or a branch, which symbolizes the cycle of birth, growth, decay, death, and rebirth.

tulip: A stylized image of a flower popular on German American gravestones.

tympanum: The triangular top of a headstone of baroque style, popular in the eighteenth and early nineteenth centuries.

undertaker: One who prepared the body for burial and often performed the related tasks of digging the grave and carrying the body to the grave. In the nineteenth century, building contractors were known as undertakers.

Upland: The Piedmont area of North Carolina and other southern seaboard states.

urn-and-willow motif: An image of a weeping willow tree over a funerary urn, sometimes with a female mourner. This bereavement image was popular during the neoclassical period of the late eighteenth and early nineteenth centuries.

vault: A burial chamber, usually of brick, containing the coffin. Generally only the top projects above ground level. Sometimes the vault top exists by itself.

vernacular: Refers to the native speech, language, or dialect of a country or place. Also used to refer to native art forms.

volute: A spiral scroll that adorns the sides of an arch or other architectural feature.

winged death's head: A skull with wings, symbol of the hope of resurrection.

winged soul: A human face with wings, symbol of the resurrected human soul.

NOTES

ABBREVIATIONS

A&H   North Carolina State Archives, Department of Archives and History, Raleigh, N.C.

SHC   Southern Historical Collection, Wilson Library, University of North Carolina, Chapel Hill, N.C.

PREFACE

1. The term "necrogeography," meaning the regionality of burial practices, is often used by cultural geographers to analyze graveyards. It was apparently coined by Fred Kniffen in his article "Necrogeography in the United States." Terry Jordan used this regional and ethnic approach for his book *Texas Graveyards*.

2. The major New England gravestone studies are Forbes, *Gravestones of Early New England*; Ludwig, *Graven Images*; and Benes, *The Masks of Orthodoxy*. See also various articles in the annual proceedings of the Dublin Seminar for New England Folklife, *Puritan Gravestone Art* and *Puritan Gravestone Art II*, and various articles in *Markers: The Journal of the Association for Gravestone Studies*, volumes 1–6.

3. Rauschenberg, "A Study of Baroque- and Gothic-Style Gravestones," 24–50. Dan Patterson at the University of North Carolina at Chapel Hill is currently working on a study of the Bigham family workshop in Mecklenburg County, North Carolina, and their Scots-Irish roots.

4. At least one other book has had the same title—*Sticks and Stones: A Study of American Architecture and Civilization*—published in 1924 by architectural critic Lewis Mumford. For Mumford, the phrase evoked the full range of American buildings, from wooden houses to stone courthouses and churches.

CHAPTER ONE

1. Watson and Laney, *The Building and Ornamental Stones of North Carolina*, plate III.

2. The so-called capitol quarry supplied stone for the state capitol. Stonecutter William Stronach bought a section of the quarry in 1839 and used the granite for walls and probably for gravestones as well. See Chapter 5.

3. Burgess, *Churchyards*, 16; see also a discussion of the undertaker's role in providing a wooden gravemarker in Rauschenberg's "Coffin Making and Undertaking in Charleston," 45–56.

4. Angus Graham, "Headstones in Post-Reformation Scotland," 6. The Frederick Weisner estate, probated May 1838, includes a payment of $7 to Thomas Fisher for "coffin, grave & tombstone" in the Davidson County Inventories, Sales, and Accounts, fol. 50, A&H.

5. Lounsbury, *Illustrated Glossary*, 255.

6. Harrelson, "Dialectic and Philanthropic Societies Burial Grounds," SHC. Minutes for January 1799 found in Appendix, 6–7. Philanthropic Society member George Clark, a student from Bertie County who died at the university in 1798, is the earliest interment in the Old Chapel Hill Cemetery adjacent to campus. Clark probably had such a railing put around his grave; the current marble ledger, a permanent monument, was placed there sometime later.

7. Cornelius Clark estate, 1824, voucher no. 19, box 25, Lincoln County Estates; Lucy Byerly estate, November 1846, fol. 484, Davidson County Inventories, Sales, and Accounts, A&H.

8. The *graveboard*, a wide wooden marker that resembles the headboard of a bed, was popular in early-nineteenth-century Charleston, but no examples in North Carolina are known. In the

early nineteenth century, Charleston artist Francis C. Hill painted a view of St. John's Lutheran Churchyard, Charleston, which shows a number of graveboards, and an individual view of a splendid late-eighteenth-century graveboard with a richly painted baroque tympanum with crown, floral decoration, and admonitory epitaph. These are in Hill's daybook, "Charleston Sketchbook," Lutheran Theological Seminary, Gettysburg, Pa.

9. White-painted head and footboards were customary in East Anglia and Surry, England, the homeland of a number of North Carolina settlers. Burgess, *Churchyards*, 16.

10. Jordan, *Texas Graveyards*. See pages 34–38 for a discussion and photographs of grave-houses. Jordan believes that this tradition is American Indian, but also cites West African precedents. A similar form of grave structure, executed predominantly in stone, occurs along the Cumberland Plateau in east Tennessee. Known locally as *comb graves*, these constitute 91 percent of all gravemarkers in 168 cemeteries in four counties. These date from 1817 to the mid-twentieth century. Artisans most commonly built them of local stone slabs, although some of the more recent examples are of wood. The oldest of the Tennessee comb graves mark the burials of North Carolina natives, suggesting that the tradition perhaps originated there, although no examples have come to light. The usual explanation given by local residents for the peculiar form is that it protected the graves from rain. Similar structures stand in Alabama, Arkansas, and east Texas. Cantrell, "Traditional Grave Structures on the Eastern Highland Rim."

11. Fries et al., *Records of the Moravians in North Carolina*, 1:417. This could refer to a clapboard railing, but more likely the clapboards were applied horizontally, as siding.

12. Roger Manley, letter to author, 16 February 1982.

13. Lounsbury, *Illustrated Glossary*, 387–88; personal communication with Bert Brooks, of Brooks Funeral Home in Morehead City, and the Reverend Matt Stockard, rector, St. Paul's Episcopal Church, Beaufort. They have extensive knowledge of vault burials in Beaufort and the coastal region.

14. William Dougal estate, fol. 231, book 2, 1835–41, New Hanover County Inventories of Estates, A&H.

15. Burgess, *English Churchyard Memorials*, figure 1.

16. Members of prominent Puritan families were buried in family tombs in early Boston. Samuel Sewall, well-known Boston diarist of the seventeenth and early eighteenth centuries, mentions his own family tomb, personalized by the family coat-of-arms, many times. Sewall, *Diary*. Cemeteries in the French Quarter of New Orleans contain row after row of such grave vaults, which have been a tradition since early settlement.

17. R. D. W. Connor described the tomb in his biographical entry "John Harvey," 42.

18. Oates, *The Story of Fayetteville*, 718.

19. Connor, "John Harvey," 42. The graveyard is located on inaccessible federal property, and knowledge of the headstone comes from this article, containing an out-of-focus snapshot of the stone.

20. Butler, "On the Memorial Art of Tidewater Virginia."

21. Welch, *Momento Mori*, 1, 9, 10.

22. Burgess, *English Churchyard Memorials*, 114.

23. For this study, the antebellum estate records of Davidson, Cumberland, New Hanover, and Lincoln Counties were sampled.

24. Elizabeth Ferguson estate, 1847, Lincoln County Estates, A&H.

25. Joseph Bass, Cumberland County, author interview, July 26, 1981.

26. Barba, *Pennsylvania German Tombstones*, 2–3.

27. Shelley, *Illuminated Manuscripts of the Pennsylvania Germans*, 83–87.

28. Interpretations of the "Pennsylvania Dutch" symbols in North Carolina gravestone art

are taken from Barba, *Pennsylvania German Tombstones*, 2–24, and Shelley, *Illuminated Manuscripts of the Pennsylvania Germans*, 83–91. Although the human figure is rare in German folk art, it appears more frequently on Pennsylvania German gravestones than on North Carolina German gravestones. Angels and cupids play a minor role in Pennsylvania German stones and are nonexistent on their counterparts in North Carolina. The significance of the various symbols used in Pennsylvania Dutch art has been debated since the 1920s, when American folk art came into public prominence. In Pennsylvania these symbols are seen on *Fraktur* (decorated certificates of birth, marriage, and so on), stoveplates, buttermolds, tinware, ceramics, textiles, kitchen utensils, architectural hardware, tombstones, and painted barns. In the Rhenish Palatinate, from which the majority of the German settlers in Pennsylvania emigrated, doors, lintels, farmyard gates, and arch keystones also contain these symbols.

29. Clark, "The Bigham Carvers of the Carolina Piedmont," 53.

30. Scorsch, *Mourning Becomes America*.

31. The earliest English funerary monument catalog in the collection of the Winterthur Library, Winterthur, Del., is Taylor and Taylor, *Designs for Monuments*, published ca. 1791.

32. The earliest American funerary monument catalog in the collection of the Winterthur Library, Winterthur, Del., is *Original Designs in Monumental Art*, by architect Paul Schulze, published in Boston in 1851.

33. Vermont Marble Company, *Children's Designs and Markers*; Nichols and Company, *Monumental Designs No. 6*, Collection of the Winterthur Library, Winterthur, Del.

34. Sears & Roebuck, *Tombstone Catalogue*. Collection of the Winterthur Library, Winterthur, Del.

CHAPTER TWO

1. Elizabeth Moore, Edenton, N.C., author interview, February 1983.

2. Ray Winslow, Hertford, N.C., author interview, 5 February 1981.

3. Map of Sir Nathaniel Duckenfield's latest patents, 1767, English Records, A&H; Parker, *The Colonial Records of North Carolina: 1697–1701*, 25 (Goddin versus Duckenfield). George Stephenson, a North Carolina archivist, brought this map and the court case regarding payment for the tombstone to my attention. It is his opinion that the landing is named for the Sothel tombstone.

4. The wealthiest planters of Chesapeake Virginia imported carved stones from English stonemasons by the second half of the seventeenth century. In 1674 a Virginia planter specified in his will that a gravestone "of Black Marble be with all Convenient Speed sent for out of England with my Coate Arms . . . engraven in brasse." Lounsbury, *Illustrated Glossary*, 166.

5. A Fayetteville newspaper, the *North-Carolina Journal*, of 2 December 1829, contains an advertisement for Henry Jones's dry-goods store in Fayetteville with such claims, typical of merchants' advertisements of the period.

6. Alexander Lillington was a patriot leader in the Battle of Moore's Creek, one of the decisive incidents in the Revolution in North Carolina. The graveyard lies in Pender County, just north of New Hanover County.

7. Cedar Grove Cemetery National Register Nomination, State Historic Preservation Office, Raleigh.

8. Catherine Bishir, "Calvary Episcopal Church," National Register nomination, listed 1971, and personal communication, December 1994.

9. M. Ruth Little and Betsy Baten, "Old Chapel Hill Cemetery," National Register nomination, listed 1994.

10. Crow and Winters, *The Black Presence in North Carolina*, 47.

11. Watson, *History of New Bern and Craven County*, 307.

12. John B. Green III, personal communication, 12 September 1996. The Christ Church (New Bern) burial registers indicated that there was a "black burying ground," perhaps Greenwood Cemetery, by 1859. A list of the decedents, dates of death, and ages at death follows: Eliza Johnson, d. 1805 aged 30; a fragmentary stone to a "Rosi . . . ," died 180_; Delia, servant of Edward Graham, d. 1816 aged 60; Sarah Rice d. 1821 aged 45; Richard Smith d. 1840 aged 44; Margaret Sawyer d. 1842 aged 61; Robert Walker d. 1846 aged 26; William Harvey d. 1855 aged 32; John Cook d. 1856 aged 65; Hannah Bremage d. 1858 aged 49; Elisha Brinson d. 1858 aged 69; and Robert Lipsey d. 1859 aged 45.

13. Green, *Fact Stranger than Fiction.*

14. A number of these in Cumberland County cemeteries follow a pattern of discoid headboards and footboards with diamond finials.

15. Frank Stephenson and Louise Boone of Hertford County; Etta Turner, Perquimans County; Wilma Spence, Pasquotank County; author interviews, February 1981. Notes in North Carolina Gravemarker Survey, Southern Folklife Collection, SHC.

16. The main-street crosswalks of Murfreesboro, Hertford County, still had ballast stone pavements in the early twentieth century, and former North Carolina secretary of state Thad Eure built porch columns on his house in Winton, Hertford County, with ballast stone from the Meherrin River banks in the 1930s. Roy Johnson, Murfreesboro, author interview, 6 February 1981; Louise Boone, Winton, N.C., author interview, 6 February 1981.

17. Ray Winslow interview. Notes in Perquimans County file, North Carolina Gravemarker Survey, Southern Folklife Collection, SHC.

18. Ibid.

19. Ledgers of similar character, as well as box-tombs, from the mid-seventeenth to the late eighteenth centuries, stand as the oldest monuments in Bruton Parish Churchyard in Williamsburg, Virginia, and in numerous other Tidewater Virginia graveyards. Clients in Williamsburg and at wealthy plantations copied London taste in monuments, with box-tombs and obelisks with armorial crests and death's heads (skull and crossbones) and paneled bases, generally made of limestone. Butler, "On the Memorial Art of Tidewater Virginia, 1650–1775."

20. Batsford, *English Mural Monuments and Tombstones*, figure 63.

21. Ibid.

22. Bill Faulk, director of the Brunswicktown State Historic Site, author interview, 4 April 1981; North Carolina Historical Highway Marker D 55.

23. Wasserman, *Gravestone Designs.*

24. Combs, *Early Gravestone Art in Georgia and South Carolina.* See especially the Nathan Bassett stone, signed by Codner, on page 132.

25. Gravestone scholar James Deetz made this attribution during an inspection of Christ Episcopal Churchyard, New Bern, on 18 March 1991. Personal communication from Catherine Bishir; Combs, *Early Gravestone Art in Georgia and South Carolina*, 11–12.

26. Ernest Caulfield, "Josiah Manning," 76–84, and "Three Manning Imitators," 1–16.

27. The highly successful Manning shop sent a number of headstones to South Carolina and Georgia graveyards as well as to those in North Carolina. Combs, 6–7, 70–71.

28. Personal communication from Jim Blachowicz, Evanston, Illinois, who has studied New England stones in the South. March 1997.

29. Wasserman, *Gravestone Designs*, 16.

30. This ledger marks the grave of Dr. Samuel Green, d. 1771. Vincent Luti, Westport, Massachusetts, letter to author, 2 January 1982.

31. Merrens, *Colonial North Carolina in the Eighteenth Century*, 56–57.

32. Bartlett, "Permanent Building Materials."

33. Vincent Cain, author interviews, July–August 1981.

34. Oates, *The Story of Fayetteville*, 16, 17, 32.

35. Pezzoni, *The History and Architecture of Lee County, North Carolina*.

36. At Old Bluff Church, a modern cairn marker was erected in 1966 in recognition of the tradition. It is inscribed in both Celtic and English, "Keep in Remembrance Our Fathers."

37. This stands at the Murchison Graveyard, Harnett County.

38. Willsher, *Understanding Scottish Graveyards*, plate 29.

39. Alexander McAllister was perhaps a descendant of Col. Alexander McAllister, who brought a group of Highlanders to the Old Bluff Church community about 1740 and became a distinguished Revolutionary leader, one of the few Highland Scots who fought for independence. Oates, *The Story of Fayetteville*, 848.

CHAPTER THREE

1. Ramsey, *Carolina Cradle*, 175.

2. Hammer, *Rhinelanders on the Yadkin*, 22, 24; Merrens, *Colonial North Carolina in the Eighteenth Century*, 61.

3. Merrens, *Colonial North Carolina in the Eighteenth Century*, 58.

4. Hammer, *Rhinelanders on the Yadkin*, 61, 95, 123.

5. Ramsey, *Carolina Cradle*, 138, 140.

6. Ibid., 151, 175, 178.

7. The stone of David McDowell, at Quaker Meadows Cemetery, Burke County, is dated 1767. The earliest known stone in the Catawba Valley is the headstone of "Elizebeth Tuck" (d. 1777) at Unity Presbyterian Churchyard in Lincoln County, one of the oldest Presbyterian churches west of the Catawba River.

8. *Raleigh Register*, 1834, quoted in Brown, *A State Movement in Railroad Development*, 23.

9. Apparently the original stone was so weathered that church officials commissioned this replacement. Arends was a native German pioneer teacher and Lutheran minister of Old White Church, established in 1788 by Lutherans and German Reformed congregations, but used for worship by every denomination in Lincolnton. Sherrill, *Annals of Lincoln County, North Carolina*, 56, 70. North Carolina Historical Highway Marker O 45, located nearby, states that Arends was first president of the North Carolina Lutheran Synod in 1803. Assuming that the stone is an exact facsimile, the style of the lettering and the eagle crest with a scroll inscribed "E pluribus unum" in the tympanum and the familiar English epitaph "Remember Man as you pass by . . ." are characteristic of the Bigham Shop (see Chapter 4).

10. Sherrill, *Annals of Lincoln County, North Carolina*, 56.

11. Swaim, *Cabins and Castles*, 10; Merrens, *Colonial North Carolina in the Eighteenth Century*, 61.

12. Soapstone is defined as a soft rock containing 10 to 80 percent talc and one or more of the minerals chlorite, serpentine, magnesite, tremolite, actinolite, diopside, enstatite, and occasionally some quartz, magnetite, or pyrite. Stuckey, *North Carolina*, 34, 455–56. See also Wilson, Carpenter, and Conrad, *North Carolina Geology and Mineral Resources*, table 3.

13. Moore and Ashcraft, "Native American Rock Art."

14. Emmons, *Geological Report*, 214–15.

15. Lewis, "Notes on Building and Ornamental Stone."

16. Stuckey, *North Carolina*, 456.

17. This belt contains metavolcanic epiclastic rocks, which include laminated argillites, graywackes, graywacke conglomerates, arkoses, and novaculites. A large lens of thin-bedded slates

and argillites is located in south central Davidson and Montgomery Counties. During the twentieth century, quarries here have produced dimension slate, flagstone, building stone, and specialty-cut stone in considerable amounts. Wilson, Carpenter, and Conrad, *North Carolina Geology and Mineral Resources*, figure 2; Stuckey, *North Carolina*, 451.

The largest quarry in operation presently in Davidson County is Jacob's Creek Blue Flatstone Quarry, located adjacent to the Uwharrie National Forest in the south end of the county. Diamond drills cut the fine-grained, blue-gray slate that is quarried here and used for flagstone and flooring tiles.

18. Watson and Laney, *The Building and Ornamental Stones of North Carolina*, 58; Stuckey, *North Carolina*, 443.

19. Willsher, *Understanding Scottish Graveyards*, 36.

20. Zug, *Turners and Burners*, 58, 355–62. Zug gives a full discussion of all the surviving ceramic gravemarkers that are known.

21. Ibid., 359.

22. Ibid., 355–62.

23. Merrens, *Colonial North Carolina in the Eighteenth Century*, 59–60.

24. Fries, *Distinctive Customs and Practices of the Moravian Church*, 45, 48.

25. Minutes of the Aufseher Collegium, April 1790, Old Salem, Inc./Moravian Archives, Winston-Salem, N.C.

26. All of these references date from the period 1793–1831. Most are taken from Rauschenberg, "A Study of Baroque- and Gothic-Style Gravestones," 24–50.

27. Minutes of the Congregational Conference of Salem, N.C., 16 January 1783, Old Salem, Inc./Moravian Archives, Winston-Salem, N.C.

28. Ibid., 1 June 1786.

29. Minutes of the Aufseher Collegium, 13 April 1790, Old Salem, Inc./Moravian Archives, Winston-Salem, N.C.

30. Ibid., 27 March 1792.

31. Ibid., 10 September 1799.

32. Minutes of the Elders Conference, Salem, N.C., 9 March 1803, in Fries et al., *Records of the Moravians in North Carolina*, 6:2738.

33. Minutes of the Elders Conference, Salem, N.C., 16 March, 1803, Old Salem, Inc./ Moravian Archives, Winston-Salem, N.C. Rauschenberg noted that the only paint found on any stone gravemarkers anywhere in North Carolina were traces of yellow paint on the base of the pierced soapstone headstone of Delia Roberts (d. 1836), Abbott's Creek Baptist Churchyard, Davidson County. Rauschenberg, "A Study of Baroque- and Gothic-Style Gravestones," 43.

34. Minutes of the Aufseher Collegium, 24 January 1820, Old Salem, Inc./Moravian Archives, Winston-Salem, N.C.

35. Ibid., 28 November 1831.

36. Minutes of the Elders Conference, Salem, N.C., 30 November 1831, Old Salem, Inc./ Moravian Archives, Winston-Salem, N.C.

37. Barba, *Pennsylvania German Tombstones*.

38. Ibid.; see also Milspaw, "Plain Walls and Little Angels," 85–95. This is a study of the south central Pennsylvania counties of Dauphin, Lancaster, and Lebanon and reveals a more consistent introduction of popular imagery and the virtual demise of the German tradition by 1815. The German Lutheran and Reformed Churchyards here were established from 1750 to 1780, and more than half the early gravestones have joyful suns, stars, and Germanic tulips and hearts, often combined with *Fraktur* writing so that "the entire tombstone resembled a pen and ink illuminated manuscript translated into stone." Milspaw frequently discovered "fat little angel faces, some moon faced and ethereal, some approaching actual portraiture." She found that

the height of German stonecarving in this area occurred between 1795 and 1811 when the "Master of the Little Angels" worked. This anonymous Anglo-German stonecutter, working in local sandstone, produced the finest group of German gravestones in the region. Although he borrowed his winged-angel trademark from the popular domain, he reinterpreted it into a pleasing linear schema of geometric shapes, with parallel-grooved wings, a large round face with tiny features, a halo that functions as a sunburst, and Germanic twelve-point stars flanking the face. Some of his headstones are decorated on the rear as well, and occasionally include epitaphs. By 1815 this stonecutter was gone, and the German congregations of the region, with one exception, adopted English and American popular style in stones, including the use of marble, ledgers, and the urn-and-willow motif. Only Bindnagle's Lutheran Church, located on the frontier of the region and isolated and conservative in its outlook, continued to develop the German *Fraktur* style, combining elegant lettering with hearts, tulips, suns, and stars.

39. Wust, *Folk Art in Stone*. See especially the pages on which figures 4 and 11 appear. Wust studied folk German gravestones in Lutheran and Reformed churchyards in the Shenandoah Valley counties of Botecourt, Wythe, Bland, and Tazewell, dating from 1798 to about 1835. Laurence Krone used the same repertoire of traditional symbols as the other carvers of the area, but his lettering style was much more assured and well proportioned, and he occasionally lettered in German Gothic. His signature stone, an eccentric sarcophagus, erected about 1808, is signed "LAURENCE KRONE STON MASON." Further research on western Virginia German stonecutters was done by Moore, "Decorated Gravestones of Wythe County, Virginia," 618–27. Most of the photographs are by Tim Buchman.

The only other German-American gravemarkers in the South that have been the subject of a published study are those of Texas. See Jordan, *Texas Graveyards: A Cultural Legacy.* German immigration in North Carolina preceded that in Texas by nearly a century, however. Aside from the generally orderly layout, the dominance of church cemeteries over private cemeteries, and a higher level of craftsmanship than in the gravemarkers of other ethnic groups, there are few parallels between Carolina and Texas German graveyards. In Texas, for example, the cross is a commonly used symbol among German Catholics and Lutherans, while it rarely occurs in the invariably Protestant Carolina German graveyards. One group of German Catholic gravestones was carved during the mid-nineteenth century out of soft white Texas limestone by German stonecutters. The Gothic and figurative imagery of these stones is akin to Catholic funerary sculpture but is not found in North Carolina. Very few of the German gravestones documented by Jordan are antebellum, whereas nearly all of the Carolina German gravestones are from this nineteenth-century period. German gravestones in Texas retain ethnic designs, such as the ancient hex symbols, into the twentieth century, while their counterparts in North Carolina had lost their ethnicity by about 1870.

40. Rowan County's diverse ethnic composition and its position as a trading center apparently gave its sizable German population greater choices of monuments than Germans in other counties. Beginning about 1800 at its two oldest Lutheran churchyards, Organ Lutheran Church and Lower Stone Lutheran Church, families erected numerous marble monuments of neoclassical style. During the same period, at Organ Churchyard, a local carver cut a group of well-formed and inscribed headstones of native stone that follow stylish marble shapes rather than traditional folk German gravestone models.

41. Dr. Benjamin Brown, personal communication with author, 1992.

42. U.S. Census, Population Schedule, 1850, Henderson County, North Carolina: John Pearson, age 55, stonecutter, born in England, A&H. For a discussion of the stone houses, such as Rugby Grange, built in the southern mountains by summer people, see Bishir, *North Carolina Architecture*, 254.

43. This stone is located at Weaver Cemetery, North Main Street, Weaverville, N.C.

44. U.S. Census, Industrial Schedule, 1880, Buncombe County; *Branson's North Carolina Business Directory*, 1884.

45. Murray, *Wake: Capital County*, 599; see also letter to author, 21 July 1991, and "The Work of an Artist," *News and Observer* (Raleigh), 15 May 1910.

CHAPTER FOUR

1. Bishir, "Traditional Building Practice," 60, 103–6.

2. *Branson's North Carolina Business Directory*, 1866–67.

3. Bishir, *North Carolina Architecture*, 484 (n. 69); Mohney, *The Historic Architecture of Davie County*.

4. Phillips, survey file for Tilley Coffin, Casket and Furniture Factory, Stokes County, A&H.

5. Most of this information comes from the work of Daniel W. Patterson, Curriculum in Folklore, Department of English, University of North Carolina at Chapel Hill, who is writing a book on the Bigham workshop.

6. Clark, "The Bigham Carvers of the Carolina Piedmont," 37. Because there were numerous Samuel Bighams living in Mecklenburg County at this time, it has been impossible to determine the familial relationship between the two Samuels, senior and junior, who carved gravestones.

7. Patterson, personal communication with author, 1981.

8. McCormick, "A Group of Eighteenth Century Clogher Headstones," 12–22.

9. Patterson, brochure for Bigham Workshop Exhibit, 1983, Center for Visual and Performing Arts, Carrboro, N.C.

10. Christison, *Carvings and Inscriptions*, 179.

11. Combs, *Early Gravestone Art in Georgia and South Carolina*, 125–26.

12. The Polly Graham ledger is located at Machpelah Presbyterian Church, Lincoln County.

13. Author's analysis based on research done by Daniel W. Patterson; see also Fairey, "Changing York County," 6–8.

14. Daniel W. Patterson, quoted in Clark, "Bigham Carvers of the Carolina Piedmont," 37.

15. Patterson, "Upland North and South Carolina Stonecarvers," 3–4; Fairey, "Changing York County."

16. Hart, "History of the Town of Yorkville," York County Public Library, Columbia, S.C.

17. During the Revolutionary War, King's Mountain was the site of the Battle of King's Mountain, a decisive British defeat in 1780 (see North Carolina Historical Highway Marker O-5, located in Cleveland County). In the nineteenth century the mountain was mined and quarried intensively for a wide variety of minerals and rocks, including iron, gold, limestone, talcose schist, manganese, and talcose slate used for whetstones and hearthstones. An 1858 geodetic survey of South Carolina diagrams intensive industrial activity at King's Mountain and mentions that a greenish variety of talcose slate, often called soapstone, was being quarried at "Caveny's quarry" in York County for gravestones. Lieber, *South Carolina Geodetic Survey*, 24.

18. Most of the biographical information on the Caveny-Crawford Shop is taken from Hart, "The Crawford Family of Bethany"; Will of John Caveny, probated 1853, York County Wills. South Carolina State Archives, Columbia, South Carolina.

19. Hart, "The Crawford Family of Bethany."

20. Will of James Crawford, Estate of James Crawford, probated 1842, York County Wills and Estates, South Carolina State Archives, Columbia.

21. Hambright's estate records contain a receipt that documents the payment of $22 to James Crawford for cutting the headstone. Fairey, "Changing York County," 15.

22. The Lincoln County Estates consist of 110 boxes of estate files, arranged alphabetically

rather than chronologically. Rather than searching systematically through each file, I searched every fifth box, e.g. Box 1, Box 5, and so on. Robert Crawford's receipts are in the following files: Estate of Daniel Finger, probated 1835, voucher no. 2 dated 1834; Estate of Tempe McNamara, probated 1841, voucher no. 4 dated 1843; Estate of Henry C. Robinson, probated 1855, voucher no. 1; Estate of John Houser, probated 1850, voucher no. 4 dated 1851; and Estate of John Loretz, receipt dated 1836. Lincoln County Estates, A&H.

23. Estate of Elizabeth Ferguson, voucher no. 30 dated 1847; Estate of Ephraim Goodson, voucher no. 13 dated 1851; Estate of Abner Goodson, voucher no. 1 dated 1877, Lincoln County Estates, A&H.

24. One Caveny-Crawford headstone, with a death date of 1853, stands at Quaker Meadows Presbyterian Churchyard in Burke County, located just west of Catawba County.

25. Estate of Elizabeth Ferguson. One receipt shows that the executor, Andrew Love, purchased "one sett of grave Stones" from Alexander Brown of Columbia for eight dollars on 29 March 1847. Another receipt, dated 29 April 1847, shows that Love paid W. N. Crawford for engraving the gravestone of Elizabeth A. Ferguson, Lincoln County Estates, A&H.

26. In the 1860 South Carolina census, William appeared as a fairly wealthy farmer, and his oldest son, Lawson James, born in 1835, may have been working with him. U.S. Census, Population Schedule, 1860, York County, South Carolina. William signed gravestones up to 1879, died in 1894, and is buried at Bethany Church.

27. Lawson James Crawford is the last known member of the Caveny-Crawford Shop. He may have carried on the business until his death in 1912. L. J. signed at least one gravestone, for Martha Bradley (d. 1880), at Olney Church. Bradley's tall marble headstone contains a round-arched tympanum with a thick Gothic beaded border and a naturalistic vine design.

28. By the 1830s, Zenas S. Hill owned land near Crowders Creek in the King's Mountain area of Gaston County and was a county resident until at least 1856, but when he died in 1877 he was buried at the home church, Bethany, in York County, South Carolina. He was living in Gaston County in 1842, because a postscript to the estate inventory of James Crawford stated this, and was still there in 1856 when Robert Crawford owed him money. Zenas S. Hill to Alexander Hill, 1838, Gaston County Deed Book 1, 502; Alexander M. Hill to Zenas S. Hill, 1866, Gaston County Deed Book 3, 510; W. N. Crawford to L. J. Crawford, 1866, Gaston County Deed Book 4, 124, A&H.

29. Estate of Hugh Gibson, voucher no. 21 dated 1843, Lincoln County Estates, A&H.

30. Robert and his wife, Margaret Quinn, had eight children born in York County between 1830 and 1849. In 1856 Robert was a resident of Lincoln County and mortgaged his crop of corn, oats, and hay to Z. S. Hill to guarantee a debt. Lincoln County Deed Book 42, 615, A&H; U.S. Census, Population Schedule, 1850, York County, S.C., A&H; U.S. Census, 1860, Lincoln County, N.C., A&H; Will of Robert M. Crawford, Estate of Robert M. Crawford, probated 1865, York County Wills and Estates, South Carolina State Archives, Columbia, S.C. At his estate sale in August 1865, the following tools were sold: a hammer, two claw hammers, one auger, one chisel, one horse rasp, one iron square, one drawing knife, two axes, a lot of irons, a crowbar, one set of saw mill irons, and two sets of mill stones. Estate of Elias Lutes, probated 1866, voucher no. 16, Catawba County Record of Settlements, 1868–85, A&H.

31. Most of the gravestones for which receipts exist in the estate records could not be located in cemeteries. The only "German" stone with a receipt that was located is the headstone of Henry C. Robinson at Trinity Lutheran Church, Lincoln County. Robert Crawford cut the headstone soon after Robinson died in 1854. Estate of Henry C. Robinson, voucher no. 1, probated 1855, Lincoln County Estates, A&H.

32. The Harmon (Herman) family, of German origin, moved to present-day Catawba

County in the late eighteenth century, and Peter was born in 1786 to William Herman Jr. (1757–1822) and his wife Mary (1757–1822). They lived near Newton, the present county seat, and both William and Mary are buried at Old St. Paul's Lutheran Church. On 10 March 1811 Peter married Lydia Simmons. They lived on the west bank of the Catawba River, where he purchased a 300-acre tract in 1822. Little, "Genealogy of Herman Family," Catawba County Historical Museum, Newton, N.C. The estate of Hugh McFelmont, probated 1833, contains a voucher to Peter Harmon in which he is referred to as a blacksmith. Lincoln County Estates, A&H.

33. Estate of Elizabeth Gross, probated 1829, voucher no. 7; Estate of George Cansler, probated 1835, voucher no. 3, Lincoln County Estates, A&H.

34. The western Catawba Valley rests on a belt of mica gneisses and schists, and the grayish-green stone Harmon used is apparently a mica schist with a high soapstone content. Wilson, Carpenter, and Conrad, *North Carolina Geology and Mineral Resources*, figure 2. The stone has mica crystals that sparkle in the sunlight and is so soft that lawn mowers have scarred it. The dimensions of the headstones vary from 12 to 20 inches wide, 18 to 50 inches high from ground level, and 1½ to 2½ inches thick.

35. This is the headstone of Margaret Clodfelter, d. 1857. Jacob Clodfelter (d. 1837) and his wife are buried side by side beneath a pair of nearly identical headstones. Margaret's stone was probably cut at the same time as that of her husband. It is still customary today to erect a double headstone when one spouse dies and to inscribe the surviving spouse's name and date of birth, leaving the death date blank.

36. Good studies of Anglo-German Protestant gravestones outside North Carolina are Barba, *Pennsylvania German Tombstones*; Milspaw, "Plain Walls and Little Angels"; and Wust, *Folk Art in Stone*.

37. Horton and Weekley, *The Swisegood School of Cabinet-making*.

38. Ibid.; Bradford Rauschenberg, personal communication with author, 21 July 1982.

39. Rauschenberg, "A Study of Baroque- and Gothic-Style Gravestones," 24–50. In this path-breaking article, Rauschenberg concluded that the stylistic similarities, geographic proximity, and overlapping dates of production of Swisegood School furniture and the pierced gravestones are strong evidence that the cabinetmakers carved the stones.

40. Sowers, "Davidson County's Pierced Gravestones," 14. Family migrations from North Carolina were typical in the first half of the nineteenth century, when backward conditions at home and economic opportunities and the freedom of the frontier lured thousands of North Carolinians to the new territories and states beyond the Appalachian Mountains.

41. Two gravestone historians and photographers, Francis Y. Duval and Ivan B. Rigby, discovered the signature and included it in their article, "Openwork Memorials of North Carolina."

42. Will of Jacob Clodfelter, Estate of Jacob Clodfelter, probated 1837, Davidson County Wills and Estates, A&H.

43. Cyril Johnson, *The Family of Noah Clodfelter*, 388–96; Will of Jacob Clodfelter, Estate of Jacob Clodfelter, probated 1837, Davidson County Wills and Estates, A&H. Joseph followed in his father's footsteps. By 1830 he was married and his household included a son, a daughter, and a male slave between fifteen and twenty years old. By 1840 his family had increased to four sons, two daughters, and six slaves. Five members of the household were employed in agriculture. The 1850 census provides a complete picture of a prosperous farmer's household: Joseph, aged 49 and worth $2,500, his wife Charity, and seven children. The three oldest sons, Adam, aged 21, Joseph, 18, and Jacob, 16, are listed as laborers. Joseph's land transactions are primarily family business. In 1828, about the time he married, he bought two hundred acres on a tributary of the Brushy Fork, adjacent to the Daniel Wagoner property, from his father for $900. In 1854 he sold a 200-acre tract to his son Adam, probably when he married and set up a household. In

1870 Joseph and Charity gave one acre to the trustees of Bethesda Methodist Protestant congregation to build a church. When Joseph died in 1872 at the age of seventy-one, he left his wife Charity his 200-acre plantation and all the furniture, his son Joseph the 197-acre plantation where he lived, a plantation to the children of his deceased son Jacob, a piece of his hometract to his daughter, and two tracts of land to his son David. U.S. Census, Population Schedule, 1830, 1840, 1850, Davidson County; Will of Joseph Clodfelter, Estate of Joseph Clodfelter, probated 1872, Davidson County Wills and Estates, A&H.

44. These tools were sold at Joseph Clodfelter's estate sale, 1872. His estate was valued at about $1,100. Estate of Joseph Clodfelter, probated 1872, Davidson County Wills and Estates, A&H.

45. In a sample of the seven volumes of Estate Inventories, Sales, and Accounts for Davidson County, covering the 1830 to 1863 period, three payments to Joseph Clodfelter were found. In 1843 he received $7.50 for an unspecified item or service from the estate of Peter Clodfelter (probated 1843, voucher no. 5); in 1849, $10.28 for an unspecified item from the estate of Peter Hedric (probated 1849, fol. 242; Hedric's gravestone, at Pilgrim Church, is a marble stone of professional workmanship); and in 1850, $9 for two coffins from the estate of Sarah Snider (probated 1849, fol. 413, voucher no. 10). Davidson County Inventories, Sales, and Accounts, 1847–51, A&H.

46. An analysis of these lyrics by Daniel W. Patterson, a southern folk music scholar, reveals a fascinating combination of oral sources. The first quatrain is apparently an oral variant of a favorite old hymn text by Watts: "Why do we mourn departing friends?" The next quatrain appears to be from a folk lyric, taken possibly from a child ballad, "The Unquiet Grave," and several love songs. The last quatrain is from another Watts hymn, "And must this body die?" Patterson, personal communication with author, September 1983.

47. Owen, "A Thousand Doors," 56, Lexington Public Library, Lexington, N.C.

48. Estate of Peter Lopp, voucher no. 4, fol. 102, Davidson County Inventories, Sales, and Accounts, 1830–32, A&H.

49. The stone rises out of a wide chunk of uncarved soapstone visible because the entire footstone is partially uprooted.

50. Estate of Philip Sink, fol. 343, voucher no. 10, Davidson County Inventories, Sales, and Accounts, 1830–32, A&H. In 1832, Pilgrim Church member Philip Leonard's estate (fol. 524, voucher no. 7, Davidson County Inventories, Sales, and Accounts, 1830–32) paid David Sowers $2.50, probably for gravestones, but these stones have disappeared from Pilgrim Churchyard.

51. Yoder, *Pennsylvania German Fraktur and Color Drawings*; Shelley, *Illuminated Manuscripts of the Pennsylvania Germans*, 22, 108; Barba, *Pennsylvania German Tombstones*; see illustrations of the bracket on Pennsylvania German headstones, 203, 215, 225.

52. Wust, *Virginia Fraktur*, 10. Wust notes that the bracket is a frequent feature on German *Fraktur* in Virginia, central Pennsylvania, and Ohio; Bivens, "Fraktur in the South." The Schwenkenfelder sect of Pennsylvania had a custom of placing the birth certificate in the coffin at burial to serve as a passport to the world beyond, and there is a Denkmal certificate that commemorates death. Shelley, *Illuminated Manuscripts of the Pennsylvania Germans*, 87–91.

53. The record book of Pilgrim Church notes the birth of David Sowers on 29 September 1794 to Valentine and Ann Maria Eva Sowers. Valentine was a son of Philip Sauer (1735–1784), who emigrated from Palatine Germany to Pennsylvania in 1749 and settled in Davidson County in 1753. Philip and his descendants lived near and attended Pilgrim Church. Valentine must have been a carpenter, for in 1831 the county court authorized him to build a bridge on Rich Fork Creek.

54. The 1820 census lists David Sowers with a wife and one child. The 1830 census shows the

couple with three additional children. The family is not listed in the 1840 census. Davidson County Marriage Bonds; U.S. Census, Population Schedule, 1820, 1830, 1840, Davidson County, A&H; Owen, "A Thousand Doors," Lexington Public Library, Lexington, N.C., 56. Sowers might have continued to carve gravestones in Indiana, although limestone was the local stone utilized by gravestone carvers in this region and Sowers's tools and traditional style might not have adapted to the change.

55. For example, the headstone of David Wear, d. 1838, at Bethany Church; the headstone of Henry Grimes, d. 1844, at Beulah Church (both in the "Pierced Style" group); and two small stones with ornamental tympana but no piercing at Abbot's Creek Church: the headstone of Healey Davis, d. 1827, and the headstone of Tobias Livengood, d. 1834.

56. Biographical information is drawn from the U.S. Census, Population Schedule, 1850, Davidson County, Southern Division; U.S. Census, Industrial Schedule, Davidson County, 1860; Davidson County Apprentice Bonds and Records, Nathan Parks, 1837; Davidson County Inventories, Sales, and Receipts, 1839–61; Estate of Nathan Parks, probated 1865, Davidson County Wills and Estates, A&H. Secondary sources on Nathan Parks are McCrary, "The Early Years of County History," 166–78; and Sink and Matthews, *Pathfinders Past and Present*, 99–100.

57. Advertisement in *Western Carolinian* (Salisbury), 31 July 1821; Sink and Matthews, *Pathfinders Past and Present*, 264.

58. McCrary, "The Early Years of County History," 177. By the 1850s, Joseph Conrad had moved far beyond furniture construction into general construction, and he and his sons operated one of the most important building firms in North Carolina, building up-to-date Italianate Revival houses and institutional buildings throughout central North Carolina until Joseph's death in 1872. His projects included Blandwood in Greensboro in 1844 and Dorothea Dix Hospital in Raleigh in 1856 from the design by A. J. Davis of New York. See Bishir, *North Carolina Architecture*, 241, 242, 244, 481 (n. 141).

59. Davidson County Court Minutes, September session, 1825, A&H.

60. Advertisement in *Western Carolinian* (Salisbury), quoted in Sink and Matthews, *Pathfinders Past and Present*.

61. Nathan Parks, 1837, Davidson County Apprentice Bonds and Records, A&H. In 1838 and 1839, Parks bought two small lots on Main Street in Lexington, perhaps for his shop, and six acres on Abbott's Creek, one mile from Lexington, perhaps for a residence. Jesse Hargrave to Nathan Parks, 1838, Davidson County Deed Book 6, 343; E. S. Caldcleugh to Nathan Parks, 1839, Davidson County Deed Book 7, 75; John Mabry to Nathan Parks, 1838, Davidson County Deed Book 6, 342. In 1854 the North Carolina Railroad came by his rural property, and he purchased a sliver of land between his land and the railroad. Jesse Rankin to Nathan Parks, 1854, Davidson County Deed Book 13, 502; see also Davidson County Deed Book 11, 279, A&H.

62. Parks and Conrad lived five households apart in south Davidson County. U.S. Census, Population Schedule, 1860, Davidson County, Southern Division, A&H. Of the some forty cabinetmakers paid for coffins in the estate records of Davidson County during the 1830s to the 1850s, Parks received the largest number of payments, Conrad the second largest. One of the payments was for "railing grave," that is, erecting a wooden fence around the grave. Estate of Lucy Byerly, probated 1846, fol. 484, Davidson County Inventories, Sales, and Receipts, 1844–47, A&H.

63. Nathan Parks died without a will or enough provisions on hand to provide his widow a year's worth of supplies. McCrary's furniture and undertaking business became known as the Davidson Funeral Home and is still in operation. McCrary, "The Early Years of County History," 166–78.

64. Jane Park was the daughter of Isaac Wiseman, pastor at Jersey Baptist Church in the

second decade of the nineteenth century. Jane married John Park in 1816, and John and Nathan are believed to have been brothers. The spelling of Nathan's name varied from Parks to Park to Parkes. Nathan joined Jersey Church in 1841 and was an active member. Hendricks, *Saints and Sinners at Jersey Settlement*, 46, 56, 58, 71, 72; Bible records of Davidson County, N.C.: John Park m. Jane Wiseman, 1 December 1816, Davidson County Historical Museum, Lexington, N.C.

65. Smalling, *The Heritage of Watauga County, North Carolina*, entry 422; Raymond Wilson, author interview, 21 June 1992.

66. Soapstone was in high demand as a fireplace lining material in the mountains, and Reverend Wilson also cut fireplace linings from his soapstone. Georgia Morris, author interview, 12 June 1992; Lewis, "Notes on Building and Ornamental Stone," 95–103.

67. Georgia Morris, author interview, 21 June 1992.

68. Watauga County Record of Accounts, 1902–14, A&H.

69. J. A. Byers, d. 1915, and E. J. Byers, d. 1918. Their grandson Billy Byers told this to Georgia Morris.

CHAPTER FIVE

1. Bishir, "Traditional Building Practice," 120.

2. McKee, *Introduction to Early American Masonry*, 15.

3. Advertisement in *Newbern Spectator*, 25 August 1835.

4. Payments were made to Lawton for funeral expenses in numerous New Hanover County estates beginning in 1837. For example, the estate of William Dougal paid him for such services in 1837. New Hanover County Inventories of Estates, book 2, fol. 229, A&H; Lawton's cabinet-making business is listed in *Kelley's Wilmington Directory, 1860–61*, but not in the next directory, *Wilmington Directory for 1865–66*.

5. This connection was traditional in other American cities as well. An article by Rauschenberg, "Coffin Making and Undertaking in Charleston," 19–63, illuminates this connection between trades in Charleston, which was a continuation of European precedent. In 1866 when the first *Branson's North Carolina Business Directory* was published, every sizable town in North Carolina had a listing for "Cabinetmaking and Undertaking," no doubt reflecting a longtime tradition. By the late nineteenth century, specialization in metropolitan areas forced the two trades apart, and undertakers and furniture stores began to have separate listings in the directories. In smaller towns and rural areas, however, the two trades continued to be connected until quite recently. See discussion of the two trades in Chapter 4.

6. Will of Henrietta Foy, in Graves, *New Hanover County Abstracts of Wills*, 42.

7. Cameron Papers, March 1842, mentioned in Anderson, *Piedmont Plantation*, 32; North Carolina State Capitol Papers, A&H; North Carolina Gravemarker Survey, Southern Folklife Collection, SHC.

8. Will of John Kelly, deceased 1842, Estate of John Kelly, Cumberland County Wills and Estates, A&H. "Italian marble" was a term used during this period to refer both to marble imported from Italy and to domestic varieties resembling the real thing. McKee, *Introduction to Early American Masonry*, 31.

9. *Carolina Observer* (Fayetteville), 3 January and 10 January 1827.

10. One David Anderson, aged 60 to 70, with a son aged 20 to 30, and 18 slaves, is in the 1830 Fayetteville census. This may be David Anderson Jr. and his father. One member of the household is employed in "commerce." In the 1840 census, only the elderly Anderson and eight slaves are listed. U.S. Census, Population Schedule, 1830, 1840, Cumberland County, A&H.

11. Christison, *Carvings and Inscriptions*, 179.

12. One member of the household, obviously Foster himself, was employed in "manufactur-

ing and trades." U.S. Census, Population Schedule, 1840, Cumberland County, A&H. Foster does not appear in the 1830 or 1850 Cumberland County census.

13. Forbes, *Gravestones of Early New England*, 51–55.

14. Information supplied in permanent display of Traugott Leinbach's silverware at the John Vogler House, Old Salem, N.C.

15. The house was demolished, but was reconstructed in the 1960s.

16. The identity and design of this stone are unknown. Minutes of the Elders Conference, Salem, N.C., 30 November 1831, Old Salem, Inc./Moravian Archives, Winston-Salem, N.C.

17. Fourteen stones are probated to Leinbach in the Davidson County estate records of the 1830s–50s. Davidson County Inventories, Sales, and Accounts, 1832–37: Estate of Marten Haines, voucher no. 11, fol. 118; Estate of Elizabeth Fry, voucher no. 11, fol. 119. Davidson County Inventories, Sales, and Accounts, 1837–44: Estate of Henry Kritefezer, voucher no. 2, fol. 89. Davidson County Inventories, Sales, and Accounts, 1844–47, A&H: Estate of Jacob Crater, voucher no. 4, fol. 100; Estate of William Bodenhamer, voucher no. 38, fol. 276; Estate of Joseph Walk, fol. 348. Davidson County Inventories, Sales, and Accounts, 1847–51, A&H: Estate of William Ledford, voucher no. 4, fol. 118; Estate of Jacob Mock, fol. 230; Estate of Magdalen Pickle, fol. 236; Estate of Jacob Lockinberry, fol. 351; Estate of David Douthil, fol. 403; Estate of Susannah Hanes, fol. 144; Estate of Hannah Hanes, voucher no. 2, fol. 331; Estate of Solomon Elrod, fol. 386.

18. Archibald Henderson Estate, voucher no. 76, 11 October 1825, from Monument Association; voucher no. 117, 1825, from Charles Fisher, Rowan County Estates, A&H.

19. Alcott, "Robert Donaldson Jr." In 1844, through arrangements made by Donaldson, Davis came to North Carolina to undertake a program of architecture and landscape design at the University of North Carolina at Chapel Hill.

20. Naturalization Paper, CR.99.301.15, August term, 1835, Wake County Court Minutes, A&H; daybooks, 1833–34, North Carolina State Capitol Papers, A&H; William Stronach's tombstone, Oakwood Cemetery, Raleigh.

21. Bishir, *North Carolina Architecture*, 165.

22. Stonecutter John Steele, writing a farewell letter to David Paton upon leaving the capitol construction project in 1838, noted that he had worked with architects and engineers of very high standing both in the British government and in the United States. David Paton Papers, A&H.

23. These meetings began in 1836 and are the first effective organized protests among the building trades in North Carolina. Bishir, "Changes in Building Practice," 187, 467 (n. 157).

24. Murray, *Wake: Capital County*, 241, 282, 324. Two of Stronach's Scottish colleagues on the capitol project, Donald Campbell and William Murdoch, remained in the Carolinas in the stone business, but diversified into construction. Donald Campbell (1808–1885) aspired, like Stronach, to put down roots. Campbell stayed in Raleigh when the Capitol was completed, and established a marble yard that was continued by his sons and grandsons into the twentieth century. Because Campbell specialized in masonry construction rather than funerary monuments, he did not compete directly with Stronach. Campbell worked on the U.S. Post Office in the 1870s and superintended the stonework for the state penitentiary in the 1880s. "Campbells Have Unique Record; Make Monuments," *Raleigh Times*, 30 November 1925, copy sent with other research notes by Elizabeth Reid Murray in a letter to author, 21 July 1991. William Murdoch moved to Fayetteville to work on the U.S. Arsenal, and to Fort Sumter, South Carolina, where he elevated himself to the role of contractor, then built masonry railroad bridges and masonry buildings in North and South Carolina during a successful career that lasted until 1893. In the 1850s he moved to Salisbury, North Carolina, and in 1858 opened one of the first sash and blind factories in the Piedmont. Davyd Foard Hood, *The Architecture of Rowan County*, 26, 31, 300, 318.

25. Wake County Deed Book 12, 510, A&H; advertisement in *Raleigh Register*, 4 June 1838.

26. "Obituary of George Lauder," *North Carolinian*, 7 June 1888.

27. U.S. Census, Population Schedule, 1850, Wake County, A&H.

28. Wake County Deed Book 14, 198.

29. Their signatures are visible on stones with death dates from 1820 to 1843.

30. Letter to author from Elizabeth Norris, citing her research in the State Auditor's Reports, 1841, 36, A&H; private communication with Jean Anderson, Orange County, July 1991.

31. This stone base and fence were moved to the City Cemetery about 1900. State Auditor's Reports, 1841, 36; Cameron Papers, March 1842, mentioned in Anderson, *Piedmont Plantation*, 33; Elizabeth Reid Murray, letter to author, 21 July 1991.

32. The Mann stone is documented in North Carolina State Auditor's Reports, 1845, 54; the Rex stone in Mitchell and Mitchell, "The Philanthropic Bequests of John Rex," 261–62 (n. 25); on 13 October 1846 Stronach received $6.48 for a "Tombstone" out of John Devereux's estate, John Devereux Estate, Wake County Estate Records, A&H. This was not necessarily the gravestone of Devereux himself, therefore I am attributing it to Stronach rather than documenting it.

33. *Raleigh Register*, 5 January 1853; 1 November 1854; 9 January 1856. One W. Stronach, denoted as "colored," is listed in the 1875–76 Raleigh city directory as a stonecutter. "W." may have been one of William Stronach's slaves whom he trained. Elizabeth Reid Murray, letter to author, 21 July 1991.

34. Elizabeth Reid Murray, letter to author, 21 July 1991.

35. North Carolina Treasurers and Comptrollers Papers, receipts in quarry accounts file, box 12, A&H; House of Eleazer Colbourn (#380), U.S. Census, Wake County Population Schedule, 1850, A&H.

36. Will of William Stronach, 1857, Wake County Wills, A&H.

37. Notes from Elizabeth Norris; "Raleigh Marble Works and Chapel in Oakwood Cemetery," *News and Observer* (Raleigh), 24 August 1899, 22.

38. "Obituary of George Lauder," *North Carolinian* (Fayetteville), 7 June 1888. Paton lived in Fayetteville for a short period in the 1830s, and Lauder may have followed him there.

39. North Carolina Historical Highway Marker I 21.

40. U.S. Census, Industrial Schedules, 1850, 1860, Cumberland County, A&H.

41. *Lexington and Yadkin Flag*, 23 November 1855.

42. It is possible that Paton supplied the design for Lauder's house; he had left North Carolina in 1840 for New York, and returned to Edinburgh until 1849, then returned to New York and spent the last thirty years of his life as a professor of architecture and engineering there. Johnson, *Hometown Heritage*, 51–53; Ashe, *"David Paton,"* 12.

43. Sarah Louise Augustus, a slave of Henrietta Clow and her husband, Scotsman James B. Smith, later reminisced to a WPA interviewer about the family. Born on James and Henrietta's plantation outside Fayetteville, she had come to work in their townhouse after the Civil War. She recalled several gifts from Europe that the Smiths brought her, and described her owners as "hard working white folks, honest, God fearing people." Augustus, "Narrative"; Johnson, *Hometown Heritage*.

44. Returns of Phoenix Lodge No. 6, Fayetteville, N.C., Records of the Grand Secretary, Grand Masonic Lodge of North Carolina, Raleigh.

45. Records of Appointments of Postmasters, United States Post Office Dept, 66.

46. U.S. Census, Industrial Schedule, 1870, Cumberland County, A&H.

47. Augustus, "Narrative."

48. *Bernard's Wilmington and Fayetteville Directory and Hand-Book of Useful Information 1866–'7*, 155.

49. Author's telephone interview with Robert Remsburg, 18 November 1983. The Western

Railroad tracks were nearby, but this railroad connected only to the coal mines in Chatham County. Fayetteville was not connected to the state's railroad network until the mid-1880s, when the Cape Fear and Yadkin Valley Railway was extended to Greensboro. Lauder's shop may have been the wooden sheds beside the tracks on Franklin Street, shown on the 1908 Sanborn Insurance Map, sheet 3. A new stonecutting shop, a brick building, appears on the San-born Map of 1914 in the same block, with an address of 107½ Maxwell Street and the initials "R & L," probably Remsburg's shop. Sanborn Map, Fayetteville, 1914, sheet 8.

50. Johnson, *Hometown Heritage*, 52.

51. Catherine W. Bishir, personal communication with author, 30 December 1991.

52. In a letter to a relative in Georgia in ca. 1848, Evans is said to have included a pen sketch of his design. William Fields, Fayetteville, author interview, 22 July 1981. The stone, broken into several pieces, has been repaired and stands in the Evans Graveyard, Cumberland County.

53. A headstone with the same tableau and quotation for a person who died in 1858 stands in the Old Town Cemetery, Hillsborough, and is signed by King and Whitelaw of Raleigh. The inexpertly carved scene contrasts strikingly with the realism of Lauder's stones.

54. The only other antebellum stones with cross imagery found in the Upper Cape Fear Valley are at the Kelly Graveyard, in Cumberland County, used by the congregation of St. Patrick's Catholic Church in the early nineteenth century. Almost all of the early-nineteenth-century headstones there, by an unknown stonecutter, have small crosses combined with urn-and-willow ornament.

55. Cross Creek Cemetery contains two of the earliest examples of obelisks in the state: for Bela William Strong (d. 1815) and Sarah Adam (d. 1819), daughter of Robert Donaldson. Both are handsome marble neoclassical monuments by unknown stonecutters. Stonecutters' advertisements from the 1820s in Fayetteville newspapers included "monuments" among the types of tombstones that they were prepared to execute, so these could have been cut by a local itinerant such as Sweetland or by an out-of-state stonecutter.

56. Mrs. E. R. MacKethan in Oates, *The Story of Fayetteville*, 290.

57. Robert Remsburg, author's telephone interview, 18 November 1983.

58. Information supplied in exhibit, "George Vogler, Gunsmith," in the John Vogler House, Old Salem, N.C.

59. Mary Jane Fowler, local historian, Salisbury, N.C., author interview, 26 March 1982.

60. U.S. Census, Population Schedule, 1850, 1860, Rowan County, A&H.

61. *Republican Banner* (Salisbury), 6 April 1855.

62. Diary of Mary S. Ferrand, SHC.

63. Estate of John Ward, voucher no. 36, fol. 66: "A. Kelogg for TombStones ($13 short) 118.00," Davidson County Inventories, Sales, and Accounts, 1857–63, A&H.

64. U.S. Census, Population Schedule, Rowan County, 1860, 1870, A&H. (George Vogler is in the 1860 census but not in the 1870 census.)

65. Bishir, "Changes in Building Practice," 145.

66. U.S. Census, Industrial Schedule, 1860, Lincoln County; Population Schedule, 1860, Mecklenburg County; *Branson's North Carolina Business Directory*, 1872.

67. The dates of operation of various monument firms were calculated using *Branson's North Carolina Business Directories*. Copies are located in the reference section, North Carolina State Library, Raleigh.

68. Cooper Brothers is listed continually in Raleigh city directories from 1896 until 1930.

69. John Thomas McLean Jr., Lincolnton, N.C., author interviews, 14 March and 27 March 1982.

70. Ibid.

71. Clarke, *The Lost Boy*, 26–27.

72. Wheaton, *Thomas Wolfe and His Family*, 90–94.

73. Murray, *Wake: Capital County*, 599; also letter to author, July 21, 1991; "The Work of an Artist," *News and Observer* (Raleigh), 15 March 1910. Wolfe signed the monument of Martha Allen (d. 1897) and the headstone of Lucy Savage (d. 1859), both at Oakwood Cemetery, Raleigh; and the ledger of Seth Jones (d. 1866), in the Jones family cemetery, Raleigh. Elizabeth Reid Murray, personal communication with author, July 1991.

74. Author interview, James W. Clarke Jr., February 1994.

75. In recent years the local monument retailer has been able to reproduce catalog designs by purchasing a full-size transfer layout, a rubber stencil, which is laid on the face of the blank monument and sandblasted to etch the carving and lettering into the stone. Monument retailers can even order a monument that is shaped, carved, and inscribed at the Elberton plant and shipped in finished form to the retailer. Older methods of quarrying and finishing the monuments have given way to automatic, computerized machines which saw, polish, and sculpt the stone into a wide variety of finished products. Now, 37 granite quarries and more than 100 manufacturing plants in Elberton, Georgia, mine and process the superior quality granite in the 35-mile-long monolith into completely finished grave monuments. Elberton is known as the "Granite Capital of the World." Elberton Granite Association brochures, Elberton, Ga.

76. Popular motifs that appear in Elberton design booklets and in hundreds of North Carolina cemeteries are generally limited to variations of a few floral and religious motifs: hearts and flowers, praying hands, stalks of wheat, the cross, entwined wedding rings, and scrolls or opened books bearing names and death dates.

77. Vincent Cain, author interviews, July–August 1981.

CHAPTER SIX

1. In his useful study, "Rural Southern Gravestones," Gregory Jeane does not distinguish between white and black graveyards and gravemarkers. This is undoubtedly because traditional black culture is concentrated in the Lowland South, the coastal areas where blacks were brought as slaves to work the plantations of the region. The two counties in North Carolina in which most of the black graveyards in the North Carolina Gravemarker Survey were recorded, New Hanover and Cumberland, are coastal counties. The Upland Piedmont counties of North Carolina have smaller black populations, and only comprehensive fieldwork, not random sampling, would record rural black graveyards there. The preponderance of churchyards among the recorded black cemeteries is explained by the survey methodology, which located graveyards using U.S. Geological Survey maps and existing cemetery inventories. Many small African American family and community graveyards do not appear in these sources.

2. Burgess, *English Churchyard Memorials*, 183.

3. Shell grave mounds are present in two black New Hanover County graveyards, Hank's Chapel AME Churchyard and the Flemington Cemetery.

4. Mrs. Lena H. Hair, author interview, 3 August 1981.

5. Ibid.

6. An example is the concrete headstone of Alman Spence (1811–1872) at the Whitney Graveyard, Pasquotank County.

7. None of the concrete headstones is signed, and the only clue to their origin is an anecdote recounted by Fayetteville stonecutter Vincent Cain. Many years ago at a monument dealers convention in Charleston, Cain met another stonecutter whose father was in the cement mortar business in the 1920s. The father traveled on the railroad, and, as a sideline, took orders for gravestones at a cost of $3 apiece. The markers were shipped back to the customers by rail. He

is said to have made a fortune through this business. Vincent Cain, author interviews, July–August 1981.

8. Joseph Bass, author interview, 26 July 1981.

9. Dennis Rogers, "He Turns Stones for the Dead into Reflections of Life," *News and Observer* (Raleigh), 11 May 1982.

10. Works dealing specifically with African American graveyards are sparse. The most useful references for African American gravemarkers are: Vlach, *The Afro-American Tradition in Decorative Arts*; Thompson, "African Influence on the Art of the United States"; Thompson and Cornet, *The Four Moments of the Sun*; and Fenn, "Honoring the Ancestors," 42–47. William Edmondson, a native of Nashville, Tennessee, was born about 1883 of parents who had been slaves. Serving as a railroad worker, fireman, and hospital orderly, he took up the carving of gravemarkers of limestone in the 1930s. He became a prominent sculptor, and his work was displayed at the Museum of Modern Art in New York and the Jeu de Paume in Paris. *William Edmondson: A Retrospective*, the catalog of an exhibit of his work organized by the Tennessee Arts Commission contains a description of his gravestone work, with a full bibliography, by John Michael Vlach.

11. Burns family, author interview, 23 October 1981.

12. Mr. Shaw, author interview, December 1982.

13. Clarence Lightner, telephone interview by author, 9 October 1996. This type of burial, known as ground-level burial, was recently outlawed by the state of North Carolina.

14. Vlach, *The Afro-American Tradition in Decorative Arts*, n. 1.

15. Hazel Culbreth, widow of Renial Culbreth, and their children, Mary Julia and Renial George, author interviews, 5 August 1981 and 9 July 1982.

16. Culbreth family interview.

17. Issiah McEachin, author interview, 9 July 1982.

18. This cemetery was relocated to the present site, which probably explains why the markers are aligned neatly in rows rather than scattered loosely in the African American tradition.

19. Beatrice Clodfelter (daughter of Emma Verdell), Petersville, N.C., verified in a telephone interview by author, on 23 June 1982, that this was her mother's grave. Mrs. Verdell moved to this community of ex-slaves in the early twentieth century from Alberton, Georgia. Mrs. Clodfelter could not recall the name of the man from Georgia who made her mother's marker.

20. Thompson, "African Influence on the Art of the United States," 152 (n. 1).

21. Thompson and Cornet, *The Four Moments of the Sun*, n. 1.

22. Roy Johnson, author interview, 7 February 1981.

23. Henry Glassie made this observation in *Patterns*, 116.

SELECTED BIBLIOGRAPHY

MANUSCRIPT AND ARCHIVAL SOURCES

Chapel Hill, North Carolina
Wilson Library, University of North Carolina
    Southern Historical Collection
        James D. Evans Papers
        Mary S. Ferrand Diary
        Dialectic and Philanthropic Societies Minutes
        Southern Folklife Collection
            North Carolina Gravemarker Survey

Columbia, South Carolina
South Carolina State Archives
    York County Wills and Estates

Elberton, Georgia
Elberton Granite Association
    Brochures, 1991

Fayetteville, North Carolina
Phoenix Lodge No. 6
    Lodge Records

Gettysburg, Pennsylvania
Abdel Ross Wentz Library, Lutheran Theological Seminary
    Hill, Francis C., "Charleston Sketchbook of Francis C. Hill" (daybook)

Lexington, North Carolina
Davidson County Historical Museum
    Bible Records of Davidson County, N.C.
Lexington Public Library
    Owen, Ruth Sowers, "A Thousand Doors: The History of Philip Sauer (Sowers) and
        His 14 Children" (typescript, 1970)

Newton, North Carolina
Catawba County Historical Museum
    Little, Pearl, "Genealogy of Herman Family" (typescript, ca. 1939)

Raleigh, North Carolina
Grand Masonic Lodge of North Carolina
    Records of the Grand Secretary
North Carolina Division of Archives and History, Department of Cultural Resources
    Archaeology and Historic Preservation Section
        National Register of Historic Places Nomination Forms (originals at National Park
            Service, Washington, D.C.)
        Survey files of historic properties, Survey and Planning Branch
    Archives and Records Section
        County Records
        English Records, Loyalist Claims

Sanborn Fire Insurance Maps

U.S. Post Office Department, Records of Appointments of Postmasters, 1832–1929

North Carolina State Government Records

Capital Building Papers

State Auditor's Reports

Treasurer's and Comptroller's Papers

United States Censuses, Population Schedules, 1820–80

United States Censuses, Industrial Schedules, 1850–80

Private Collections

David Paton Papers

Phillips, Laura. Tilley Coffin, Casket, and Furniture Factory file, Stokes County Survey, 1981

Cedar Grove Cemetery National Register Nomination, 1972

Salisbury, North Carolina

North Carolina Lutheran Synod Office

Record Book of Pilgrim Reformed Lutheran Church, Davidson County, N.C.

Wilmington, North Carolina

Local History Room, New Hanover County Public Library

McCoy, Elizabeth F. "Inscriptions Copied in St. James Graveyard and Oakdale Cemetery, April 1939" (typescript)

Winston-Salem, North Carolina

Old Salem, Inc./Moravian Archives

Aufseher Collegium, Minutes, 1790, 1792, 1799, 1820, 1831 (trans. by Erika Huber)

Congregational Conference of Salem, North Carolina, Minutes, 1783 (trans. by Erika Huber)

Elders Conference, Salem, Minutes, 1803 (trans. by Erika Huber)

Elders Conference, Salem, Minutes, 1831 (trans. by Edmund Schwarze)

Winterthur, Delaware

Winterthur Library

Funerary monument catalogs

Children's Designs and Markers. Proctor, Vt.: Vermont Marble Company, ca. 1910.

Monumental Designs No. 6. Chicago: Nichols and Company, 1908.

York, South Carolina

York County Public Library

Hart, John R. "History of the Town of Yorkville" (typescript; written before 1942)

Hart, Joseph E., Jr. "The Crawford Family of Bethany" (typescript, 1969)

INTERVIEWS

Unless otherwise noted, all interviews were conducted by the author.

Bass, Joseph. Cumberland County, N.C. 26 July 1981.

Blachowicz, Jim. Evanston, Illinois. March 1997.

Boone, Louise. Winton, N.C. 6 February 1981.

Brown, Dr. Benjamin. Raleigh, N.C. 1992.

Briggs, Jack. Lanier-Briggs Funeral Home, Denton, N.C. 8 June 1981.

Burns family. Cumberland County, N.C. 23 October 1981.

Cain, Vincent. Eastover, N.C. July–August 1981.

Clarke, James W., Jr. Raleigh, N.C. February 1994.

Clodfelter, Mrs. Beatrice. Petersville, Davidson County, N.C. 23 June 1982.

Culbreth, Hazel, Mary Julia Culbreth, and Renial George Culbreth. Roseboro, N.C. 5 August 1981 and 9 July 1982.

Deetz, James. Interview with Catherine Bishir, New Bern, N.C., 18 March 1991.

Faulk, Bill. Brunswicktown State Historic Site, N.C. 4 April 1981.

Fields, William C. Cumberland County, N.C. 22 July 1981.

Fowler, Mary Jane. Salisbury, N.C. 26 March 1982.

Green, John B., III. New Bern, N.C. 12 September 1996.

Hair, Mrs. Lena H. Cumberland County, N.C. 3 August 1981.

Johnson, Roy, Johnson Publishing Company. Murfreesboro, N.C. 7 February 1981.

Lightner, Clarence. Lightner Funeral Home, Raleigh, N.C. 9 October 1996.

McEachin, Issiah. Eastover, N.C. 9 July 1982.

McLean, John Thomas, Jr. Lincolnton, N.C. 14 March, 27 March 1982.

Moore, Elizabeth. Edenton, N.C. February 1983.

Morris, Mrs. Georgia. Boone, N.C. 12 June 1992.

Murray, Mrs. Emma Yopp. Ogden, N.C. 13 November 1981.

Patterson, Daniel W. Chapel Hill, N.C. September 1983.

Rauschenberg, Bradford. Winston-Salem, N.C. 21 July 1982.

Remsburg, Robert. Fayetteville, N.C. 18 November 1983.

Shaw, Mr. Shaw Funeral Home, Wilmington, N.C. December 1982.

Spence, Mrs. Wilma. Elizabeth City, N.C. 6 February 1981.

Stephenson, Frank. Murfreesboro, N.C. 6 February 1981.

Turner, Mrs. Etta. New Hope, N.C. 6 February 1981.

Wilson, Raymond. Boone, N.C. 21 June 1992.

Winslow, Ray. Hertford, N.C. 5 February 1981.

NEWSPAPERS AND DIRECTORIES

Bernard's Wilmington and Fayetteville Directory and Hand-Book of Useful Information. 1866–'7. Wilmington, N.C.: William H. Bernard, 1866.

Branson's North Carolina Business Directory. Raleigh, N.C.: N.p., 1866–67, 1867–68, 1869, 1872, 1877–78, 1884, 1896, 1897.

Boyd's Wilmington, N.C., Directory & General Advertiser, 1881–82. Wilmington, N.C.: P. Heinsberger, 1882.

Cape-Fear Recorder (Wilmington)

Carolina Observer (Fayetteville)

Directory of the City of Wilmington, N.C. 1889. Wilmington, N.C.: Julius A. Bonitz, 1889.

Directory and General Advertiser of the City of Wilmington for 1894–'95. Wilmington, N.C.: H. Gerken, 1895.

Fayetteville Gazette

Haddock's Wilmington, N.C., Directory. T. M. Haddock, comp., 1871.

J. L. Hill Printing Co.'s Directory of Wilmington, N.C. 1900. Richmond, Va.: J. L. Hill, 1900.

Kelley's Wilmington Directory, 1860–61. T. Tuther Jr., comp., Wilmington, N.C.: Geo. H. Kelley, 1861.

Lexington and Yadkin Flag (Lexington)

Messenger (Fayetteville)

Newbern Spectator (New Bern)

News and Observer (Raleigh)

North-Carolina Journal (Fayetteville)

North-Carolinian (Fayetteville)

Raleigh City Directories, 1896–1930

Raleigh Register

Republican Banner (Salisbury)

Richmond Commercial Compiler (Richmond, Va.)

Sheriff's Wilmington City Directory for 1877–8. Sheriff Benj. R., comp., n.d.

Western Carolinian (Salisbury)

Wilmington Advertiser

Wilmington Directory for 1865–66. Frank D. Smaw Jr., comp., Wilmington, N.C.: P. Heinsberger, 1866.

BOOKS, ARTICLES, THESES, AND PAPERS

Alcott, J. V. "Robert Donaldson Jr." In *Dictionary of North Carolina Biography*, edited by William S. Powell. Vol. 2. Chapel Hill: University of North Carolina Press, 1986.

Anderson, Jean B. *Piedmont Plantation: The Bennehan-Cameron Family and Lands in North Carolina*. Durham, N.C.: Historic Preservation Society of Durham, 1985.

Ashe, Samuel A. *"David Paton": An Address Delivered by Samuel A. Ashe on March 12, 1909*. Raleigh: E. M. Uzzell, 1909.

Ashton, John. *Social Life of the Upper Classes, 1702–1714*. Vol. 3 of *Social Life in the Reign of Queen Anne Taken from Original Sources*. London: Chatto and Windus, 1882.

Augustus, Sarah Louise. "Narrative of Sarah Louise Augustus." In *North Carolina Narratives*, edited by George P. Rawick, part 1, 51–57, vol. 14 of *The American Slave: A Composite Autobiography*. Westport, Conn.: Greenwood Publishing Company, 1976.

Barba, Preston. *Pennsylvania German Tombstones*. Allentown, Pa.: Pennsylvania German Folklore Society, 18 (1954).

Bartlett, Charles, Jr. "Permanent Building Materials in Some Ante-Bellum Structures of Moore Co., North Carolina." Term paper, University of North Carolina, Chapel Hill, May 1966.

Batsford, B. T. *English Mural Monuments and Tombstones*. London: n.p., 1916.

Benes, Peter. *The Masks of Orthodoxy: Folk Gravestone Carving in Plymouth Co., Massachusetts*. Amherst: University of Massachusetts Press, 1977.

———, ed. *Puritan Gravestone Art*. Annual Proceedings of the Dublin Seminar for New England Folklife. Boston: Boston University Scholarly Publications, 1976.

———, ed. *Puritan Gravestone Art II*. Annual Proceedings of the Dublin Seminar for New England Folklife. Boston: Boston University Scholarly Publications, 1978.

Bishir, Catherine. *North Carolina Architecture*. Chapel Hill: University of North Carolina Press, 1990.

Bishir, Catherine W., Charlotte V. Brown, Carl R. Lounsbury, and Ernest H. Wood III. *Architects and Builders in North Carolina: A History of the Practice of Building*. Chapel Hill: University of North Carolina Press, 1990.

Bivens, John. "Fraktur in the South: An Itinerant Artist." *Journal of Early Southern Decorative Arts* 1, no. 2 (November 1975): 1–23.

Brown, Cecil Kenneth. *A State Movement in Railroad Development*. Chapel Hill: University of North Carolina Press, 1928.

Burgess, Frederick. *English Churchyard Memorials*. 1963. Reprint. London: SPCK, 1979.

Burgess, Pamela. *Churchyards*. London: SPCK, 1980.

Butler, Patrick. "On the Memorial Art of Tidewater Virginia 1650–1775." Master's thesis, University of Delaware, 1969.

"Campbells Have Unique Record; Make Monuments." *Raleigh Times,* 30 November 1925.

Cantrell, Brent. "Traditional Grave Structures on the Eastern Highland Rim." *Tennessee Folklore Society Bulletin* 47, no. 3 (September 1981): 93–103.

Caulfield, Ernest. "Josiah Manning (1725–1806)." *Connecticut Historical Society Bulletin* 27, no. 3 (July 1962): 76–84.

———. "Three Manning Imitators." *Connecticut Historical Society Bulletin* 43, no. 1 (January 1978): 1–16.

Christison, D. *The Carvings and Inscriptions on the Kirkyard Monuments of the Scottish Lowlands.* Edinburgh: Neill and Co., 1902.

Clark, Edward W. "The Bigham Carvers of the Carolina Piedmont: Stone Images of an Emerging Sense of American Identity." In *Cemeteries and Gravemarkers: Voices of American Culture,* edited by Richard E. Meyer, 31–59. Ann Arbor, Mich.: UMI Research Press, 1989.

Clarke, James W., Jr., ed. *The Lost Boy: A Novella by Thomas Wolfe.* Chapel Hill: University of North Carolina Press, 1992.

Combs, Diana Williams. "Eighteenth-Century Gravestone Art in Georgia and South Carolina." Ph.D. diss., Emory University 1978.

———. *Early Gravestone Art in Georgia and South Carolina.* Athens: University of Georgia Press, 1986.

Connor, R. D. W. "John Harvey." *The North Carolina Booklet* 8, no. 1 (July 1908): 3–42.

Crow, Jeffrey J., and Robert E. Winters Jr., eds. *The Black Presence in North Carolina.* Raleigh: North Carolina Museum of History, 1978. Exhibition catalog.

Deetz, James, and Edwin Dethlefsen. "Death's Head, Cherub, Urn and Willow." *Natural History* 76 (March 1967): 28–37.

Duval, Francis Y., and Ivan B. Rigby. "Openwork Memorials of North Carolina." *Markers: The Journal of the Association for Gravestone Studies* 1 (1979–80): 62–75.

Emmons, Ebenezer. *Geological Report of the Midland Counties of North Carolina.* Raleigh: Henry D. Turner, 1856.

Fairey, Wade B. "The Changing York County, South Carolina, Tombstone Business, 1750–1850." *Journal of the Museum of Early Southern Decorative Arts* 16, no. 2 (November 1990): 1–29.

Fenn, Elizabeth A. "Honoring the Ancestors: Kongo-American Graves in the American South." *Southern Exposure* 13, no. 5 (1985): 42–47.

Forbes, Harriet M. *Gravestones of Early New England and the Men Who Made Them.* 1927. Reprint. New York: Da Capo, 1967.

Fries, Adelaide L. *Distinctive Customs and Practices of the Moravian Church.* Winston-Salem, N.C.: Commenius Press, 1949.

Fries, Adelaide, Douglas LeTell Rights, Minnie J. Smith, and Kenneth G. Hamilton, eds. *Records of the Moravians in North Carolina.* Vols. 1 and 6. Raleigh: North Carolina Historical Commission, 1922–43.

Glassie, Henry. "Folk Art." In *Folklore and Folklife: An Introduction,* edited by Richard M. Dorson, 253–79. Chicago: University of Chicago Press, 1972.

———. *Pattern in the Material Folk Culture of the Eastern United States.* Philadelphia: University of Pennsylvania Press, 1968.

Graham, Angus. "Headstones in Post-Reformation Scotland." *Proceedings of the Society of Antiquaries of Scotland* 91 (1957–58): 1–9.

Graves, Mae B. *New Hanover County Abstracts of Wills.* Vol. 1. Wilmington, N.C.: Privately printed, 1981.

Green, John L. *Fact Stranger than Fiction.* Cleveland, Ohio: Riehl Printing Co., 1920.

Guide to North Carolina Historical Highway Markers. 7th ed. Raleigh: Department of Cultural Resources, 1979.

Hammer, Carl, Jr. *Rhinelanders on the Yadkin.* Salisbury, N.C.: Rowan Printing Co., 1943.

Hendricks, Garland A. *Saints and Sinners at Jersey Settlement.* N.p., 1964.

Hood, Davyd Foard. *The Architecture of Rowan County.* Salisbury, N.C.: Rowan County Historic Properties Commission, 1983.

Horton, Frank L., and Carolyn J. Weekley. *The Swisegood School of Cabinet-Making.* Winston-Salem, N.C.: Museum of Early Southern Decorative Arts, 1973.

Jeane, Gregory. "Rural Southern Gravestones: Sacred Artifacts in the Upland South." *Markers IV: The Journal of the Association for Gravestone Studies* 4 (1987): 55–84.

Johnson, Cyril L. *The Family of Noah Clodfelter.* Russellville, Ind.: N.p., 1954.

Johnson, Lucille Miller. *Hometown Heritage: Fayetteville, North Carolina.* Fayetteville, N.C.: Daughters of the American Revolution, Col. Robert Rowan Chapter, 1978.

Jordan, Terry G. *Texas Graveyards: A Cultural Legacy.* Austin: University of Texas Press, 1982.

Kniffen, Fred. "Necrogeography in the United States." *Geographical Review* 57 (1967): 426–27.

Lee, Lawrence. *New Hanover County: A Brief History.* 2d ed. Raleigh: Department of Cultural Resources, 1977.

Lefler, Hugh Talmage, and Albert Ray Newsome. *North Carolina: The History of a Southern State.* Chapel Hill: University of North Carolina Press, 1963.

Lewis, J. V. "Notes on Building and Ornamental Stone." In *First Biennial Report of the State Geologist, 1891–92,* 95–103. Raleigh: The Survey, 1893.

Lieber, Oscar M. *South Carolina Geodetic Survey.* Columbia, S.C.: N.p., 1858–59.

Lounsbury, Carl R. *An Illustrated Glossary of Early Southern Architecture and Landscape.* New York: Oxford University Press, 1994.

Ludwig, Allan I. *Graven Images: New England Stonecarving and Its Symbols, 1650–1815.* Middletown, Conn.: Wesleyan University Press, 1977.

McCormick, Finbar. "A Group of Eighteenth-Century Clogher Headstones." *Clogher Record* 9, no. 1 (1976): 5–16.

McCrary, J. W. "The Early Years of County History as Seen by J. W. McCrary." In *Centennial History of Davidson County, North Carolina,* edited by Rev. Jacob Calvin Leonard, 168–79. Raleigh, N.C.: Edwards and Broughton, 1927.

McEachern, Leora H., and Isabel M. Williams, eds. *Wilmington–New Hanover Safety Committee Minutes, 1774–1776.* Wilmington, N.C.: Wilmington–New Hanover County American Revolution Bicentennial Association, 1974.

McKee, Harley J. *Introduction to Early American Masonry: Stone, Brick, Mortar and Plaster.* Washington, D.C.: Preservation Press, 1980.

Merrens, Harry Roy. *Colonial North Carolina in the Eighteenth Century.* Chapel Hill: University of North Carolina Press, 1964.

Milspaw, Yvonne. "Plain Walls and Little Angels: Pioneer Churches in Central Pennsylvania." *Pioneer America* 12, no. 2 (May 1980): 85–95.

Mitchell, Memory F., and Thornton W. Mitchell. "The Philanthropic Bequests of John Rex of Raleigh: Part 1." *North Carolina Historical Review* 49, 3 (July 1972): 254–79.

Mohney, Kirk Franklin. *The Historic Architecture of Davie County, North Carolina.* Mocksville, N.C.: Davie County Historical and Genealogical Society, 1986.

Moore, David G., and A. Scott Ashcraft. "Native American Rock Art in Western North Carolina." Paper presented at the annual meeting of the Southeastern Archaeological Conference, Knoxville, Tenn., November 1995.

Moore, J. Roderick. "Decorated Gravestones of Wythe County, Virginia." *Antiques* 140, no. 4 (October 1991): 618–27.

Murray, Elizabeth Reid. *Wake: Capital County of North Carolina.* Vol. 1. Raleigh: Capital County Publishing Co., 1983.

Oates, John A. *The Story of Fayetteville and the Upper Cape Fear.* 1950. Reprint. Charlotte, N.C.: Dowd Press, 1972.

"Obituary of George Lauder." *North Carolinian,* 7 June 1888.

Parker, Mattie Erma Edwards, ed. *The Colonial Records of North Carolina: 1697–1701.* Raleigh, N.C.: State Department of Archives and History, 1971.

Patterson, Daniel W. "Upland North and South Carolina Stonecarvers." *Newsletter of the Association for Gravestone Studies* 6 (Summer 1982): 3–4.

Pezzoni, J. Daniel. *The History and Architecture of Lee County, North Carolina.* Sanford, N.C.: Railroad House Historical Association, 1995.

Ramsey, Robert W. *Carolina Cradle: Settlement of the Northwest Carolina Frontier, 1747–1762.* Chapel Hill: University of North Carolina Press, 1964.

Rauschenberg, Bradford L. "A Study of Baroque- and Gothic-Style Gravestones in Davidson County, North Carolina." *Journal of Early Southern Decorative Arts* 3, no. 2 (November 1977): 24–50.

———. "Coffin Making and Undertaking in Charleston and Its Environs, 1705–1820." *Journal of Early Southern Decorative Arts* 16, no. 1 (May 1990): 45–56.

Rogers, Dennis. "He Turns Stones for the Dead into Reflections of Life." *News and Observer,* 11 May 1982.

Schulze, Paul. *Original Designs in Monumental Art.* Boston: Paul Schulze, 1851.

Scorsch, Anita. *Mourning Becomes America: Mourning Art in the New Nation.* Harrisburg, Pa.: William Penn Historical Museum, 1976. Exhibition Catalog.

Sears & Roebuck. *Tombstone Catalogue.* Chicago: 1902.

Sewall, Samuel. *The Diary of Samuel Sewall, 1674–1729.* Boston: Massachusetts Historical Society, 1878.

Shelley, Donald A. *The Fraktur-Writings or Illuminated Manuscripts of the Pennsylvania Germans* Vol. 23. Allentown, Pa.: Pennsylvania German Folklore Society, 1961.

Sherrill, William L. *Annals of Lincoln County, North Carolina.* Baltimore, Md.: Regional Publishing Company, 1967.

Sink, M. Jewell, and Mary Green Matthews. *Pathfinders Past and Present: A History of Davidson County, North Carolina.* High Point, N.C.: Hall Printing Company, 1972.

Smalling, Curtis, ed. *The Heritage of Watauga County, North Carolina.* Vol. 2. Boone, N.C.: Southern Appalachian Historical Association, 1987.

Sowers, Betty K. "Davidson County's Pierced Gravestones." *Homespun* 3, no. 3 (Spring– Summer 1976): 7–16.

Stuckey, Jaspar. *North Carolina: Its Geology and Mineral Resources.* Raleigh: Department of Conservation and Development, 1965.

Sutton, Brett. "Primitive Baptist Hymns of the Blue Ridge." 33⅓ rpm sound recording. Chapel Hill: University of North Carolina Press, 1982. Album Notes.

Swaim, Douglas, ed. *Cabins and Castles: The History and Architecture of Buncombe County, North Carolina.* Asheville: City of Asheville and North Carolina Department of Cultural Resources, 1981.

Taylor, J., and I. Taylor. *Designs for Monuments.* England: N.p., 179?.

Thompson, Robert Farris. "African Influence on the Art of the United States." In *Black Studies in the University: A Symposium,* edited by Armstead L. Robinson et al., 122–70. New Haven, Conn.: Yale University Press, 1969.

Thompson, Robert Farris, and Joseph Cornet. *The Four Moments of the Sun: Kongo Art in Two Worlds.* Washington, D.C.: National Gallery of Art, 1982. Exhibition Catalog.

Vlach, John M. *The Afro-American Tradition in Decorative Arts.* Cleveland, Ohio: Cleveland Museum of Art, 1978.

——. *William Edmondson: A Retrospective.* Nashville, Tenn.: Tennessee Arts Commission, 1981. Exhibition catalog.

Wasserman, Emily. *Gravestone Designs.* New York: Dover, 1972.

Watson, Alan D. *A History of New Bern and Craven County.* New Bern, N.C.: Tryon Palace Commission, 1987.

Watson, Thomas L., Francis B. Laney, and George P. Merrill. *The Building and Ornamental Stones of North Carolina.* North Carolina Geological Survey Bulletin 2. Raleigh: E. M. Uzzell, 1906.

Welch, Richard F. *Momento Mori: The Gravestones of Early Long Island, 1680–1810.* Syosset, N.Y.: Friends for Long Island's Heritage, 1983.

Wheaton, Mabel, with LeGette Blythe. *Thomas Wolfe and His Family.* Garden City, N.Y.: Doubleday, 1961.

Willsher, Betty. *Understanding Scottish Graveyards.* Edinburgh: Council for Scottish Archaeology, 1990.

Wilson, William F., P. Albert Carpenter III, and Stephen G. Conrad. *North Carolina Geology and Mineral Resources: A Foundation for Progress.* Raleigh: North Carolina Department of Natural Resources and Community Development, 1980.

"Work of an Artist, The." *News and Observer,* 15 May 1910.

Wust, Klaus. *Folk Art in Stone: Southwest Virginia.* Edinburg, Va.: Shenandoah History Publishers, 1970.

——. *Virginia Fraktur: Penmanship as Folk Art.* 2d ed. Edinburg, Va.: Shenandoah History Publishers, 1975.

Yoder, Don. *Pennsylvania German Fraktur and Color Drawings.* Lancaster, Pa.: Pennsylvania Farm Museum of Landis Valley, 1969.

Zug, Charles G., III. *The Traditional Pottery of North Carolina.* Chapel Hill, N.C.: Ackland Art Museum, 1981. Exhibition Catalog.

——. *Turners and Burners: The Folk Potters of North Carolina.* Chapel Hill: University of North Carolina Press, 1986.

INDEX

Page numbers in italics refer to illustrations.